FREUD AND THE DESIRE
OF THE PSYCHOANALYST

THE CENTRE FOR FREUDIAN ANALYSIS AND RESEARCH LIBRARY

Series Editors:
Anouchka Grose, Darian Leader, Alan Rowan

CFAR was founded in 1985 with the aim of developing Freudian and Lacanian psychoanalysis in the UK. Lacan's rereading and rethinking of Freud had been neglected in the Anglophone world, despite its important implications for the theory and practice of psychoanalysis. Today, this situation is changing, with a lively culture of training groups, seminars, conferences, and publications.

CFAR offers both introductory and advanced courses in psychoanalysis, as well as a clinical training programme in Lacanian psychoanalysis. It can provide access to Lacanian psychoanalysts working in the UK, and has links with Lacanian groups across the world. The CFAR Library aims to make classic Lacanian texts available in English for the first time, as well as publishing original research in the Lacanian field.

OTHER TITLES IN THE SERIES

www.cfar.org.uk

FREUD AND THE DESIRE
OF THE PSYCHOANALYST

Serge Cottet

Translated by
Beatrice Khiara, John Holland, and Kate Gilbert

Routledge
Taylor & Francis Group

LONDON AND NEW YORK

First published 2012 by Karnac Books Ltd.

Published 2018 by Routledge
2 Park Square, Milton Park, Abingdon, Oxon OX14 4RN
711 Third Avenue, New York, NY 10017, USA

Routledge is an imprint of the Taylor & Francis Group, an informa business

The first edition of this work was published by Editions Navarin in 1982 as *Freud et le désir de psychanalyste.*

Liberté • Égalité • Fraternité
RÉPUBLIQUE FRANÇAISE

This book is supported by the French Ministry of Foreign Affairs, as part of the Burgess programme run by the Cultural Department of the French Embassy in London.
www.frenchbooknews.com

CFAR Library
Series Editors
Anouchka Grose, Darian Leader, Alan Rowan

The Centre for Freudian Analysis and Research

CFAR was founded in 1985 with the aim of developing Freudian and Lacanian psychoanalysis in the UK. Lacan's rereading and rethinking of Freud had been neglected in the Anglophone world, despite its important implications for the theory and practice of psychoanalysis. Today, this situation is changing, with a lively culture of training groups, seminars, conferences and publications.

CFAR offers both introductory and advanced courses in psychoanalysis, as well as a clinical training programme in Lacanian psychoanalysis. It can provide access to Lacanian psychoanalysts working in the UK, and has links with Lacanian groups across the world. The CFAR Library aims to make classic Lacanian texts available in English for the first time, as well as publishing original research in the Lacanian field.

www.cfar.org.uk

ISBN-13: 9781855755925 (pbk)

Typeset by Vikatan Publishing Solutions (P) Ltd., Chennai, India

CONTENTS

Occasionally something stirs toward synthesis, but I am holding it down.

—Freud, letter to Wilhelm Fliess, 16 April 1900.*

The truth is perhaps simply one thing, namely, the desire of Freud himself, the fact that something, in Freud, was never analyzed.

—Lacan, *The Four Fundamental Concepts of Psycho-analysis.***

*Masson, *The Complete Letters of Sigmund Freud to Wilhelm Fliess 1887–1904*, p. 409.
**Seminar XI, p. 12.

INTRODUCTION

The modern interpretation of psychoanalysis has been oriented for some years towards a more or less sceptical relativism: Freud's work has been relativized with respect to the prejudices of his time, such as those towards women. It has also been relativized in terms of his dealings with his students; and today his work is being placed in a new perspective by Lacan's teaching.

It is fashionable now to relativize Freud by blunting the sharp edge of his discovery; in my opinion, this approach derives its consistency from its failure to ask a question about psychoanalysis: the question of Freud's desire and of the origin of psychoanalysis. Through Lacan, we have learned how to apply to Freud's work the principles that originated in it and the rules of interpretation that it formulated. Thus, Freud is relative even in connection with himself. This is, indeed, a consequence of Freud's own discourse: it does not exempt its inventor from speaking from a place of which he is unaware. Since this place is that of his own desire, the problematic that I am bringing up has, naturally, been dictated to us by its own inventor. *What is the desire of the analyst?* I am going to direct this crucial question to Freud's own work. There is something in Freud that, according to Lacan, has not been analysed and which must be deciphered (*déchiffré*).

I propose here to "inject" into the body of Freud's texts an essential Lacanian category—the desire of the analyst—in order to test a thesis of Lacan's: "[I]t is ultimately the analyst's desire that operates in psychoanalysis" (*Écrits*, p. 724).

This key should allow a reading of Freud's work that is guided by Lacanian principles.

Emphasizing what has never been analysed in Freudian psychoanalysis raises formidable methodological problems. I would like, therefore, to dissipate any equivocations concerning this project. The reader will not find, in the following work, that I have used psychoanalysis to make deductions about the unconscious of its inventor. Various authors have already made this attempt, and the result is a psychological reduction of Freud's discovery, which clearly shows that they have not understood his work. Freud, indeed, believed that psychoanalysis could eventually be included within the problematic of science. Consequently, only demonstrations that are more radical than his own can be allowed into this field.

Freud's biography, the avatars of his personal history, and even the elements of his self-analysis ought not to exempt authors from analysing his work with the same rigour that he transmitted to us. The goal of such attempts is always to return Freud's discovery to the embrace of psychology. My point of view is entirely opposed to such a project. Not only do I consider Freud's desire to be essential in order to explain and enter into his work, but I also believe that insofar as psychoanalysis becomes confused with the desire of its inventor, this discipline loses all consistency, seeking to conceptualize itself by objectifying the analytic experience.

For the same reason, I shall avoid reducing the desire of the analyst to his fantasy. This orientation leads, in general, to a conception of analysis as a two-body relation, a conception that is criticized in this work.

It is clear, furthermore, that the advocates of a psychological approach to Freud are the same people who rank as the most faithful guardians of the psychological sciences. I shall argue, on the contrary, that the psychoanalyst's desire can be read less in his dreams than in his technical writings.

If I have the impertinence to ask this question, it may be because, on the one hand, Lacan had already asked it, but also because it becomes unavoidable from the moment that Freud is treated as someone other than one author among many: as the inventor of the concepts and operations that have propagated and diffused psychoanalysis. When psychoanalysis forgets the origin and the history of the concepts that it conveys or unveils, it misunderstands the nature of its object, by taking it to be objective.

To claim that the entire theoretical and technical operation that Freud produced is relative to his desire does not invalidate his work. It is, on the contrary, by accentuating this dependence that psychoanalysis can still avoid the growing bastardization of its concepts. It is always necessary to highlight, in Freud's orientation, the extreme virulence of his thought and the radical character of his topics, all of which are being stifled today by improper conceptualizations of psychoanalysis. The problematic of the desire of the analyst, however, does not derive its legitimacy from the Lacanian operation and from the cuts that Lacan effected in Freud's texts. Although Freud does not thematize the desire of the psychoanalyst, this category can be taken to be equivalent to a number of problems that he did mention. The goal of my work is to bring the following problems together and to avoid treating them as scattered and unrelated, as readers of Freud usually do: suggestion, the ideals of the analyst, the idea of the end of analysis, and Freud's ethic. All these questions are internal to psychoanalysis, and their vectors originate from one point: the desire of the analyst. This decrypting of Freud by means of Freud himself makes him a symptom in psychoanalysis.

Yet is it legitimate to treat a written text as material to be interpreted? Can psychoanalytic texts be treated as if they were an immense slip of the tongue? Psychoanalysis teaches us that only the enunciation authorizes interpretation; statements (*énoncés*) themselves do not, especially those that claim to provide the keys to interpretation. A Lacanian reading of Freud can, however, relax this prescription a bit. Such a reading can highlight the way in which the meaning (*sens*) of concepts slips within Freud's work, to the point that they can be treated as pure signifiers: their meaning is relative to Freud's use of them at a given moment of his practice. In these very slippages and in the gap between a term's various significations, Freud appears as a subject; such a subject is manifested in the effects of the cut itself.

Thus, to take literally Freud's analogy between scientific and psychoanalytic work, the insistence of certain signifiers can be followed in the scansions that punctuate his writings. The stumbling blocks, the pauses, and even Freud's theoretical resistance and his relation to truth will illustrate this thesis.

INTRODUCTION TO THE SECOND EDITION

This work explores, in a way that conforms with the canons of the university, a question that is far from academic; the desire of the psychoanalyst ought to invalidate the claims of scholarly argument if they are cut off from a certain sphere: that of the analytic experience and of the procedures invented by Lacan in order to encompass and evaluate it.

In 1982, the date of this book's first appearance, it was not considered too haughty, however, to present and analyse this concept by starting with Freud himself. From this perspective, the desire of the analyst was taken to be almost identical to Freud's desire. This is the general thrust of this work. This orientation was justified at that time because it dissipated a confusion: then, people frequently mistook the question of the analyst's desire for that of her subjectivity and, in its most popularized version, with the countertransference. It was therefore not useless to return to the source and to analyse Freud's desire as the cause of psychoanalysis itself.

In 1964, Lacan brought up the desire of the scientist, and indeed the desire of science, by issuing an invitation to construct a new epistemology.

Furthermore, it had not yet become a habit, as it has today, to deal with this problem by approaching people one by one, as is the rule in the pass, an operation that intended to throw light on the analyst's analysis. There was not yet any classifying and evaluating in the institution. Finally, in places that were external to the Lacanian field, the question of analytic training was raised in an atmosphere of complete ignorance of the pass.

Fifteen years ago, people could claim that the desire of the analyst was a rather disembodied function with one exception: Freud himself. Through him the universal function that was isolated by Lacan between 1964 and 1967 took on a certain consistency. It became, if not a paradigm of the desire of each analyst, at least a model, a norm in relation to which each and every one could be challenged.

Therefore, it was tempting to apply the instrument that Lacan had offered us—the desire of the analyst—to Freud's case histories, and to make this phenomenon both the "pivot" of the treatment and the law to which Freud's desire to know was subjected; it would thus be central to both theory and practice.

In "The Direction of the Treatment", Lacan makes the desire of the analyst appear as pivotal, since the end of analysis, like its stagnation or resistance, are subordinated to it.

Defining this function only requires drawing a corollary from the concept of the desire of the Other: the desire of the analyst is presupposed from the outset by the subject, who is called upon to decrypt his own desire through the mediation of the desire of the Other. After Lacan created the notion of the "subject supposed to know" at the end of his seminar, *The Transference*, it became possible to deduce the desire of the analyst as a "subject supposed to desire" from the desire of the Other. The two suppositions are complementary. Analytic practice makes the desire of the subject emerge as the desire of the Other. The latter is the cause of the subject's desire.

This function, however, neither brings with it any particular existence nor names anyone specifically. Desire is understood in the generic sense: that of the universal nature of the function. This universal quality is necessary to the dynamic of the treatment and to the handling of a transference that is specific to each analysand: it is well and truly a supposition.

Now, we move to a question which relates to existence itself: does there exist at least one agency that satisfies this function, and can its operation be verified? That appeared to be impossible to demonstrate during a certain period: the period that it took to invent the operation that could verify the emergence of this desire. Such a verification can only be made with each specific person.

Before the invention of the pass in 1964, Freud's desire was the exception about which one could wonder to which rule it conformed; it was the only desire that could claim to be able to respond to the question of the cause of psychoanalysis, since Freud's desire is psychoanalysis itself.

This desire is therefore in an exceptional position for a number of reasons: first, Freud was not a "subject supposed to know"; he *did* know.

Next, he desired psychoanalysis and made it exist as a new signifier within civilization: he married it for better or worse. Did he not say to Ferenczi at the time when he was working on *Totem and Taboo*: "Sometimes I feel as though I only wanted to start a little liaison and at my age discovered that I had to marry a new wife" (Brabant-Gerö, Falzeder & Giampieri-Deutsch, p. 317)? Finally, he loved this cause and wanted it just as it was. Lacan goes so far as to hypothesize that he wanted it even in what, from the institutional point of view, was its deadliest form: the International Psychoanalytical Association (IPA).

We are thus confronted, according to Lacan, with the question of the relation between Freud's desire and the "desire of the psychoanalyst". For the singularity of Freud's desire, in both its historical contingency and its absolute character as the condition for the birth of psychoanalysis, raises the problem of the model, the paradigm. Yet this element of identification, which leads back to the identification with the dead father, also constitutes a reason for being repelled by it. We know all too well the pernicious consequences that such identifications engender in the analytic community.

It is thus necessary to ask what the place of Freud's desire is in the history of psychoanalysis.

For convenience, I am distinguishing here three moments, which are more logical than chronological, and which can be found dispersed in the various chapters of this work.

1. The first concerns the elaboration of the concept of the "desire of the analyst" as an operative function; the logic of the treatment imposes this, and other relations are implied within it: the transference, the

end of the analysis, and the pass. These relations can be described without any need to base them on one person's desire rather than another's.

2. We have defined the desire of Freud in its singularity: as the very condition for this experience, it constitutes an exception to this function. It is the ex-centricity of the desire of its inventor in relation to this very function.

3. The particularity of the desire of each psychoanalyst, taken one by one, in its difference from that of other analysts. This raises the question of the fit between the desire of a particular analyst and this universal; more precisely, it is a question of how each person, on the basis of his unconscious, is able to convert his own desire in such a way that it can fit into this category.

This schema can look much too Aristotelian. It seeks to contrast the universal nature of a function with the particularity of Freud's individual position. The question is whether he himself was adequate to this function or whether, on the contrary, the singularity of his desire has not marked, in a strange way, the history of psychoanalysis. Whether Freud's position can serve as a model or should be avoided at all costs, its origin should be decrypted and clarified.

Like the famous logical paradoxes, Freud's desire exists in a state of internal exclusion from its own discovery.

Our work therefore follows a path: that of extracting Freud's desire from an enunciation, which can be decrypted as a desire to know in its particularity. Freud's desire has thus been broadly understood as a desire to know, but also as a subjective position in relation to his passion for truth. This has been done on the basis of his case histories, as well as of the totality of his work. What Lacan referred to as the sum of Freud's prejudices has not been ignored, especially those that emerge in his treatment of Dora and his examination of the question of femininity and the sexual relation in general.

Thus, what is at stake is a re-evaluation of Freud's desire. This re-evaluation was often effaced by the return to Freud that Lacan began from 1953. However, in 1964, a critical note became perceptible in his work on this subject: "Something in Freud was never analysed" (*Seminar XI*, p. 12).

In the 1980s, there was a tendency to *interpret* this judgement in a positive way. I myself saw in it an invitation to analyse Freud's desire as a pure desire to know, one that exists beyond the limits imposed by the master discourse.

Today, however, I would emphasize more the tension that exists between the principles implicit in Freudianism and the Lacanian orientation. It is as if Lacan, during the latter part of his teaching, divided the structure inherent in the experience from the fiction by which Freud apprehended it.

The present study, which does not quite reach this new perspective, limits itself to describing the characteristics of Freud's desire in terms that tend to emphasize the identity between the universal component of the function and Freud's paradigm. This approach remains valid.

A large part of Lacan's teaching assumes that there is a quasi-identity between structure and Freud's desire. The latter is, at this point, the model for a new form of knowledge and of a "novel desire" that appears at the limit of the discontents of civilization and from which a new ethic arises.

Before Lacan discovered that something was wrong with Freud's desire, he came close to promoting him as the Ideal founder of the analyst's subjective position. Through its lyricism, the last page of "The Direction of the Treatment" constitutes a real hymn to Freudian heroism:

> Who was more able than him, when avowing his dreams, to spin the thread on which the ring that unites us with being slides, and make its brief shine glow in closed hands, passing it from the one to the other in the swiftly shifting game of human passion?
>
> Who has inveighed as much as this scholar against the monopolization of jouissance by those who load the burden of need onto others' shoulders?
>
> Who, as fearlessly as this clinician, so firmly rooted in the everydayness of human suffering, has questioned life as to its meaning—not to say that it has none, which is a convenient way of washing one's hands of the matter, but to say that it has only one, that in which desire is borne by death?
>
> A man of desire, a desire he followed against his will down pathways where it is reflected in feeling, dominating, and knowing, but whose unparalleled signifier he and he alone—like an initiate at the defunct mysteries, succeeded in unveiling the phallus, the receiving and giving of which are equally impossible for the neurotic (*Écrits*, pp. 536–537).

Many passages from this text point to the division at the very heart of desire. Against his will, Freud defines his path—as the inaugural dream of Irma's injection shows—as one in which his desire to know, before recoiling in the face of feminine castration, is inscribed in a Molièresque identification with the position of physician. The absence of any "solution" that would allow the sexual relation to succeed leaves open only one path for elucidating the real: through a symbolic formula. Lacan in the commentary that he gave on this topic (*Seminar II*) situates the navel of the dream at this point; here, one finds something that is located beyond Freud's desire, and especially beyond therapeutic desire.

There are many other examples, all of which signal a point at which the theory stumbles, a fading away of the desire to know. Until the discovery of the death drive in 1921, we can see Freud following, against his will, a fate that doomed both him and his invention to being the pariah of civilization.

As witness to that which in psychoanalysis is foreign to the scholar's (*savant*) desire, he wrote to Binswanger that "In truth there is nothing for which man's disposition befits him less than occupying himself with psychoanalysis" (Fichtner, p. 69).

Forcing this position of being the exception, a position in which he confronts what is intolerable, Freud, moreover, writes in 1925 in a Jewish journal: "As a result of these criticisms [of the repression of desire by civilization] psycho-analysis is regarded as 'inimical to culture' and has been put under a ban as a 'social danger'" ("The Resistances to Psycho-Analysis", p. 220).

Identifying more with Abelard or Kepler than with Copernicus, Freud assumes the prestigious but sacrificial function of subverting psychic life. In de-centring the subject of the unconscious from the ideals of mastery and of the understanding (*connaissance*) of the self, he inscribes himself in the place of the Jew within civilization, thereby refinding a destiny from which he had vainly tried to escape, through the quest for a universal recognition by the scientific community: "Nor is it perhaps entirely a matter of chance that the first advocate of psychoanalysis was a Jew" ("The Resistances to Psycho-Analysis", p. 222).

Some years before *Civilization and its Discontents*, Freud reveals that his position is one that has been cut away from the master discourse, and, indeed, has been placed in absolute opposition to it. From this point of view, the specific character of the Freudian ethic as antagonistic to the ideals of the master can be radicalized.

Thus the return to Freud that Lacan carried out until 1964 can be situated as the ethic of a "purified" desire: it is essentially in this that Freud's advice to doctors consists in 1912: that *"Purifiezierung"* ("purification") is opposed to the physician's prejudices and resistances.[1]

This cleansing is taken up again by Lacan, following Ferenczi, who had described this ascesis of the analyst in terms closely resembling the Taoist's principles of "non-activity".

In his commentary on Ferenczi's 1928 paper, "The Elasticity of Psycho-analytic Technique", Lacan confirms the necessity for this ascesis in the name of the need to annul the analyst's ego (see "Variations on the Standard Treatment", *Écrits*, pp. 269–302).

This subjective division of the analyst, a theme dear to Ferenczi, culminated in the 1930s in the institutionalization of a personal treatment as a necessary precursor of the analytic act. The separation of the subject's being from his act cannot, however, be reduced to an ideal of objectivity; it is still as the desiring subject that the analyst operates. This first version of the desire of the analyst already anticipates the article in 1967, in which the abolition of the ego will be the very condition of interpretation (*"La psychanalyse: raison d'un échec"*, pp. 345–346).

This move towards curtailment is evocative of the sculptural metaphor that was so dear to Freud, who practised *"via per levare"*.

Rediscovering the charm of the precepts of non-activity, Lacan defined this position, indeed, in terms of its negative qualities: "reduction of one's personal impact; knowledge relegated to a subordinate position; authority that knows not to insist; goodness without indulgence; distrust at the altar of good deeds; the only resistance to be attacked being that of indifference" (*Écrits*, p. 283).

It is true that this description is still inscribed in terms of the analyst's subjectivity. The categories that inform this were seriously undermined after 1968. The analyst would no longer be considered as subject but rather as object *a*, which plugs up the analysand's subjective gap.

The reversal of the relations between knowledge and truth in *"Radiophonie"* no longer allows the humanistic prestige of learned ignorance to be analysed. The question of the psychoanalyst's knowledge was going to be given priority. On this matter, there is a perceptible difference between Freud's and Lacan's thinking concerning the desire to know.

If we were to enumerate the high points of Lacan's correction of this matter, it would be necessary to give a special place to the *Écrits*, in which the concept of the "desire of the psychoanalyst" is used, on the contrary, to show the value of Freud's work. In his seminar *The Other Side of Psychoanalysis*, however, Lacan clearly separates the analytic discourse from Freud's desire.

Once one has taken into account the paradigmatic virtues—which are even close to the ideal—that Freud's position has in Lacan's eyes, the fall of such an ideal raises an historical problem. The change in perspective is consistent with a re-elaboration of the fundamental concepts of psychoanalysis. The desire of the analyst itself undergoes a conceptual reworking. It is not surprising that this shift took place in 1964, the moment at which Lacan instituted the pass, a procedure that examines the analyst's analysis. The logic implicit in his own concepts had finally led Lacan to revise his conception of Freud's desire.

If we add that in the 1970s, there is a questioning of the guarantee offered by the Other and even an examination of its inconsistency, we can then grasp the existence of another dialectic of desire: the desire of the analyst comes to exist in a state of tension with the desire of the Other. The analyst's desire is no longer adorned with the virtues of intersubjectivity. It designates the paradox of a desire that seeks the place of the discarded object, a bit of rubbish.

Finally, it is necessary to reformulate the relation between psychoanalysis and the discourse of science; a de-centring of the Freudian ideal has turned out to be necessary.

Freud does not undermine the notion of science as the ideal for knowledge. Lacan, moreover, does not object to this scientism and regards this adhesion to the ideas of nineteenth-century positivism as an essential element in the discovery of psychoanalysis. We know that the cut made by Galileo is essential to the constitution of psychoanalysis, even if we do not know whether the latter is scientific or not. Freud, indeed, considers the scientific ideal to be external to his field and to be the model upon which he could rely. For example, he based the technique of interpreting dreams on the signifier in order to escape from obscurantism, and to keep well away from religious or paranoiac interpretations.

In contrast, Lacan establishes that science structures the Freudian field from within, that the signifier is the point at which, from the start, psychoanalysis is connected to science (*"Introduction à l'édition allemande"*, p. 558). Psychoanalysis thus has nothing of a normative ideal (see Milner's "Lacan and Modern Science").

The evaluation of Freud's desire to know depends on the relationship between science and truth. Lacan, it is certain, always clearly distinguished truth from exactitude, and favoured truth; however, in "*Radiophonie*" and in the seminars that follow, he locates knowledge in the real, without regard for truth.

When Lacan claims that the original sin of psychoanalysis was "Freud's amorous adventures with truth", he also undermines the claim that science has anything whatsoever to say about the order of truth ("*Note italienne*", p. 309).

Presumably one would not question Freud's ethical standards, when he instructs his patient not to lie and, in the name of love of the truth, to renounce "any kind of sham or deceit" ("Analysis Terminable and Interminable", p. 248).

Nevertheless, what can be questioned is Freud's obstinate determination to lift primary repression, to put his hands on the real, with the passion of a detective caught up in the mystery of the bedroom's primal scene. From this perspective, Freud's passion for truth has more in common with Sherlock Holmes's than with that of Edgar Allan Poe's Dupin. The latter reference, so dear to Lacan, implies a completely different conception of truth: it is right in front of everyone's eyes, no one actually sees it, and no one wants to know anything at all about it.

It is true that in the 1930s, Freud had a less absolute conception of truth and gave a place to myth, which Lacan calls the fictional structure of truth. Analytic "constructions", in particular, only touch the real tangentially; they substitute for both the repressed and for memory. As Freud puts it, citing Hamlet's Polonius, "Our bait of falsehood had taken a carp of truth." My chapter on "constructions" should be read as Freud's renunciation of both direct proof and catharsis. The real can only be touched with signifiers. Proof of the unconscious can only be obtained indirectly. Thus, knowledge is constructed in the context of ignorance and not in the light of truth. This is why Freud warns his students against the idea of a "mysterious unconscious" and its power to spellbind them ("Remarks on the Theory and Practice of Dream-Interpretation", p. 112).

It remains no less true that Freud's desire to know, which has one foot in science, limps along as a result of his passion for truth, which his own Oedipal myth reveals. Lacan locates the origin of this myth in Freud's relationship with the father and in the religious aspect of the

Oedipal register, which had remained unthought. At stake is nothing less than Freud's neurosis: in a sense, Lacan's formalization returns here, as Jacques-Alain Miller has shown, "to purge the paternal function from the intension of psychoanalysis" ("*Petite introduction à l'au-delà de L'Œdipe*", p. 9).

The constructions of *Totem and Taboo* are sustained by religious necessities that need to be made explicit: what kind of father would deserve even more love by being the great castrator of the horde of his sons (see Lacan, *Seminar XVII*, Chapter Seven)? These religious foundations, however, belong more to Christianity than to Judaism. Freud, indeed, does not predict the conquest of a promised land; the dark continent of feminine sexuality serves as an obstacle to this. Yet we can, with Lacan, see evidence of Christocentrism in Freud: Freud saves the father and protects him from castration. In this sense, love of the truth and the myth of the father converge.

It is here that Lacan reinterprets the Oedipal myth: it is not a crime against the father but rather a forcing of the limits imposed upon truth. Oedipus blinds himself because he has forced these limits, and this is the fundamental position of the neurotic. Lacan thus suggests that such a love is confused with an appeal for castration.

Furthermore, Freud's "phallic cause"—his belief in the sexual relation—is related to this requirement of truth.

This critique of Freud, which dates from the 1970s, is rather severe. It does not always take into account the different rectifications Freud proposed, in particular those concerning the limits of interpretation, the residual character of the end of analysis, and the importance of psychic knots which are inaccessible to symbolic interpretation. The result of these rectifications is that Freud's desire is not exhausted by his passion for decrypting and for archaeological investigation, nor by his obsession with the primal scene. Nevertheless, Lacan does hold the latter's passion at least partially responsible for triggering the Wolf Man's psychotic break.

In 1923, in his "Two Encyclopaedia Articles", Freud situates the desire to know beyond the jouissance of an encounter with the unconscious. In this text, the satisfaction of decryption itself is called into question. When investigating a case, the analyst cannot be contented with satisfying his "desire to know" (*Wissbegierde*); the latter term is very rare in this context (p. 249).[2]

By replacing interpretation with the work of construction—a radical change in technique introduced in the 1920s—Freud refuses to abandon himself to the seductions of decryption, as well as to the aptitudes of the patient's supposed resistances.

He thus confirms the decline of interpretation, which was due as much to the way in which his students had abused it as to its relative inefficacy at that time.

By recognizing a non-symbolizable part in the famous "residue" (*reste*) of interminable analysis, Freud refuses the idea that there can be a totalization without a residue. There is a real that cannot be symbolized and which is beyond meaning; it is the real of jouissance and has no demonstrable link with the unconscious. Freud here is on the terrain of the logic of his era, which recognized inconsistency and undecidability.

By freeing himself from the myths of depth psychology and by anticipating structuralism with his method of decrypting, as Lévi-Strauss himself says (see *The Jealous Potter*), Freud raises the piece of waste (*déchet*) that science casts away to the level of knowledge inscribed in the real.

"Scientific knowledge has transmitted into the scrapheap of learned ignorance a knowledge hitherto unknown" ("*Note italienne*", p. 309).

Commenting on this statement, Jacques-Alain Miller shows that there is a relation between scientific knowledge and the discontents of civilization. Freud spares science from the accusation of being an ideology that suppresses the subject, without always understanding the consequences of the subordination of science to the master discourse (see "*La passe de la psychanalyse vers la science*").

However, as already stated, psychoanalysis is not part of a revolt of humanistic discourse against science. It takes into account the scraps (*rebuts*) of science and what is foreclosed from this discourse: the relation between desire and an object that is not by nature desirable. In *Seminar XI*, Lacan radicalizes this absolute difference between a servitude to the ideal that has been subjected to the law of the same and the absolute singularity of desire.

To conclude, it must be added that the vast field opened up by the question, "What did Freud want?" leads us naturally to approach psychoanalysis in terms of its extension: the politics of psychoanalysis. Our work at the time was limited to the intension of psychoanalysis. It was completed, nevertheless, amid the thunderclaps provoked by the crisis and dissolution of the Freudian School of Paris.

With hindsight, this crisis, like so many others in the history of psychoanalysis, carries the traces of an institutional question that has remained latent, and even unthought in Freud's work.

What did Freud want for psychoanalysis? He most certainly wanted it to endure beyond his name, as the *Aufklärung* (Enlightenment) of modernity.

What did Freud want for psychoanalysts? That is more difficult to answer. He wanted there to be a group in which there was solidarity for "the cause". What sort of group, however, did he have in mind? Church, army, political party?

He certainly did not succeed in inventing an original social bond that would be capable of transmitting psychoanalysis.

Suspicious of physicians and priests in their ambition to subjugate psychoanalysis to either a technique or a vision of the world, he was unable to recognize the seeds of self-destruction in analysts themselves. Perhaps he thought that the ideal of the scientific method would carry the day over all other considerations; after all, he told Pfister that he believed that "the purely medical importance of analysis is outweighed by its importance to science as a whole" (Meng & Freud, p. 120).

Imaginary group-effects, however, did not cease with his death. The model of the Freudian horde made its presence felt within the IPA where the official religion of the dead father proved to be compatible with the abandonment or the bastardizing of his teaching.

Did he intend to prevent that from happening with the seven members of his secret committee, united in fidelity by their rings?

At the end of his life, as Kardiner recounts, he reproached himself for having taken up too paternal a place in his analyses: could he not also have recognized the consequences of such a position on the institution (see *My Analysis with Freud*)? Perhaps Freud, as leader of the School took the place, for followers of his Cause, of the Other of the law. Yet in being so unseeing with regard to the teaching of his pupils, he was also quite blind to the deviations that were clearly on their way. What matters in reality was not each pupil's love for Freud, but each person's relation with the unconscious. (On these questions, see *Le tumulte: dossier.*)

Moreover, it would seem unthinkable today to opine on the question of the desire of the analyst outside this institutional reference: the pass, the School, Schools ....

Do analysts want psychoanalysis to continue? In what way do they want to associate with one another?

If it is true that, by the time of the third generation after Freud, the unconscious was already on the way to closing up again, then this is because it is not eternal. Lacan warned us about this. Analysts have a responsibility towards both the existence and the very future of the unconscious. Correlatively, it is always to be feared that there will be an aphanisis of the desire of the analyst, which can succumb to the requirements of the master discourse. If the unconscious, as Lacan suggests, implies that we listen to it, the voice of reason can become so quiet that the unconscious may end by being silenced.

Such is the ethical axis of a desire that would try to be equal to the Freudian ideal of transmission.

This requirement cannot be deduced directly from analytic discourse itself, nor from the practice that claims to represent it. It requires a decisive choice on the part of each and every analyst.

Serge Cottet,
July 1995

Notes

1. "It is not enough for this that he himself should be an approximately normal person. It may be insisted, rather, that he should have undergone a psycho-analytic purification and have become aware of those complexes of his own which would be apt to interfere with his grasp of what the patient tells him" ("Recommendations to Physicians Practising Psycho-Analysis", p. 116).
2. The *Standard Edition* renders "*Wissbegierde*" as "curiosity" rather than as "desire to know"; in the French translation to which Cottet refers, the text reads "*désir de connaître*" (see Freud's *Résultats, Idées, Problèmes*, p. 67) (translator's note).

PART I

FROM THE HYSTERIC TO FREUD'S DESIRE

Psychoanalysis is like a woman who wants to be seduced but knows she will be underrated unless she offers resistance.

—Freud, *Letter to Stefan Zweig*, 20 July 1939.*

---

*Freud, E. L., *Letters of Sigmund Freud 1873–1939*, p. 303.

CHAPTER ONE

Freud's analytic act

Freud was not always Freudian. The changes that punctuate his work point both to moments of discovery and periods of inhibition. His time for understanding was not regulated by a will to knowledge, however obvious the latter may have been. Nor is the light thrown on his desire by his transference to Fliess enough to define the specificity of his orientation in relation to those of other physicians of his time.[1] If my concern here is to grasp Freud's analytic act *in statu nascendi*, this is because no prehistory of psychoanalysis can account for this absolute beginning, which grants full power to speech by stating a fundamental rule: "Say everything."

That Freud wanted his patients to say everything and to follow this rule has not been without consequences, which have necessarily created questions that must be addressed by all those who have followed in his path.

What does an analyst want?

Apathy, ataraxia, and silence were for a long time considered to be the cardinal virtues of a psychoanalyst: wanting nothing, doing nothing, and desiring nothing seemed to be not only the necessary guarantees

3

4 FREUD AND THE DESIRE OF THE PSYCHOANALYST

for "axiological neutrality" in conducting the treatment, but were also the only foil against both spiritual guidance and suggestion. Freud had always wanted to remove psychoanalysis from the discourse of mastery, yet does this mean stifling the desire of the analyst?

It would certainly be paradoxical, and perhaps even fraudulent, for an analyst to claim to be neutral. After all, she has been led to her current position along paths that she now intends to clear for someone in her care. Can an analyst really forget who and what have set her up? If so, the ascesis that she is supposed to show is merely a semblance in which she has dressed herself up; she can thus offer to the other an even surface that reflects the speaker's message and restores it to him, so that he can understand to whom he is actually addressing it. Even if this experience is forgotten by the very person whose task is to take another through it, it cannot be claimed that such indifference underlies Freud's invention: "Psycho-analysis is seeking to bring to conscious recognition the things in mental life which are repressed" ("Five Lectures", p. 39).

Is it really possible for an analyst to accept such a programme precisely by disengaging herself from it? Since each analyst can only base her practice on the transmission of something that has been bequeathed to her by Freud, can she forget his heritage? Her own connection with Freud is all the more unavoidable since there is no guarantee or third party that can endorse the scientific nature of the experience. Its nature remains not only ineffable but also unverifiable. Moreover, this experience cannot find its reason for existence anywhere else than in the desire of its inventor: Freud himself. No other necessity than Freud's passion can account for the invention of this "plague", for which the general public has no need.

Towards the end of his life, when his pioneering spirit had somewhat abated, Freud wrote to Binswanger that "In truth there is nothing for which man's disposition befits him less than occupying himself with psychoanalysis" (Fichtner, p. 69).

These lines prove that Freud, who occupied the place of the at-least-one person who did not recoil from analysis and who showed a certain aptitude for it, had little idea about how it could be transmitted. The gap he opened up has no real reason to stay open, unless someone with a will as strong as his own decides to open it up again. One only has to consider the number of articles and works about Freud's life to conclude that none of them is able to say why he invented psychoanalysis rather than something else. This is not even a failure on their part, for it is quite simply impossible to do so. A work cannot be psychoanalysed, Freud's no less so than anyone else's.

The inventor of psychoanalysis, however, did not lack passions, not the least of which was a burning ambition to make a name for himself. Yet it is clear that the sum of Freud's passions could not be extinguished by inventing psychoanalysis. It also cannot seriously be denied that Freud far from being the conservative bourgeois that André Breton, to his astonishment, thought that he had discovered in Vienna was a man of desire. The fact that the future of psychoanalysis depends on Freud's cause would only be obvious if the passionate element that he committed to it could be determined. When we consider the enormous weight of this heritage, it is difficult to imagine to what other source an analyst can trace back her filiation.

It is legitimate, then, to consider the question of Freud's desire in terms of the sum of his passions. If, however, following Lacan, we speak of "the desire of the psychoanalyst", this is because there is a certain community between this desire and the patient's. Does this imply that the same properties can be applied to both? If we refer to the psychoanalyst's desire, we cannot eliminate its erotic dimension: if desire, for Freud, is "lust" (*Seminar II*, p. 65), then the psychoanalyst's desire cannot escape this definition. We can even claim that the metaphor of the sexual relation was the only formula by which Freud could account for this curious encounter:

> The analyst's power over the symptoms of the disease may thus be compared to male sexual potency. A man can, it is true, beget a whole child, but even the strongest man cannot create in the female organism a head alone or an arm or a leg; he cannot even prescribe the child's sex. He, too, only sets in motion a highly complicated process, determined by events in the remote past, which ends with the severance of the child from its mother. ("On Beginning the Treatment", p. 130)

The fact that the context of psychoanalysis, from the start, was not the doctor–patient relation but Freud's relation with a woman and in particular a woman with an hysterical complaint gives a supplementary consistency to this claim. By excluding from this setting "all his feelings, even his human sympathy" ("Recommendations to Physicians", p. 115), Freud lays bare the reality of the unconscious: sexuality.[2]

At the same time, the sexual relation is ruled out, and Freud thus provokes a question in his partner: "What does he want? What does he want to do?"

We see that the analyst's desire is split into two parts, based upon whether something is supposed about it or whether something is said that allows his desire to be located. These two aspects "subjective" desire and the function that Lacan referred to as x must not be confused. Furthermore, what analyst worthy of Freud and with at least some awareness of his own desire could be unaware of these sadder passions? Hate also plays a role. If we assume that an analyst is better aware of his desire than most, then how can he not know that the essence of love is deception, a deception that is conditioned by self-love? This is often the motive for misunderstandings between analysts: if one wants to make an analyst the equal of God, one cannot suppose that he is capable of hate. Yet it can hardly be said that Freud was incapable of hatred.

Horror of the act

It would be wrong to think that Freud had a simple love relation with the unconscious. His 1905 programme could not fail to lead to many surprises and disappointments: "Neurotics are a nuisance and an embarrassment for all concerned—including the analysts" ("The Question of Lay Analysis", p. 241).

This disappointment is at the heart of the analytic framework. The fundamental rule and its corollary, free-floating attention (*gleichswebende Aufmerksamkeit*), imply that the analyst agrees to let himself be taken by surprise ("Recommendations to Physicians", pp. 114–115). Now, unpleasant surprises were soon to appear, less from the discovery of the sexual aetiology of the neuroses than from transference love; less from the repetition-compulsion than from the negative therapeutic reaction. Yet in allowing himself, on every occasion, to be surprised, Freud necessarily had to wonder about the legitimacy of his act. As he states, with regard to the *Unheimlich* that is the unconscious, "One feels inclined to doubt sometimes whether the dragons of primaeval days are really extinct" ("Analysis Terminable and Interminable", p. 229).

It was thus in the wake of a certain failure that Freud moved forward on the analytic scene, the very place where one might say that Breuer—who fled psychoanalysis at the moment when things started to go wrong—had succeeded. Breuer avoided the sexual transference, the irrefutable proof of the sexual aetiology of the neuroses. This "untoward event" (*On the History of the Psycho-Analytic Movement*, p. 12) became Freud's point of departure. He did not shy away from the consequences that had to be drawn from the sexual aetiology of hysteria. Breuer's flight when his patient, Anna O, brought him the symptom of his own desire in the flattering form of an imaginary child, was a bungled action, and was therefore a successful discourse against psychoanalysis. Breuer did not recognize this first-born child of psychoanalysis as his own, and left the scene. "With all his great intellectual gifts there was nothing Faustian in his nature" (E. L. Freud, p. 413) added Freud, who himself had no qualms about taking on the gods of the underworld.

In order for an act not to be an *acting out*—which implies exiting the scene—but rather a passage to the act, one must risk failure, something Freud certainly did not avoid: "What is needed, as in the establishment of any right, is a passage to the act, and [...] it is from this that that the psychoanalyst today is in retreat" (Lacan, "Response to Students of Philosophy", p. 108, translation altered).[3]

This is what has aroused the indignation of the sociologist Robert Castel, who has not been duped by "analytic neutrality", and who considers the instituting of the analytic method to be an assertion of power (*Le psychanalysme*, p. 38). It is true that this valid remark exempts the author from questioning the foundations of psychoanalysis in terms other than those of intellectual arbitrariness or the abuse of power, since he does not see that it is only the symbolic that can offer consistency to any material. One cannot say, however, that Freud carried out this feat of genius light-heartedly; he predicted that his act would lead to the most fearful consequences, even if he did not suspect the nature of the plague he was about to unleash: "Such is the fright that seizes man when he discovers the true face of his power that he turns away from it in the very act—which is his act—of laying it bare" (*Écrits*, p. 201).

It would be futile even to try to account for the history of psychoanalysis without considering the risk Freud took. The history of psychoanalysis, indeed, raises the question of Freud's resistance to his own discovery. Before his hysterical patients, from whom he learned everything, sent back to him, in inverted form, his message—his own desire to make them talk about "everything" Freud could perhaps believe that both the science and the truth that he uncovered could cohabit very well. How an intellectual (*savant*)—someone who equates serving truth with the service of goods and social duty—was able not to compromise his desire is the mystery that this work shall try to elucidate.

From the hysteric's desire to Freud's passion for origins to his ethics, Freud's work consists of a series of links in a chain, but without this desire, his work is condemned to the realm of non-sense.

Notes

1. This is Octave Mannoni's thesis in "L'analyse originelle" (see *Clefs pour l'imaginaire: ou l'autre scène*). See chapter V below.
2. "Real sexual relations between patients and analysts are out of the question" (Freud, *An Outline of Psycho-Analysis*, p. 176).
3. The outcome is a split in the principle of the act. With regard to Freud, Lacan recognizes in him: "a man of desire, a desire he followed against his will" (*Écrits*, p. 537). At the time of the dissolution of the *École Freudienne de Paris*, Lacan still asserts: "Yes, the psychoanalyst holds his act in *horror*" ("The Other is Missing", p. 135). See also p. 179 below.

CHAPTER TWO

Capturing the unconscious

Freud's first works on hysteria stand as the "primal scene" of psychoanalysis. In his *Studies on Hysteria*, Freud's desire can be read in terms of his request: "I am asking you to remember; I am asking you to speak." Since what his patients told him was in answer to this appeal, we can argue that everything they said was related to it. It should be noted, however, that this relativity is connected less to the truth of the material than to its exactitude; in other words, the different scenes that the patient has remembered, and which may well conform to the physician's expectations in terms of their chronology, are not entirely created. The same cannot be said of the historical exactitude of the material, since, in this case, all certitude is undermined by the intercession of the phantasy. Freud was not yet aware of this fact, just as he did not grasp the quite striking homogeneity between his theoretical preoccupations and the way in which his hysterical patients told their stories.

I shall establish that the structure of these hysterical accounts is connected with the structure of medical discourse. In relation to Charcot's method, however, Freud establishes a cut by supposing the existence of knowledge in the other and by allowing her to take the initiative to gain access to it; his message is "You are the one who knows", rather than "I already knew that". He therefore supposes the existence of a knowledge that does not know itself and which the patient possesses. This knowledge, which causes the analyst's desire, can be called the *unconscious*. Freud only knows what his patients are able to tell him; his love for the subject's unconscious must also be valuable enough for her to offer it to him as a gift. This is not the same structure as that of suggestion, even if it is clear enough that the hysteric only says what the other wants to hear.

What, then, did Freud want to hear? What did he not already know? A hysteric's docility in telling her secrets, her reticence or, on the contrary, her bad temper, her hesitations, her resistance—in a word, the signifying breaks in her enunciation—are subject to variations in which the analyst's implication cannot always be read; there are, however, cases in which the hysteric is clearly seducing her psychoanalyst. Who seduces whom, however, when the master orders the hysteric to produce the knowledge she possesses?

It seems that Freud's hysterical patients considered his artifice of applying pressure to the forehead as an amorous support, of which they had been imaginarily deprived. In the real of the treatment, it was a sign of Freud's desire: a sign that he loved the knowledge they possessed.

It is easy to give an example of how the hysteric, on being questioned by Freud, leads him by the hand, by making her choice of memories conform to what the master has repeatedly insisted upon. In his chapter, "The Psychotherapy of Hysteria", Freud specifies how a therapist, confronted with the phenomenon of "resistance", should intervene: "The hysterical patient's 'not knowing' was in fact a 'not wanting to know'—a not wanting which might be to a greater or lesser extent conscious. The task of the therapist, therefore, lies in overcoming by his psychical work this resistance to association" (*Studies on Hysteria*, pp. 269–270). He emphasizes the unequal character of the struggle between a "resistance to association" and the "insistence on the part of a strange doctor who is unfamiliar with what is happening". It is therefore a quantitative factor, a difference in degree between the two forces that leads Freud to resort to what he calls a "small technical device". This consists in annulling the pressure exercised by the will over the pathogenic idea:

> In these circumstances, I make use in the first instance of a small technical device. I inform the patient that, a moment later, I shall apply pressure to his forehead, and I assure him that, all the time the

pressure lasts, he will see before him a recollection in the form of a picture or will have it in his thoughts in the form of an idea occurring to him; and I pledge him to communicate this picture or idea to me, whatever it may be. He is not to keep it to himself because he may happen to think it is not what is wanted, not the right thing, or because it would be too disagreeable for him to say it. There is to be no criticism of it, no reticence, either for emotional reasons or because it is judged unimportant. Only in this manner can we find what we are in search of, but in this manner we shall find it infallibly. Having said this, I press for a few seconds on the forehead of the patient as he lies in front me; I then leave go and ask quietly, as though there were no question of a disappointment: "What did you see?" or "What occurred to you?" (*Studies on Hysteria*, p. 270)

The schema in question is as follows: a patient, in response to Freud's questioning, evokes the absence of a pathogenic memory by maintaining that she knows nothing about it. He then applies pressure to her forehead, thus making a thought come to her. For instance, a patient suffering from a nervous cough tells him, "Now I am quite alone in the world. No one here loves me. This creature was my only friend, and now I have lost him." "She continued her story," writes Freud: "'The cough disappeared when I left my aunt's, but it came on again eighteen months later.' 'Why was that?' 'I don't know.' I pressed again" (*Studies on Hysteria*, p. 273).

We finally reach the pathogenic idea: "No one loved her." This is not enough, but Freud can get nothing more out of her: "But there was something attaching to the idea of 'love' which there was a strong resistance to her telling me. The analysis broke off before this was cleared up" (*Studies on Hysteria*, p. 273).

It is clear that what Freud calls resistance is precisely the measure of his disappointment. It appears likewise that the proximity of his desire—or his passion—for truth, causes the hysteric to draw back, in a reaction that Freud soon afterwards qualifies as a negative transference. This does not mean, however, that he has correctly understood that its source is his own insistence on always asking her for more, while also maintaining his distance from her.

Thus he makes the following confession, an extraordinary misunderstanding of the way in which the transference responds to the physician's desire:

> It is quite common for the patient to complain of a headache when
> we start on the pressure procedure; for her new motive for resistance
> remains as a rule unconscious and is expressed by the production
> of a new hysterical symptom. The headache indicates her dislike of
> allowing herself to be influenced. (*Studies on Hysteria*, p. 302)

How could such a result be avoided when Freud, as he himself admits,
considers that the price that must be paid for his patient's sacrifice,
in agreeing to deliver her erotic thoughts, is his own consent to offer
her a substitute for love? "The trouble taken by the physician and his
friendliness have to suffice for such a substitute" (*Studies on Hysteria*,
p. 301). I have already briefly discussed this artifice. In the words of
Pierre Kaufmann:

> Let us, as Freud suggests, separate this "small technical device",
> this "deft use of his hand", from its primary support and restore it
> to its pure mediating function. To the analysand's free expression—
> her expression freed from the requirement for appropriation that is
> inherent in enunciation—the analyst responds by assuming a cer-
> tain tone, a certain position of rest in his voice. The whole art of
> intervention is already to be found here. (*Psychanalyse et théorie de la
> culture*, pp. 48–49)

It seems to me that the ideas of capturing and controlling are better
suited to convey this function of mediation than the calm tone used in
the *Studies*, a work that does not yet convey the ideal of passiveness later
defined as "free-floating attention". It is, rather, Freud's *uneven* manner
of listening that characterizes his mode of intervention at this time. His
insistence on extracting confessions reveals the extent to which he misunderstands that what is really at stake in the patient's silence is the
presence of the Other: the transference.

How could it be otherwise, when Freud, having asked his patients
to say everything, and making "a careful collection of the occasions on
which [resistance] was particularly marked", claims to have acquired a
total confidence in his technique (*Studies on Hysteria*, p. 154). Elisabeth
von R relates her life to him, page by page, scene after scene, as if it
were a novel; he assumes that she leaves a gap in her account only
when she is confronted with an unbearable representation, one that
is linked to her account of a primal scene: the first seduction that she

experienced becomes the cause of the ensuing conflict. Freud declares that "I put the situation dryly before her with the words: 'So for a long time you had been in love with your brother-in-law'" (*Studies on Hysteria*, p. 157). Since the patient does not admit this herself, and as she, on the contrary, rejects his "explanations," attributing them to suggestion, we can conclude that this forcing of love is an effect of Freud's "counter-transference", which "forc[es] the call for love onto the object of identification" (*Écrits*, p. 534).

It is not surprising then, that Lacan emphasizes that the "springs of aggressiveness" are triggered by the overly well-intentioned therapist. The role of prophet or saviour not only contradicts an ethic that repudiates suggestion, but also triggers the patient's hostile reaction, since there is an aggressive response to charity. Misunderstanding not what he wants but rather what he desires, he ends up arousing a transference that can be called negative, in the sense of a negative therapeutic reaction; such a reaction inevitably results when an intervention moves too quickly towards curing the patient:

> What appears here as the proud revenge of suffering will show its true face—and sometimes at a moment decisive enough to enter the "negative therapeutic reaction" that interested Freud so much—in the form of that resistance of *amour-propre*, to use the term in all the depth given it by La Rochefoucauld, and which is often expressed thus: "I can't bear the thought of being freed by anyone but myself." (*Écrits*, p. 87)

Freud, trapped in a misunderstanding, employs a seduction technique that will ensure that the patient will fall in love with him; the only possible result is that the treatment will fail, or at least that her associations will cease. His intervention "in the real", and in particular his method of applying pressure, both symbolizes a "capture" of the unconscious—thus revealing his desire for mastery—and provokes the patient's reciprocal love.

As soon as a patient's associations stop, transference, as Freud was not yet aware, can be said to exist; it is then that he applies pressure to his patient's forehead. Inevitably, however, his gesture functions either as a suggestion or as an invitation to resistance. Freud is not wrong in saying that transference is an obstacle that can be equated with resistance. His error, however, lies in having unknowingly created this effect, a true declaration of impatience and a confession of his desire to possess the Other.

This process differs radically from that of suggestion, however, since no representative content has been offered to the patient: "I was set the task of learning from the patient something that I did not know and that he did not know himself," he claims in 1905, in his "Five Lectures on Psycho-Analysis" (p. 22).

Freud's process, which marks a transition between hypnosis, which he had recently abandoned, and free association, aims at giving rise to memories that could ensure a continuity in the patient's discourse:

> When I reached a point with them at which they maintained that they knew nothing more, I assured them that they did know it all the same, and that they had only to say it; and I ventured to declare that the right memory would occur to them at the moment at which I laid my hand on their forehead. In that way I succeeded, without using hypnosis, in obtaining from the patients whatever was required for establishing the connection between the pathogenic scenes they had forgotten and the symptoms left over from those scenes. ("Five Lectures", p. 23)

Freud then gives his reason for abandoning hypnosis: it was "a laborious procedure, and in the long run an exhausting one" ("Five Lectures", p. 23). In other words, the modifications he has made to his technique—the movement beyond the cathartic method—were not entirely based on questioning the use of suggestion. Indeed, he believes that "the cathartic method had already renounced suggestion" ("Freud's Psycho-Analytic Procedure", p. 250). The procedure of applying pressure to the forehead may not fundamentally be a technical artifice, one that serves as a provisional replacement for a technique that would be better adapted to the dynamics of transference and resistance. Instead, it is a permanent sign of Freud's desire to discover secrets and obtain confessions.

It would be going too far to claim that this was his preoccupation from the beginning of his analytic work to the end. It is the case, however, that analytic treatment at that time was modelled on an interrogation; the latter, however, has little in common with a police interrogation since, as we know, the patient is asked to say not just what she knows but also, and more importantly, what she does not know ("The Question of Lay Analysis", p. 189). This supposition that the other possesses knowledge may be what best defines his relation to the hysteric at this time. For the psychoanalyst, the patient is a subject supposed to know, and his desire is to pierce through to the mystery beyond the wall of language.

This identification of the unconscious with a knowledge that does not know itself leads to a practice that directs patients to reveal a secret. Freud promises to disclose his patients' objects of desire to them by unveiling this secret. In other words, during this period, he equates the unconscious with a knowledge about jouissance that had been barred by repression, and from which he intends to disencumber the subject. "Psycho-analysis is seeking to bring to conscious recognition the things in mental life that are repressed" ("Five Lectures", p. 39).

The following formula may consequently be applied to the *Studies*: "Man's desire is the desire of the Other". We know that, for Lacan, it was the experience with hysterics that proves this expression to be justified, for according to the hysteric, human desire locates desire in the place of an object, which implies two consequences:

1. Her desire remains unsatisfied, since it is not her own desire that she is seeking to satisfy by means of what is often called her "intrigue". It is according to the determination by the genitive that we should understand Lacan's formula: her object is her father's desire.
2. The second meaning of the phrase exceeds the use of the genitive. It refers to the desire of the Other, insofar as this desire originates in the place of the Other. The intervention of a third party is determinant here. It should be noted that only a signifier can produce this effect: it starts at the place of the little other and creates a symbolic position there. For example, while it is clear that Dora is interested in a man because of his desire for a woman, the essence of her intrigue is intended to maintain the man's desire. This desire is not just any man's desire, but her father's—although any man can occupy this place if he desires a woman other than herself.

I shall not develop this point further, but will apply the formula to the question of Freud's desire, whose structure we perceive in his wished-for organization of things, to which his first patients lent themselves so willingly. It is worth noting that, without forcing the interpretation of his texts, the hysteric directs and realizes Freud's desire, at least in the first sense given to the formula. As has often been remarked, what Freud's patients say is not interpreted, for it is not yet the aim of cathartic treatment at this stage to reveal a hidden sexual meaning, but simply to bring out a knowledge that only the hysteric possesses. It appears, indeed, that Freud's hysterical patients' submission to his procedure realizes this desire just as well. Freud's desire does not precede the establishment of the analytic procedure, but rather reveals itself as an unconscious desire through his patients' confessions and resistance.

Freud's insistence that his hysterical patients recall a scene of seduction shows that the major indices of desire are to be found essentially in moments of resistance. This reminds us of Lacan's commentary on the relations between Breuer and Anna O ...: "Why is it that we do not consider Bertha's pregnancy, rather, according to my formula man's desire is the desire of the Other, as the manifestation of Breuer's desire?" (*Seminar XI*, pp. 157–158).

If the above formula is applied to Freud's analytic treatments, then what he hears is exactly what he has been wanting to hear: the seduction scene, as a real element that has been waiting to be unveiled, comes right on cue. It can easily be observed how sexuality enters the analytic scene: through the "original sin", according to Lacan, of Freud's desire:

> So hysteria places us, I would say, on the track of some kind of original sin in analysis. There has to be one. The truth is perhaps simply one thing, namely, the desire of Freud himself, the fact that something, in Freud, was never analyzed. (*Seminar XI*, p. 12)

Far from considering that this desire infects psychoanalysis with an historical or psychological relativity that would destroy its theoretical purity, I shall argue, on the contrary, that psychoanalysis would be nothing without it. The entire Freudian field must accept this heritage. Lacan adds:

> I have said that the Freudian field of analytic practice remained dependent on a certain original desire, which always plays an ambiguous, but dominant role in the transmission of psychoanalysis. The problem of this desire is not psychological, any more than is the unsolved problem of Socrates' desire. (*Seminar XI*, p. 13)

Therefore, just as Breuer's desire for a child impregnated Bertha, so too was it in response to Freud's desire as master that the hysterics gave their confessions to Freud, confessions that could be called "seduction", "trauma", the "bad encounter", or the fright produced by sexuality (see Melman, "*À propos des Études sur l'hystérie*").

A desire to know, therefore, manifests itself in a lack of satisfaction, a lack that takes the form of never obtaining the final word about a history whose storyline becomes ever more complicated the more Freud tries to pick out the thread that would link all its scenes together.

Freud's curiosity, eagerness, and insatiable demand, which inevitably leaves him hungry for more, are, indeed, indicated on one occasion, by a patient, Emmy von N, who has been infuriated by his talkativeness: "I requested her to remember by tomorrow. She then said in a definitely grumbling tone that I was not to keep on asking her where this and that came from, but to let her tell me what she had to say. I fell in with this" (*Studies on Hysteria*, p. 63).

By putting Freud in his place, Emmy actually gives him a place that he has not himself invented: that of the psychoanalyst. Furthermore, in teaching him how to be quiet, she unwittingly points to what, unknown to him, has triggered his burning, indiscreet, and insatiable curiosity: his own unknown desire.[1]

Note

1. It is not possible to locate this displaced desire, and Freud's later formula would particularly apply to himself: "Thus past, present and future are strung together, as it were, on the thread of the wish that runs through them" ("Creative Writers and Day-Dreaming", p. 148, emphasis added).

CHAPTER THREE

Between two passions:
the real and the signifier

The abandonment of hypnosis in 1896,[1] following the discovery of resistance, led Freud to go beyond the ideology of the secret and the confession, neither of which had always been extorted without violence.

The arbitrary character of interpretation, and even suggestion pure and simple, become most apparent in Freud's revelation to Elisabeth von R: "She cried aloud when I put the situation drily before her with the words: 'So, for a long time you had been in love with your brother-in-law.'" (*Studies on Hysteria*, p. 157). At about the same time, Freud also gives up his "neurotica"[2]— his theory of trauma—in favour of the Oedipus complex and infantile sexuality. The abandonment of these two theories is a turning point in the progress of his discoveries, but it also means that Freud's desire and psychoanalysis were now linked in a common orientation towards a real that is independent of facts and events. It is this change in perspective that I wish to illustrate.

From one secret to another

From the moment when the theory of the phantasy takes over from that of the trauma, the real is no longer considered to be the actual.

This shift—which, in fact, hardly alters the role played by seduction (see *The Wolf Man*)—now becomes another secret, and behind the mask, there is another mask. This process of looking further and further back in search of the event—the primal scene—thus has an historical thrust:

> One was drawn further and further back into the past; one hoped at last to be able to stop at puberty, the period in which the sexual impulses are traditionally supposed to awake. But in vain; the tracks led still further back into childhood and into its earlier years. (*On the History of the Psycho-Analytic Movement*, p. 16)

Thus Freud is led to pay attention to the traumatic scenes recounted by his patients. Yet, once again, the real becomes suspect: "If hysterical subjects trace back their symptoms to traumas that are fictitious, then the new fact which emerges is precisely that they create such scenes in *phantasy*, and this psychical reality requires to be taken into account alongside practical reality" (pp. 17–18). Why do the narrative, the fictional account now acquire a supplementary truth-value and why do they become the indices of a real that is to be discovered? What is implausible becomes the index of the real for Freud, who has been "helplessly bewildered" by this discovery; for him, "the firm ground of reality was gone" (p. 17).

At this point, Freud, tired of waiting for a confession that was taking too long in coming, takes the risk of making a false construction by presenting his theory of infantile masturbation to Dora, a theory that would remain his primal scene until his analysis of the Wolf Man, and which would attract his curiosity in relation to any question connected with infantile sexuality. "This reflection was soon followed by the discovery that these phantasies were intended to cover up the auto-erotic activity of the first years of childhood, to embellish it and to raise it to a higher plane" (p. 18).

It is clear that, at the time of his letters to Fliess, Freud was looking for a "suitable point of attack" in order to reconsider his theory of sexuality. His analysis of dreams had made this reformulation necessary. In his book on dreams, as in his letters to Fliess, his concern was only to identify "early sexual incidents" or "events occurring between the ages of one and a half and four years", or between four and eight (letter 52) in obsessional neurosis and paranoia; once he abandons his theory of trauma, however, his orientation changes. Thus, concerning the choice of neuroses, he believed until 1897 that it depended on the age at which a trauma had occurred. Next, he considers that much deeper layers or "sexual phases"[3] are involved.

The concept of depth always designates a temporal dimension in Freud's work: through the phantasy, one reaches a history that must be reconstituted down to its smallest details, and then, beyond this history, there is a real, on the basis of which the law of repetition functions. With regard to this passion for the real, Lacan writes that Freud

> … applies himself, in a way that can almost be described as anguish, to the question—what is the first encounter, the real, that lies behind the phantasy? We feel that throughout this analysis [that of the Wolf Man], this real brings with it the subject, almost by force, so directing the research that, after all, we can today ask ourselves whether this fever, this presence, this desire of Freud is not that which, in his patient, might have conditioned the belated accident of his psychosis. (*Seminar XI*, p. 54)

Freud's passion for the real leads him, as we shall see, to conclude that "an inherited constitution" exists (*On the History of the Psycho-Analytic Movement*, p. 18). Thus does the real of jouissance irrupt, beyond the series of supposed traumas, and it becomes the guiding principle of Freud's technique for deciphering the unconscious.

On love declarations or the secret of masturbation

In *Dora*, Freud writes that "I believe that Dora only wanted to play 'secrets' with me, and to hint that she was on the point of allowing her secret to be torn from her by the doctor" (*Dora*, p. 78). Freud's intention is to relate both her hysterical symptoms and her contempt for doctors to yet another secret, which she has also kept from herself:

> The reproaches against her father for having made her ill, together with the self-reproach underlying them, the leucorrhoea, the playing with the reticule, the bed-wetting after her sixth year, the secret which she would not allow the doctors to tear from her—the circumstantial evidence of her having masturbated in childhood seems to me complete and without a flaw. (*Dora*, p. 78)

Freud's obstinate attempt to impute most of her symptoms to masturbation does not conform entirely to observation and he constructs the neurotic's history, as he always does during this period, by privileging object relations over identifications. For example, with regard to her brother's role in transmitting disease, he says:

> Dora's brother must have been concerned in some way with her having acquired the habit of masturbation; for in this connection she told me, with all the emphasis which betrays the presence of a "screen memory", that her brother used regularly to pass on all his infectious illnesses to her. (*Dora*, p. 82, note 1)

Freud uses the term "screen memory" to refer to a deformation of memory or even to a phantasy, one that is meant to "hide" something that has been repressed. He thus, once again, uses the model of a secret, one that is betrayed by speech. There is no need, however, to look beyond speech—in this case, Dora's speech about her illnesses—for the truth revealed by the analogy in question. Freud makes conclusions about Dora's masturbation from her account of her "identification" with a cousin who suffered from gastric pains. "Dora gave me two facts from her conscious knowledge: she herself had frequently suffered from gastric pains, and she had good reasons for believing that her cousin was a masturbator" (*Dora*, p. 79). A bit earlier, we have learned that her identification with her cousin is based on love affairs involving not just one but two of her female cousins, and two men: in one case their love was happy, in the other, unhappy. The cousin who has seen the other's successful marriage suffers from stomach aches. Freud, at this point, only concludes that an imaginary identification is at work: "Whom are you copying now?" (*Dora*, p. 38).

He later "forgets" this symbolic element, however, on drawing the equation: gastric pains = masturbation. The point here is not that he was wrong, but that he gives up just as much from his hypothesis of masturbation as he gains. His obsession with masturbation blinds him to everything else, particularly to the two types of identification that he has been able to distinguish but cannot conceptualize: first, copying or imitating a model—Dora's father, her brother, or her cousin—as love-objects, and second, identification with the desire of the other, as in the case of her cousin's unhappy love.

It is, without doubt, Fliess's model of bisexuality that Freud is again putting to the test, and this model hides Dora's masculine identification from him. In a letter to Fliess about her, he writes that "… the principal issue in the conflicting thought processes is the contrast between an inclination toward men and an inclination toward women" (Masson, p. 434). It is obvious to us now, however, that the object of her inclination was woman, and that she liked to create a romantic novel, a love story, concerning the relations between men and women.

Freud, who notes that Dora "had been able to keep abreast with her brother" until her first illness, claims that she was able to embark upon the "normal" path of femininity once asthma had replaced incontinence: "After the 'asthma' she became quiet and well-behaved. That illness formed the boundary between two phases of her sexual life, of which the first was masculine in character, and the second feminine" (*Dora*, p. 82, note 1).

If, following Lacan, however, one emphasizes the hysteric's masculine identification—more precisely, her identification with the unary trait of the ego ideal—one can see that Dora's master signifier is the impotent father, while her symptoms point to his phallic deficiency. It seems, indeed, that all her symptoms, those of her childhood as well as those of her present illness, inscribe phallic jouissance on her body. Freud, however, in attempting to account for her persistent masturbation, simply uses her leucorrhoea as proof of the latter; the signifier "wet" supposedly confirms the connection between masturbation and incontinence.

> Dora knew that there was a kind of getting wet involved in sexual intercourse, and that during the act of copulation the man presented the woman with something liquid *in the form of drops*. She also knew that the danger lay precisely in that, and that it was her business to protect her genitals from being moistened. (*Dora*, p. 90)

Might we not rather say that it was an attempt by Dora to symbolize the feminine sexual organ? In her first dream, her sexual organ, which cannot be named immediately, is represented only by metaphors of waste and stains, thus showing the imaginary effect of castration on a girl who can only cathect her sexual organ if it has been cut off from any symbolic trait.

Freud's technique should therefore be considered, within the general perspective of his theory of hysteria, as a defence against sexuality. To list the "sum of his prejudices" in this context would lead us, however, to question his conception of femininity and would involve a number of other developments. Freud himself recognizes that the interest of the case lies less in his account of Dora's analytic work than in the light that it casts on the relation between symptoms and structure. As a consequence, except in the case of dreams—and in a very few other places—he does not unveil the technique used in their analytic work: "My object in this case history was to demonstrate the intimate structure of a neurotic disorder and the determination of its symptoms" (*Dora*, p. 13).

The direction of the treatment is clearly a direct consequence of this claim. One must, of course, not forget, during this period—in 1900—Freud had only just established the sexual aetiology of neurosis. His first article dealing in depth with this question only dates from 1898.[4] *Dora* was published in 1905, and thus provided some of the key observations that premised his *Three Essays*.

The practice of the letter in Dora

Freud occasionally refers to his *Three Essays on the Theory of Sexuality* in *Dora*. This book and *The Interpretation of Dreams* are the two theoretical pillars whose hypotheses are put to the test in this particular case of hysteria. The presentation, in this case history, of the ideas developed in these books is not, however, absolutely exact, since these three works were not written at the same time. While a part of *The Interpretation of Dreams* was written during Dora's analysis, an account of which could have figured as one of its chapters, the *Three Essays* were written and published in 1905.

These temporal coordinates are important for understanding both the trajectory that Freud intended to pursue and his particular method of demonstration. Two axes, which connect at certain points are emphasized: the *referential axis* and the *axis of the letter*. This terminology establishes two places: on the one hand, that of the signification of symptoms and, on the other, that of the dream text, whose key is the phantasy. The two modes of interpretation in question are not, however, situated at the same level.

Deciphering dreams allows Freud, who takes non-sense as his starting point, to isolate the over-determination of the text, its variety of meanings. Then, at another stage, he enables the multiple meanings of a symptom to coincide with the different unconscious phantasies that underlie and support it. This task, of course, requires the patient to follow the rule of free association, which was not yet the case for

Dora. She does, admittedly, choose to pursue her analytic work on an everyday basis, but the rule of free association has not yet been formulated as such.

Freud now no longer takes the analysis of the symptom as the goal of analysis:

> At that time the work of analysis started out from the symptoms, and aimed at clearing them up one after the other. Since then I have abandoned that technique, because I found it totally inadequate for dealing with the finer structure of a neurosis. I now let the patient himself choose the subject of the day's work, and in that way I start out from whatever surface his unconscious happens to be presenting to his notice at the moment. (*Dora*, p. 12)

He then concludes: "But on this plan everything that has to do with the clearing-up of a particular symptom emerges piecemeal, woven into various contexts, and distributed over widely separated periods of time" (*Dora*, p. 12).

Freud considers the dream to be a scene that provides a simultaneous inscription of all the layers of "superimposed" meanings—to employ the expression used in *The Interpretation of Dreams*—that a "symbol" has had since childhood (p. 376). The function of the signifier can be recognized through its ability to lend itself to equivocation. The unconscious, in playing upon the equivocation, also acts to fix the meaning of the signifier.

This is the case, for example, in the case of the signifier "wet", the meaning of which varies according to the "period" in which the subject employs the term: sometimes, if it is connected to enuresis, it is the equivalent of masturbation, and sometimes the equivalence between white discharge and sperm points to an identification with a man. Freud, as ever the conscientious archaeologist, collects together elements that could, one piece at a time, like a jigsaw puzzle, disclose the outline of the phantasy and the signifying chains that compose it. He emphasizes the innovative nature of this conception in the following terms:

> According to a rule which I had found confirmed over and over again by experience, though I had not yet ventured to erect it into a general principle, a symptom signifies the representation—the realization—of a phantasy with a sexual content, that is to say, it

signifies a sexual situation. It would be better to say that at least *one* of the meanings of a symptom is the representation of a sexual phantasy, but that no such limitation is imposed upon the content of its other meanings. (*Dora*, pp. 46–47)

Since the symptom is thus intrinsically bound to a phantasy, the best means for decrypting it is through the dream, the royal road to the unconscious. In other words, if a symptom can be decrypted like a dream, it is because it has a number of meanings—not because it is hiding a secret.

Freud's preoccupation is thus no longer with extracting a secret. On the one hand, he now admits that unconscious insincerity is more important than conscious insincerity, and that a gap in memory or a modification in chronological order point to a structure or labour of forgetting, the key to which is not in the subject's possession. Now more than ever, Freud, the decipherer of enigmas, becomes destined to take on the role of Oedipus.

The referential axis, on the other hand, is established in the *Three Essays*, and leads to the theory of the Oedipus complex, which closes this work. Hysteria, as Freud remarks in *Dora*, remains "as great a puzzle as ever" (*Dora*, p. 24). What does this mean and how is this enigma to be resolved?

Let us put forward the following hypothesis: Freud was disappointed by the mediocre results of his therapeutic work with hysterics. Indeed, he tells us that, before discarding the theory of seduction, he often fell into complete confusion. He is then oriented towards the love lives of children by his own self-analysis. Next, he obtains results that connect the sexual life of children with the figure of the father, which will clearly mark his reflections at the end of the *Three Essays on the Theory of Sexuality*. Neurotics "are *in love* with [...] these blood-relations of theirs" (p. 228); this conclusion is precisely what was lacking in the *Studies*, a lack that had made his theory of trauma unsatisfactory. It is without any doubt the not-very-distant echo of Dora's recent analysis that enables Freud to write that "In cases in which someone who has previously been healthy falls ill after an unhappy experience in love it is also possible to show with certainty that the mechanism of his illness consists in a turning-back of his libido onto those whom he preferred in his infancy" (*Three Essays*, p. 228).

The ending of the *Three Essays* is concerned with incest and the "after-effects of infantile object-choice" (see pp. 228–229). Freud's intention is to separate these effects from their causes, and, in Dora's case, he makes all her phantasies converge on her incestuous love for her father. The sole purpose of his long detour through infantile sexuality is to demonstrate that primal object choice persists after an unhappy love experience.

Freud then attempts to solder onto the oral phase of sexuality the repression of genital sexuality that is manifest in the young woman: "Instead of the genital sensation which would certainly have been felt by a healthy girl in such circumstances, Dora was overcome by the unpleasurable feeling which is proper to the tract of mucous membrane at the entrance to the alimentary canal—that is by disgust" (*Dora*, p. 29). Here, Freud assumes from the beginning the theory he wants to prove: the principle of a "reversal of affect" and a "displacement of feeling". According to him, disgust is a negative pleasure, one that cannot be felt as such. He later says the same thing of phobias (see *Beyond the Pleasure Principle*).

The repression of genitality leads to the eroticization of the mouth, and Dora's symptoms are said to symbolize an oral satisfaction related to sucking. Lacan, on the other hand, argues that disgust is a desexualization that occurs when "the sexual object moves towards the side of reality" (*Seminar XI*, p. 172). For Lacan, "It is precisely to the extent that adjoining, connected zones are excluded that others take on their erogenous function and become specific sources for the drive" (*Seminar XI*, p. 172).

Freud attempts here, in a confused way, to show the oral drive's dependence on genital sensation. By means of the mechanism of displacement, the oral drive migrates: the genital sensation is 1) displaced and then 2) reversed. This, however, is an obsessional rather than a hysterical mechanism, since in this case repression of sexuality is far from perfect.

What Freud does not wish to say is that the hysteric feels real disgust for sexuality; the displacement of sexual energy from one zone to another—from the clitoris to the mouth or the throat—does not shed any light on the question of disgust itself. The lack of sexual satisfaction appears in the place of the failure of the sexual relation.

We thus have two models at our disposal: the Freudian model of a displacement of sensation, which implies that the latter had once existed, and the Lacanian model of something that takes the place of the lacking sexual relation. What the hysteric translates as (oral) disgust is her impossibility of experiencing jouissance as long as she is "in love with" her father (*Dora*, p. 57). If Freud's desire is to enable the hysteric to recognize the object of her desire, then it turns out, as later results would show, that he has lost his way. In situating the love for the father as the origin of repression, however, he is erring in the right direction.

This passion for the signifier, however, clearly had its drawbacks. The therapeutic descent into hell leads either to an impasse—a limit— or to an asymptotic conclusion to treatment.[5] A patient's secret is only partially disclosed. The succession of scenes related by a patient reveals a sameness that, in its very repetition from scene to scene, *insists*, without there being any jettisoning of the ballast of the real from this very repetition.

Freud was clearly seeking something beyond the knot of signifiers. Introducing a cut, which would not be located in the symbolic, but which would, instead, have an object as its stake, would, however, have meant eliminating the conception of transference as an obstacle, and Freud would therefore have had to situate himself as an object *a* in the treatment. When interpretation is made simply in terms of either the signifier or sexual meaning, the real is not brought into play.

The dichotomy of the signifier and the object of desire relativizes the objection that is made about Freud, and for which he also reproached himself: that he had misunderstood the nature of the transference. What I hope to throw light on is the way in which this stumbling block of transference was itself related to the place that that he himself occupied in it.

Notes

1. "The history of psycho-analysis proper, therefore, only begins with the new technique that dispenses with hypnosis" (*On the History of the Psycho-Analytic Movement*, p. 16).
2. Until 1897, Freud uses this term to designate his conception of sexual trauma as caused by seduction in early childhood. See the letter of 21 September 1897 in *The Complete Letters of Sigmund Freud to Wilhelm Fliess* (pp. 264–266).
3. For example, see the discussion of auto-eroticism in the *Five Lectures on Psycho-Analysis*, pp. 42–48.
4. See S. Freud, *Sexuality in the Aetiology of the Neurosis*.
5. In his letters to Fliess, Freud refers at length to the eventful treatment of the case of Herr E .... He mentions for the first time "the asymptotic conclusion of the treatment" to which, as such, he is quite indifferent (Masson, p. 409).

CHAPTER FOUR

On Freud's transference

L acan states in *Seminar I* that Freud tried to mould Dora's ego (p. 184), and in the *Écrits* he describes her negative transference as a response to Freud's countertransference (p. 183). This is a mirror relation because Freud, misunderstanding Dora's masculine identification, favours this dual relation in his treatment. He is not yet aware of the distinction, which he would make later, between the object of love and the object of identification. If he fails to understand the object of Dora's desire—let's call her Frau K—it is because of the prejudice, which was not peculiar to him, that "girls like boys".

More deeply, one can observe that if Freud considers Dora's obvious interest in Herr K as proof of her undeclared love, it is only because her masculine identifications have escaped his notice. His insufficient understanding of Dora's "homosexual" relation and his error concerning the nature of the transference amount to the same thing, so that his "counter-transference" results from his misunderstanding of the hysteric's desire. Indeed, by "forcing the call for love onto the object of identification" (*Écrits*, p. 534)—in Dora's case Herr K—Freud actually misunderstands several things.

It is important, in this context, to distinguish between error and prejudice. Concerning Dora, Lacan writes that "When the analyst's biases (that is, his countertransference, a term whose correct use, in my view, cannot be extended beyond the dialectical reasons for his error) have misled him in his intervention, he immediately pays a price for it in the form of a negative transference" (*Écrits*, p. 252).

It is precisely the relation between these two forms of transference that we propose to examine.

Let us now reverse these positions and assume that Freud supposes in Dora the existence of a knowledge of his own unconscious. What, then, does Freud know and what does he want? In Lacan's opinion, "It is because he put himself rather too much in Herr K's shoes that Freud did not succeed in moving the Infernal Regions this time around" (*Écrits*, p. 182).

This statement should be considered in the light of another observation: because Dora identifies with a man—Herr K—she is also able to identify with Freud. This is why Lacan could observe that Freud's error about the smell of smoke does not point to a love relation in which Dora sees the two men—who were both smokers—as a matched set, by whom she wanted to be kissed. Instead, the smell designates the unary trait, which although meaningless in itself, supports her masculine identification. The smell of smoke is a trait common to three people: her father, as Dora herself points out, Herr K, and Freud (*Dora*, p. 73).

Lacan concludes from this that Dora's olfactory hallucination on waking up, rather than indicating an infantile oral demand, points to the "twilight stage of the return to the ego" (*Écrits*, p. 181). Does Freud, then, play no role in producing this effect? Once again, one can see that Freud's whole account is governed by a law—the law of his desire—that predestines the feminine creature to what is good for her.

Further still, if an hysteric's masculine identification—the (imaginary) matrix of which for Dora lies in her identification with her elder brother—does not correspond to any form of constitutional bisexuality, one can say that at this date (in 1900), Freud's view is still way off the mark.

Prejudices, however, are not necessarily errors, as Freud himself teaches us in *The Future of an Illusion*.[1] Where a desire prevails, misconceptions regarding a particular structure cannot simply be shed when new discoveries are made, especially in relation to the "dark continent". This is why the importance of the homosexual connection, which he finally accepts in 1925, does not deal a blow to Freud's construction of the Oedipus complex; this is the case because he does not yet recognize that the primordial object for both sexes is the mother, and that in the case of little girls, the father holds a symbolic rather than an imaginary place, as he does for little boys.

In his "Presentation on Transference", Lacan puts forward an interpretation of Freud's desire that is clarified by his later theory that "There is no sexual relation": "I would say that this has to be ascribed to a bias, the very same bias that is expressed simply in the well-known refrain, "Thread is to needle as girl is to boy" (*Écrits*, p. 182).

Lacan, at the time, points out that this observation implicates Freud in a fashion that "brings the whole case alive in a way which, vaulting the theoretical digressions, elevates this text, among the psycho-pathological monographs that constitute a genre in our literature, to the tone of a Princesse de Clèves bound by an infernal gag" (*Écrits*, p. 182). Today, however, one cannot be contented with an estimate founded on the predominant role played by Freud's countertransference, which would be based on his presumed sympathy for Herr K, and which would supposedly have led him to dream of the "victory of love" (*Écrits*, p. 182).[2]

What is essential, I believe, lies instead in Freud's theory of the Oedipus complex, which makes the vicissitudes of the drives depend on the desire for the father, rather than on the desire *of* the father, to which Dora, however, has sacrificed her masculine object. Freud is not yet able to demonstrate that the hysteric can be interested in the relation between a man and a woman provided that she slip away from it as object, to the detriment of her desire for a sexual partner.

The sum of Freud's prejudices

In order to relate the hysteric's discourse to Freud's desire, we can reverse the terms of the relation; if the modulations in the transference can be deciphered in terms of Freud's countertransference, nothing prevents us from correlating the variations and modulations in Dora's transference with Freud's desire to convince her. Let us posit that Freud's desire was homogeneous with his interpretation of the transference, the obstacle that will break the analysis: "I will attempt," says Lacan, "*to define in terms of pure dialectic the transference* that is said to be negative on the part of the subject as the doing [operation] of the analyst who interprets it" (*Écrits*, p. 178).

If one supposes, furthermore, that a certain "transference love" is established in this relation, then Freud's mistake is to break it off for reasons that are no more rooted in affect than is the transference itself. His error lies in not distinguishing the love-object from the object of identification—in slipping from an imaginary identification to a symbolic identification. The latter extends beyond the person's narcissistic interests, from which love and hate spring, and points to a place from which he can perceive himself as being loveable and can identify with signifiers that, according to Lacan, result in the formation of the ego ideal.

Dora's masculine identification in no way implies that she is in love with Herr K, but only that he takes up the position of a master who does not renounce his desire; she can identify with him on the condition that she is not his object. It is thus his desire, rather than his person, that she loves. In his "Presentation on Transference", Lacan explains that Herr K plays the role of ego for Dora: the masculine image through which, by playing the part of the man, she is able to accomplish two objectives. She can both attempt to symbolize an exit from the Oedipus complex through an identification with the ideal, and also stand up to men in an imaginary rivalry, one that expresses her rage at being a love object and a phallic signifier.

At the same time as she sustains her own desire as unsatisfied, she also calls upon the man to desire the woman who contains "the mystery of [her] own femininity": Frau K, who is her love object by proxy, since Dora works to procure her for her own father, whose desire she sustains through her intrigues (*Écrits*, p. 180). Herr K then upsets the equilibrium and provokes passionate protests, which Dora makes while occupying her father's place. Herr K allows Dora to understand that he has sacrificed his wife to her father in exchange for Dora herself. Her rage at being thus treated as an object of an "odious exchange" leads to the memorable slap that she gives him (*Écrits*, p. 178).

Freud's error concerning Herr K's place proves to be the stumbling block that puts an end to the analysis. The basis of this error is his prejudice that girls are supposed to love boys. There is a big difference, however, between taking a certain amount of time to realize that "homosexuality" is the stronger tendency in the young woman, and failing to differentiate between two types of identification, one of which excludes desire. It is the hysteric's masculine identification that bars the road to sexual love for her. Freud develops this point in the

1920s, particularly in chapter VII of his *Group Psychology*, in which he distinguishes between the two forms of identification.

Dora's identification with the man's desire, and indeed, identification with it insofar as it is an impotent, and thus impossible, desire, is expressed by her cough and her dyspnoea, which commemorate her father's jouissance. Her aphonia, meanwhile, clearly indicates the place Herr K occupies in her phantasy. Freud tells us that that when the latter is absent, Dora's symptoms, especially her aphonia, return. The oral drive is particularly intense when Dora is alone with Frau K. In other words, her aphonia mimes a cunnilingus with her father's mistress. She takes Herr K's place when he is away.

We can guess, in retrospect, that Dora's interest in Herr K is not a "true love" but is instead a point of hysterical identification, from which she could perceive Frau K as desirable; in other words, it operates as a signifier. If Freud's prejudice concerning a woman's relation with a man is now emphasized, one can then ask what his main illusion is and what his biggest mistake is.

Both of them can be found in his statement that Dora is in love with Herr K (*Dora*, p. 39). His mistake, as we have seen, concerns the identity of the person involved, especially since, as he knows, the object in question is actually Frau K. Behind this error is a prejudice: that there is a sexual relation between girls and boys, and beyond even this prejudice lies the fact that his Oedipal theory takes it for granted—rather than considering it a norm—that girls love their fathers. To quote Lacan: "I would say that this has to be ascribed to a bias, the very same bias that falsifies the conception of the Oedipus complex right from the outset, making him consider the predominance of the paternal figure to be natural, rather than normative" (*Écrits*, p. 182).

Freud considered the "early partiality [...] on the part of a daughter for her father, or on the part of a son for his mother" to be self-evident, and was thus in line with the orthodox position, one that his theory of sexuality would subsequently counter; to do so, however, he would first have to recognize the complexity of the girl's Oedipus complex and its lack of symmetry with the boy's (*Dora*, p. 12). Freud's theoretical resistance can therefore be measured in terms of the time he takes to understand that a girl's Oedipal phase must be considered in relation to the acquisition of the phallic signifier, of which her mother has frustrated her and which she must seek elsewhere (see "Female Sexuality").

Freud's resistance

Lacan explains that Freud takes up the case of Dora:

> ... on the plane of what he himself calls resistance. What does that
> mean? I have already explained it to you. It is absolutely obvious
> that Freud brings into play his *ego*, the conception he himself has
> of what girls are made for—a girl is made to love boys. (*Seminar I*,
> p. 184)

In an age when the analysis of resistance had become a paragon of analytic technique, Lacan turned the tables by focusing on the analyst's
resistance, rather than on the patient's.

Thus, the love for Herr K, which Freud imputes to Dora, becomes
the object of "violent feelings of opposition" and he adds that "Dora
persisted in denying my contention for some time longer, until, towards
the end of the analysis, the conclusive proof of its correctness came to
light" (*Dora*, pp. 58–59).

Freud thus situates himself as the master of truth, and he thereby
prevents Dora from recognizing that Frau K is the object of her desire.

Lacan suggests that instead of "putting his own *ego* into play with
the aim of remoulding, of modelling that of Dora", Freud could have
shown her that "it was Frau K whom she loved" (*Seminar I*, p. 184).

Lacan's hypothesis leads us to think that if Freud had done so, the
transference relation would have been changed radically: the truth-effect
produced by such an intervention would have given Freud the very prestige that she puts to a harsh test, so that the reversal of the sign that the
transference has taken on—its positive or negative character—depends
on the interpretation of the cause of desire. Lacan, accordingly, asks:

> If, therefore, in a third dialectical reversal, Freud had directed Dora
> towards a recognition of what Frau K was for her, by getting her to
> confess the deepest secrets of their relationship, couldn't that have
> contributed to his prestige (I am merely touching on the meaning of
> positive transference here), opening up a pathway to her recogni-
> tion of the virile object? (*Écrits*, p. 181)

In his 1923 note, Freud tells us that "Before I had learnt the importance
of the homosexual current of feeling in psychoneurotics, I was often
brought to a standstill in the treatment of my cases or found myself
in complete perplexity" (*Dora*, p. 120, note 1). Had he detected this

"strongest unconscious current in her mental life", he feels, the outcome would have been different. Dora would not have taken her revenge on him as she did with Herr K. Her acting out is thus a consequence of Freud's ignorance on this matter.

According to Lacan, "This is how theory translates the way in which resistance is engendered in practice. It is also what I am trying to convey when I say that there is no other resistance to analysis than that of the analyst himself" (Écrits, p. 497).

Freud thus mistakenly accuses Dora of resisting, showing thereby that he is unaware of his own resistance, which is an effect of his own incomprehension; these are the terms by which he himself generally qualifies resistance to psychoanalysis: "There is only one resistance, the resistance of the analyst" (Seminar II, p. 228).

Lacan says in his "Presentation on Transference" that transference is "nothing real in the subject if not the appearance, at a moment of stagnation in the analytic dialectic, of the permanent modes according to which she constitutes her objects" (Écrits, pp. 183–184). This statement shows us how Freud encourages Dora's "aggressiveness" by not understanding the true motivation of her relation to men: an imaginary identification structuring her narcissistic relation. Lacan's formula can also, however, be applied to resistance, which has nothing to do with what is real in the subject, but is an effect of interpretation. There is only one resistance because there is only one transference.

Lacan reverses the order of the relation between transference and interpretation that was commonly accepted in the 1960s (see Lebovici et al.). "The problem", he says, "is that contemporary authors seem to have gotten the sequence of analytic effects backward. According to them, interpretation is but hesitant stammering compared to the opening up of a broader relationship in which, at last, we understand each other ('from the inside', no doubt)" (Écrits, p. 497).

In other words, transference does not ensure "the analyst's security", on the basis of which any possible interpretation could be made. Once the transference has been established it ought not to "[serve] as an alibi for a sort of revenge the analyst takes for his initial timidity, that is, for an insistence that opens the door to all kinds of forcing, placed under the banner of 'strengthening the ego'" (Écrits, p. 498).

This statement should, of course, be considered in the context in which it was made. It nevertheless sheds light on Freud's divergence from such an option, as well as on what, in his technique, leads to this theoretical aim. In Freud's style of intervention with Dora, it is noteworthy that his interpretations create an obstacle to a positive transference, for they favour the dual relation. In attempting to put Dora on the right track, Freud only fuels her desire for vengeance, a desire that is a consequence of her narcissistic alienation: her identification with Herr K and himself. Her negative transference is thus an effect of Freud's interpretation of the transference and is relative by it. "Desire, in fact, is interpretation itself" (*Seminar XI*, p. 176). We can therefore claim that Freud's desire coincides with his interpretation of the cause of desire; this is a more explicit formula than that of the countertransference. According to Lacan, "It has nothing to do with counter-transference on the part of this or that analyst; it has to do with the consequences of the dyadic relation, if the therapist does not overcome it, and how could he overcome it when he views it as the ideal of his action?" (*Écrits*, p. 498).

There is thus a complex combination of Freud's prejudices and errors, to which his theoretical inhibitions can be added; the latter can be seen, after the fact, to have arisen because his theory had progressed too slowly. It was not yet able to account for Dora's unconscious knowledge of the absence of a sexual relation.

Freud tells us that he did not discover the signs of the transference in time. Is there any need to emphasize that it is a question of a negative transference? In his words,

> I did not succeed in mastering the transference in good time. Owing to the readiness with which Dora put one part of the pathogenic material at my disposal during the treatment, I neglected the precaution of looking out for the first signs of transference, which was being prepared in connection with another part of the same material—a part of which I was in ignorance. (*Dora*, p. 118)

This "unknown factor" is the fact that Freud reminds Dora of Herr K (p. 119). As a result, she takes revenge on him, just as she has done on her father and on Herr K: out of scorn. All men are the same to her. The universal character of her revenge on men and her narcissistic rivalry with them reminds us of Lacan's reference to Freud's "all-mannishness" ("*touthommie*" in *L'étourdit*, p. 462). He is unable to make himself an exception to the negative transference and thereby to constitute himself as the "at least one" man who, by renouncing his position of mastery, could introduce her to the object of her desire.

Not all difficulties in handling the treatment, however, stem from the analyst's desire. Resistances are structural if they are the resistance of speech rather than of the subject's ill will.

The hysteric's displays of hostility and aggressiveness are reactions that are directed less towards the "person of the analyst", as Freud believes, than towards the signifier of the analyst to which his person gives consistency. To the extent that he wishes to cure or to acquire knowledge, the master reactivates the hysteric's castration; her purpose, in unleashing her aggressiveness on him, is to provoke him to desire and to love her because she is castrated.

This is why both negative transference and acting out implicate the psychoanalyst in his action, although in different ways. Indeed, to the extent that the analysis "has already led the subject toward an authentic recognition", the price to be paid will be all the greater if he makes a wrong interpretation (*Écrits*, p. 252). On the other hand, if the signifier of the analyst implies a desire to heal or even to save the subject, the response will be no better.

This is the case with the young female homosexual, who tries to capture Freud's desire by bringing him dreams that involve her in what she supposes to be *his* own phantasy; he does not, however, become her dupe.[3]

One ought therefore to bear in mind that a negative transference implies the subject's resistance to suggestion, rather than indicating any bad intention on her part. The latter conception, as we know, motivated the "analysis of resistances". The reason for the hysteric's mistrust[4] would eventually appear with the reactivation of the seduction scene; the treatment itself will come to mimic this scene when "the patient is seized by a dread of becoming too much accustomed to the physician personally, of losing her independence in relation to him, and even of perhaps becoming sexually dependent on him" (*Studies on Hysteria*, p. 302).

Freud admits to his disappointment in the following terms: "I do not know what kind of help she wanted from me, but I promised to forgive her for having deprived me of the satisfaction of affording her a far more radical cure for her troubles" (*Dora*, p. 122).

Making oneself the agent of the all-mighty, and thus reconciling the subject with her desire does not amount to not being the "at least one" man who could stand as the exception to the hysteric's general repulsion for men. Freud thus exposes himself to the aggressive after-effects of the indoctrination to which he generally subjects patients; he does so, with Dora, by "forcing the call for love onto the object of identification" and by giving solidity to a signifier (Herr K) whose role in supporting desire implies "the object's indifference" (*Écrits*, p. 534). The hysteric's "beautiful indifference" is therefore aimed at Freud's interpretation itself; by the same token, it annuls the signifier of the psychoanalyst, after Freud has implicated himself in the real by manoeuvring in such a way that she "disputed the fact no longer" (*Dora*, p. 104).

Freud's confusion of his person with the signifier of the analyst is even more evident in the case of the young female homosexual: "In reality she transferred to me the sweeping repudiation of men which had dominated her ever since the disappointment she had suffered from her father. Bitterness against men is as a rule easy to gratify upon the physician" ("Psychogenesis of a Case of Homosexuality", p. 164). When she later brings Freud dreams that are meant to deceive him, he concludes that "She intended to deceive me just as she habitually deceived her father" ("Psychogenesis of a Case of Homosexuality", p. 165).

Freud, it seems, believes that he is being targeted in the real: the person of the physician catalyses both his patient's scorn and her error: "The two intentions, to betray and to please her father, originated in the same complex" ("Psychogenesis of a Case of Homosexuality", p. 166).

Likewise, the female homosexual intends both to deceive and to please him; both of these intentions have an Oedipal source. The fact that he is her analyst does not provide her with a new signifier by which she can distinguish him from a "supposed" father, who wants to turn her away from her perversion. Freud, however, does perceive that the young girl has dreams *for* her analyst; she supposes in him the existence of the same desire that her father has. It is therefore justifiable to ask what role Freud is playing with this interpretative technique. In *Dora*, he declares that he is not playing a part:

> I have always avoided acting a part, and have contented myself with practising the humbler arts of psychology. In spite of every theoretical interest and of every endeavour to be of assistance as a physician, I keep the fact in mind that there must be some limits set to the extent to which psychological influence may be used, and I respect as one of these limits the patient's own will and understanding. (*Dora*, p. 109)

This is rather hard to believe. Later, while drinking to its dregs the bitter cup of his memories of his analyses of hysterics, Freud writes:

> [The patient] will of himself form such an attachment and link the doctor up with one of the imagos of people by whom he was accustomed to be treated with affection. It is certainly possible to forfeit this first success if from the start one takes up any standpoint other than one of sympathetic understanding, such as a moralising one, or if one behaves like a representative or advocate of some contending party —of the other member of a married couple, for instance. (pp. 139–140)

It is precisely because he does introduce himself as a third party into the real, however, that Freud lends substance to Dora's interpretation that all men are complicit in her father's betrayal.

This gives us the opportunity to clarify an idea: if the patient's desire gains consistency from encountering her analyst's desire, this can point to a convergence within the Freud/Dora couple: the failure of the sexual relation. Let's recall that Dora's main symptom was a series of "all-powerful"[5] ideas: the "incessant repetition of the same thoughts about her father's relations with Frau K" (*Dora*, p. 54).[6] The persistence of this idea can be attributed to the jouissance that the hysteric derives from the Other's (the woman's) knowledge about her father's jouissance. Freud, unbeknown to himself, pays the price for competing with the master of desire—the signifier of the neurotic—with which he identifies.

The obstacle of the "negative transference" reveals where Freud positions himself: in the place of the master of desire, who competes with a knowledge about sex that Dora possesses. Transference love is not lacking but does not develop as expected. Dora, Freud's object *a*, transforms him into a case.

Notes

1. "An illusion is not the same thing as an error; nor is it necessarily an error. […] We call a belief an illusion when a wish-fulfilment is a prominent factor in its motivation" (pp. 30–31).
2. In *Dora*, Freud notes that "Incapacity for meeting a *real* erotic demand is one of the most essential features of neurosis. Neurotics are dominated by the opposition between reality and phantasy. If what they long for

the most intensely in their phantasies is presented to them in reality, they none the less flee from it; and they abandon themselves to their phantasies the most readily where they need no longer fear to see them realised" (p. 110).

3. "For the young homosexual woman in the case of female homosexuality, he [Freud] sees the problem more clearly, but errs when he regards himself as the object aimed at in reality (*réel*) by the negative transference" (*Écrits*, p. 534).

4. In *Dora*, Freud recounts that Dora forgot to relate that she had smelled cigarette smoke upon awakening from a dream and that she refused Freud's interpretations of this element; the author seems to be referring to this in speaking of the "hysteric's mistrust" (see *Dora*, p. 73) (translator's note).

5. "*Überstarker*", "*überwertiger Gedanke*". See S. Freud, *G. W: V*, pp. 214–215.

6. There is an abundant literature on Freud and Dora. For example, see "*L'interruption de la cure*" in *La conclusion de la cure* and "*Problématique freudienne de la sortie d'analyse*" in *Comment finissent les analyses*.

CHAPTER FIVE

The case of Freud

If my argument is justified, then the unconscious that we have been encountering does not fit with Freud's description of it at the time. Indeed, his case histories, especially that of Dora, tell us that the unconscious can no longer be treated as an external and objectifiable object; if it is not an "internal" object that can be exhibited, or which can be transformed from potentiality into an act, this is because the analyst's act commits him to being a part of the phenomena of which his artifice is a product. Like the unconscious, the analyst is himself in a relation of internal exclusion to her object; in other words, there is no better illustration of the fact that the observer is himself a part of what he observes than the transference. This is the least we can say, considering that Freud always implicitly admits to his choices, preferences, and disappointments, with the result that his patients' responses, dreams, and transferences appear to have been prompted by his demand.[1]

The signifier of the analyst is already present in the hysteric's speech as soon as she opens her mouth, thus providing an opening for his finger either to open it more fully or to stop her from talking altogether. When Lacan writes that "the transference alone is an objection to intersubjectivity", this forces us to renounce any hope of establishing a dual relation, one in which two unconsciousnesses might interpret or homogeneously interpenetrate each other, thus rediscovering how to communicate (Lacan, *Proposition of 9 October 1967*, p. 4). If, on the other hand, a case is never external to the analyst who is relating it, this is because Freud's resistance to recognizing the object of desire defines precisely the structure of the unconscious. Indeed, if the psychoanalyst is included in the very "existence" of the unconscious, no text can illustrate Freud's relation to women more explicitly than *Dora* (Lacan, *Television*, p. 14).

It is not Freud's unconscious that is implicated here, but rather the negation of the unconscious, which, as he explains in 1914, "ignores contradiction" and is unaware of sexual difference. In Lacanian terms, there is no sexual relation in the unconscious. Freud, however, at least in this case, believes that there is a relation between men and women. To be more precise, this case indicates not so much that Freud's unconscious has a parasitic relation to Dora's own, but that his ego has intervened by idealizing Dora's sexual partner.

Jacques-Alain Miller has discussed this point in *"El caso Dora es también el caso Freud"* ("Dora's case is just as much Freud's case") (*Cinco Conferencias*, p. 85), and Octave Mannoni had already pointed out that Dora's first dream about a fire illustrates the fact that Freud was implicated both in her very act of saying (*les dires mêmes*) and in her unconscious formations (*Clefs pour l'imaginaire*, pp. 150–160). It is quite clear, especially in the light of Freud's later texts on femininity, that this case is also the case of the person relating it, in the context of Freud's relation to Woman, and despite the fact that he insists he is not "acting a part" (Dora, p. 109).

Freud's phallic cause

In the course of the stages that he desires to make Dora pass through, it becomes clear that Freud's interpretations concern the cause of desire: Herr K, as a substitute for the father. The fact that the hysteric supports this desire at the cost of her own lack of satisfaction does not escape Freud's notice, for contingent reasons. He does not, however, consider the question of the girl's castration complex at the time, since he assumes that girls had been castrated from the beginning. Lacan emphasizes this problem in the following terms: "Freud, for his part, takes off from his phallic cause, in order to deduce castration from it. Which does not take place without smudges that I am undertaking to mop up" ("The Other is Missing", p. 134).

Can we find traces of the stumbling block of castration in both Freud's patients' dreams and their interpretation? Castration gives Freud the wrong orientation, one in which woman "fits it to a 't'" ("*L'étourdit*", p. 465).

Early on, his patients' dreams reveal to Freud that the analyst is present in their speech. The case of the young female homosexual shows us that one dreams for one's analyst, and does so in order to deceive his desire, which she equates with a demand to change her behaviour. According to Freud, the signifier of the analyst, if it must be distinguished from his person, is always a desiring subject, a "subject supposed to desire" (See Miller, *L'orientation lacanienne*).

We can also mention, as an example, the "market dream", which may be interpreted as intending to fall short of the analyst's demand. Freud had explained to his patient the previous day that the events of our earliest childhood are no longer accessible as such, but are "replaced in analysis by 'transferences' and dreams" (*The Interpretation of Dreams (I)*, p. 184). We can accordingly consider her dream to be a symptom of Freud's desire or, in other words, an interpretation. Here is the dream:

> *I dreamt that I arrived too late at the market and could get nothing either from the butcher or from the woman who sells vegetables*. An innocent dream, no doubt; but dreams are not as simple as that, so I asked to be told it in greater detail. She thereupon gave me the following account. *She dreamt she was going to the market with her cook, who was carrying the basket. After she had asked for something, the butcher said to her: "That's not obtainable any longer," and offered her something else, adding "This is good too." She rejected it and went on to the woman who sells vegetables, who tried to get her to buy a peculiar vegetable that was tied up in bundles but was of a black colour. She said: "I don't recognize that; I won't take it."* (*The Interpretation of Dreams (I)*, p. 183)

Freud takes particular note of the expression, "That's not obtainable any longer." This phrase, which he himself had uttered the day before, attracts his attention in accordance with his method. The metaphor of vegetables has a dual function, and they signify a lack for more than one reason.

The desire of the Other, in this case Freud's desire, is evoked by the German metaphor of the closed butcher shop which Freud translated as his flies. Thus, the phrase, "I won't take it" in the dream requires two explanations, which are confirmed by a second dream:[2]

1. I don't understand that; I don't know what that is.
2. Don't take me; there's no point.

In both cases, the young woman's refusal of substitutes obviously indicates her refusal of phallic jouissance in place of the non-existent "sexual harmony". She also refuses to give Freud the satisfaction that she legitimately imagines he will obtain, by refusing to provide him with any memories.

She expresses herself in a language of double entendres using vocabulary suggestive of the geography of the female body (the box, the piano …). She had been dissatisfied with her figure in childhood and now repudiates the insignia of her femininity, to the extent that they cause the desire of the Other—her husband—which she denies herself. Above all, she does not want these signs. She "doesn't know what that is" and asks another woman to explain (Frau K had provided Dora with dictionaries). It seems that Freud's patient is interpreting his desire in terms that go beyond what he was demanding of her. Their exchange can be imagined in something like the following terms: "As you have no childhood memories, I am asking you to dream and to transfer …." "So you want sexual meaning do you? No problem, you shall have it. But you can't have the phallus."

What is striking in this dream is the continuity between this patient's theory of transference and Freud's own, which at the time of *The Interpretation of Dreams* consisted in the mere displacement of a signifier. Freud gives her "explanations" that she does not want. Her resistance occurs precisely where Freud has said it would: "So *I* was the butcher and she was rejecting these transferences into the present of old habits of thinking and feeling" (*The Interpretation of Dreams (I)*, p. 184).

The desire expressed in the dream is therefore not to dream of substitutes. She dreams that she does not desire transferences, dreams, and substitutes. Her dream, however, also transposes a sexual meaning onto Freud's request for dreams and transferences. He makes her propositions. Since "That's not obtainable any longer," she must make do with substitutes, an ersatz of satisfaction that she does not want. The butcher says, "This is good too," and the woman selling vegetables wants to sell her vegetables that she has never seen before. One might formulate her position as follows: "I won't take what I don't know." Clearly the knowledge in question is not good enough to take. Like Irma, this young woman does not want the replacement solutions that Freud (the butcher) offers her. More precisely, the inferior substitutes for memories in the dream activate memories of a lack, which is the patient's imaginary castration. To Freud's proposition, "There are substitutes," she replies not by producing childhood memories, but by refusing to accept his offer. She tells him not to bother.

To whom would this discouraging formula be addressed if not to masters who are offering their services to her? The young woman's dream shows that the imaginary castration is reactivated whenever a false equivalent for what she does not have is proposed to her. She dreams that she desires neither dreams nor propositions. Freud's demand is transposed into an offer that, in the dream, she refuses. The dream transposes a sexual request onto his demand, thus reproducing the "initial trauma from which her neurosis had arisen" (*The Interpretation of Dreams (I)*, p. 185, note 1). Thus she dreams of the transference in terms that conform to the "explanations" that Freud had given her in around 1900: in terms of the transposition of a scene of seduction. Freud adds in a note that "I have since then come across the same behaviour in other patients; having been exposed to a sexual assault in their childhood, they seek, as it were, to bring about a repetition of it in their dreams" (*The Interpretation of Dreams (I)*, p. 185, note 1).

Traumatic dreams clearly did yet not pose a problem with regard to Freud's theory of wish fulfilment in dreams. Repetition was considered only to obey the pleasure principle.

Does this mean then that Freud's patients dreamt according to his conception of trauma and the aetiology of hysteria? This seems to have been the case. Trauma, disgust, and the seduction scene all figure in these dreams. Nevertheless, beyond the interpretation of the dream according to the schemas of 1897 (the "neurotica") we see something else here: just as in Dora's second dream, there is a contradiction between knowledge about sex and jouissance, a contradiction that Lacan will emphasize. The young woman deprives herself of genital satisfaction because "she does not know what that is", a formulation that clearly indicates both the repression of the phallic signifier and an opposition between knowledge and jouissance.

The ideal father

Freud therefore came to understand at his own expense that there was a price to pay for speaking to a patient from the position of a master. On this subject, Lacan tells us that one of the pitfalls that the analyst must avoid is that of incarnating the ideal father: "The Father the neurotic wishes for is clearly the dead Father—that is plain to see. But he is also a Father who would be the perfect master of his desire—which would be just as good, as far as the subject is concerned" (*Écrits*, p. 698).

In other words, the analyst's learned ignorance must be accompanied by a questioning of the ideal:

> How the analyst must safeguard the imaginary dimension of his non-mastery and necessary imperfection for the other, is as important a matter to deal with as the deliberate reinforcement in the analyst of his nescience regarding each subject who comes to him for analysis, of an ever renewed ignorance so that no one is considered a typical case. (*Écrits*, p. 699)

This is the sense in which one can speak of neutrality: what is neutralized is the signifier of a father who would turn a blind eye to desires. How can the analyst occupy this place?

There are clearly two ways in which one can turn a blind eye. Not wanting to know is the equivalent of authorizing, to giving one's assent to every desire, and this is how it functions in the unconscious. The father who prohibits desire does not, contrary to general belief, stop the neurotic from desiring, and it is the latter's phantasy of the dead father that protects him from castration. This figure, which is not made explicit in Freud, is, nevertheless, not absent from his work, since dreams of the dead father show his position in relation to prohibition and desire. The dead father, furthermore, symbolizes a place: that of the phallus. As such, it can adapt to being occupied by knowledge about sexuality; for Dora, this knowledge functions as a substitute for the dead father. Yet does this knowledge about sexuality not come into conflict with Freud's own knowledge? He sees very well that it is Dora's desire to avenge herself on her father that leads her to take revenge on Herr K and then, through the transference, on himself. Yet was this not, in fact, precisely because Freud had also set himself up as knowing about sexuality?

Dora "had gone away from home by her own choice; her father was ill, and then dead …. Then she went home; all the others were already at the cemetery. She went to her room, not the least sadly, and calmly began reading the encyclopaedia" (*Dora*, p. 110, note 1). Lacan refers to this passage in order to emphasize that the hysteric makes a substitution; she puts knowledge in the place of jouissance. "Since you have treated me like a servant, I shall take no more notice of you, I shall go my own way by myself, and not marry" says her dream (*Dora*, p. 110, note 1). It is thus not simply revenge but knowledge that is in question here. Hysterics are well placed to tell the truth about the sexual relation.

Freud does not always, it seems, reject the figure of the ideal father, and we observe how the latter emerges in *Dora* when he explicitly steps in as the master of truth: "Thus the discourse of the master finds its justification in the discourse of the hysteric, for in becoming the agent of the all-mighty, he gives up responding as a man to what he is called upon to be, the hysteric thus obtaining only knowledge" (Lacan, *Radiophonie*, p. 445).

To the hysteric's call—"Show me whether you are a man"—Freud more or less replies that "I have the ultimate weapon, knowledge." Yet since this knowledge is constantly undermined by Dora's ectopic responses to his requests, Freud remains a castrated master.

> There are several procedures for avoiding castration; the hysteric has a simple one: she unilateralizes it on the other side, that of the partner. Let's say that for the hysteric, there must be a castrated partner. It is very clear that his being castrated is what makes the hysteric's jouissance possible. He must only be what responds from the place of the phallus. (Lacan, *Le séminaire XVIII*, pp. 174–175)

In speaking to her from the place of a master, Freud inevitably fuels Dora's lack of satisfaction, since he does so by identifying, unknown to himself, with Herr K, an identification that entails a number of drawbacks. Demeaning himself by declaring his love to Dora, and thus admitting that he was not a master, Herr K had provoked an aggressive reaction. Freud, similarly, wondering what he can possibly have in common with Herr K, is unaware of his own desire to reunite the supposed lovers. Freud is thus mistaken about the hysteric's desire, for she prefers knowledge about truth to jouissance. He gets taken in by her intrigue, and finds himself playing the role of Faust, for which he has to face the consequences. "No one who, like me, conjures up the most evil of those half-tamed demons that inhabit the human breast, and seeks to wrestle with them, can expect to come through the struggle unscathed" (*Dora*, p. 109).

He reaffirms this opinion on other occasions, such as in *The Resistances to Psychoanalysis* and in *Analysis Terminable and Interminable* in which he compares the analyst's actions to those of someone who handles dangerous X-rays.

Once Freud can no longer legitimately believe that patients can be cured through love, other passions will follow, which we will now consider.

Notes

1. "As it needs to be said, the unconscious is a fact in as much as it supports itself on the very discourse that establishes it" ("*L'étourdit*", p. 478).
2. "Her husband asked her: 'Don't you think we ought to have the piano tuned?' And she replied: 'It's not worth while; the hammers need reconditioning in any case'" (*The Interpretation of Dreams (I)*, p. 185).

PART II

THE PASSION FOR ORIGINS

I have an impression that analytic practice has not always avoided errors and over-estimations on this point, partly owing to an exaggerated respect for the "mysterious unconscious".

—Freud, *Remarks on the Theory and Practice of Dream-Interpretation* (1923).*

---

*S. E., 19, p. 112.

CHAPTER SIX

Questioning the desire for truth

In a letter to Jung, Freud declares that the only valid motivation for research is the "love of truth" (McGuire, pp. 5–6). Perhaps he was only expressing the reverence, which is compulsory for the scholar, towards a truth that lies beyond partisan prejudices and considerations. "Hats off to truth" is a part of the intellectual's ethic.[1] This postulate, however, for a psychoanalyst—if there is a psychoanalyst cannot—be accepted unquestioningly. If psychoanalysis has displaced the philosophical question of truth from the domain of thought to things, as Lacan tells us, it is because the truth in question is not good to say (*Écrits*, p. 342). The whole edifice of philosophy is subverted by this antipathy between desire and truth. This raises the question of whether Freud did in fact love the truth and wanted his patients to desire it. Clearly he was not left speechless by the splendour of truth. And yet, if he was not duped by truth, could he have been duped by the real? A distinction ought to be made here. The metaphor of unmasking may well suit Freud's undertaking: it is better to lift the veil of Maya rather than let well enough alone. Yet he does so not to provide the subject with access to his own good but rather to weave together a fatal truth. Thus, his ethical imperative not to let sleeping dogs lie was not motivated by a wish to liberate the subject from vain fictions, which had been able to act precisely because they had remained unknown and inexpressible. On the contrary, awakening the subject meant laying bare a real that was not only far from reassuring, but with which he would thereafter have to reckon.

Thus, contrary to the formula that Freud puts forward in the case of the *Rat Man*, it does not seem quite so certain that: "The destruction of Pompeii [begins once it has] been dug up" (p. 176). In other words, looking truth in the face means neither that one will love it, nor that it will love you. Its effect of dissolving the symptom has to be reconsidered entirely. For Freud abandoned catharsis at the moment when he understood that the task of liberating speech was linked to the problem of transference: to the new and artificially created reality of analytic treatment. Does Freud's realism concern truth?

It is important to note that when Freud invented psychoanalysis he did not suggest that the unconscious was a wonderful thing. This is the meaning of his work on Irma's dream. Indeed, considering the unspeakable nature of Oedipus's discovery, it is paradoxical that Freud identified with his preoccupation with solving enigmas. What, after all, did Oedipus discover if not the unnameable? He paid the price, not for his inability to see, but for desiring to see and know the truth. Such then is the essence of neurosis: the neurotic must learn to "half-say" (*mi-dire*) the truth, just as the psychoanalyst must learn to malign (*médire*) it.

When Freud outlines the qualities of a psychoanalyst, he does not portray the latter as a faultless human being, but on the contrary and along the same lines as Abelard, considers that psychoanalysis renders the psychoanalyst detestable to others.

> Well, then, I think your *Analysis* suffers from hereditary vice of—virtue; it is the work of too decent a man, who feels himself bound to discretion. Now, these psycho-analytical matters are intelligible only if presented in pretty full and complete detail, just as an analysis really gets going only when the patient descends to minute details from the abstractions which are their surrogate. Thus discretion is incompatible with a satisfactory description of an analysis; to provide the latter once would have to be unscrupulous, give away, betray, behave like an artist who buys paints with his wife's house-keeping money or uses the furniture as firewood to warm the studio for his model. (Meng & Freud, p. 38)

What ferocious desire inheres in Freud's technique, if it obliges the neurotic to confront her desire directly? The entire movement of the treatment is animated by a patient's resistance to confessing, by truth's resistance to being said.

Psychoanalysis does not introduce us to a pleasant or desirable truth. Rather, Freud's discoveries seek to move towards a limit, to go beyond—in a word, to transgress—a prohibition. This is why his dream about Irma is paradigmatic of his desire: it introduces us to a concept of truth as a point of horror.

Irma

Freud's dream about Irma's injection testifies that there is something beyond truth. If, following Lacan's example, we consider the polysemous character of the word *Lösung* (solution), it seems that Freud's burning passion for extracting confessions from Irma was not the best way to go about sorting out her life. Indeed, Freud's immediate conclusion is to blame someone else for this blunder: the doctor who used a "dirty syringe" to inject her with the wrong solution (*The Interpretation of Dreams (I)*, p. 118).

In answer to Abraham's question as to whether the sexual meaning of Irma's dream had been completely exhausted by his interpretation, Freud responds that: "Sexual megalomania is hidden behind it, the three women, Mathilde, Sophie and Anna, are the three godmothers of my daughters, and I have them all!" (Falzeder, p. 21, see p. 19).

It is both easy and tempting to note the double meaning of "syringe" and of the "solution" that it contains. If the syringe provides the wrong solution this is not only because Freud does not agree with Schrobak's remedy: "*Penis normalis dosim repetatur*" (*On the History of the Psycho-Analytic Movement*, p. 15). The foolishness of the remedy—genital happiness promised by specialists in hysteria—was equalled only by their hypocritical refusal to accept the sexual aetiology of this neurosis.

Freud's alternative solution is to provide the sexual meaning of symptoms, which spared the analysand from making any further comment:

> It was my view at that time (though I have since recognized it as a wrong one) that my task was fulfilled when I had informed a patient of the hidden meaning of his symptoms: I considered

> that I was not responsible for whether she accepted the solution or
> not—though this was what success depended on. (*The Interpretation
> of Dreams (I)*, p. 108)

Freud's wish for absolute power, which he expressly acknowledges in
his answer to Abraham, says a great deal about his identification with
the father of the primal horde, who possesses all women: the totally
unrepentant *jouisseur* who rapes his own daughters (Freud's three
daughters had the same names as the three women on his list …).

It was only later that Freud learns that the curative power of analysis
is "not complete" ("*pas toute*").

The mistaken doctor in his dream also stands for all the doctors of
truth, whatever their solution, who exert their mastery over the desire
of others while remaining completely unaware of their own:

> Instead of me, there are all the others. Here I am only the repre-
> sentative of this vast, vague movement, the quest for truth, in
> which I efface myself. I am no longer anything. My ambition was
> greater than I. No doubt the syringe was dirty. And precisely to
> the extent that I desired it too much, that I partook in this action,
> that I wanted to be, myself, the creator, I am not the creator. (Lacan,
> *Seminar II*, pp. 170–171)

In this dream, which serves as a paradigm for all the other dreams in *The
Interpretation of Dreams*, Freud points an accusing finger, beyond his own
ambitious ego, at all the other alter egos queuing up for knowledge.
This shows the extent to which the *Wissentrieb* can occupy the place of
a fundamental misunderstanding. In what can be called a "diffraction"
of the ego and an "in-mixing" of subjects, the subject disappears behind
the doctors in the amphitheatre—who are hunched over the enigma
of what woman desires—thus establishing a distinction between the
desire of the psychoanalyst and the desire of the master (see *Seminar II*,
pp. 155–160). Freud thus both admits to his guilt and traces out the paths
by which this passion for truth will later be eased (see *Seminar II*, p. 170).
In this place, the "passion for the signifier" will come to punctuate the
void element in signification, to the benefit of the jouissance of encrypt-
ing (*chiffrage*), of non-sense and of the dream-work; in contrast with this
jouissance, the dream's meaning expresses purely "normal thoughts".
Freud's dream might therefore suitably be considered a warning to

every Oedipus who adores enigmas. When he interprets this dream, he "is already addressing himself to us" (*Seminar II*, p. 170).

Lacan's interpretation of this dream, meanwhile, seeks to combine a dual process: on the one hand, the analyst's ego must be effaced or annulled so that an unconscious desire can emerge beyond his own narcissism; on the other hand, there is a desire that is situated at the origin of psychoanalysis and which inaugurates the analytic act, and which is therefore both inhuman and transgressive (see *Seminar II*, pp. 245–246). The meaning of this dream thus concerns the signification of all the other dreams, and indeed the "direct confrontation with the secret reality of the dream, the quest for signification as such" (*Seminar II*, p. 160).

In his discussion of Irma, Lacan outlines a theory of what is beyond the desire to know:

> … in the style of the passionate quest, too passionate we would say, and it is indeed one of the meanings of the dream to say formally, since at the end that is what it comes down to—the syringe was dirty, the passion of the analyst, the ambition to succeed, were here too pressing, the counter-transference was itself the obstacle. (*Seminar II*, p. 164)

What makes the quest for x—the analyst's desire—homogeneous with the real is that the analyst annuls and dissipates the imaginary springs of the ego. This "spectral decomposition" clears the way towards a "final real", wherein the *subject* resides (*Seminar II*, p. 165).

In Irma's dream, "finally another voice is heard", one to which Freud gives up his place and which is not the voice of the community of learned men (*Seminar II*, p. 159). This is the voice of the imaginary decomposition of the ego, which represents the obverse (*envers*) of psychoanalysis.

Freud's original sin, which is also the original sin of psychoanalysis, is thus situated beyond the ego that analytic training aims to eradicate (*Écrits*, p. 282).

At the same time, this very dehiscence only measures the *nothing* of the dream's signification: the word itself. "There is no other word, no other solution to your problem, than the word" (*Seminar II*, p. 158). In Lacan's splendid analysis, the "word" prevails over the thing. In the light of his later theoretical developments, especially with regard to the question of the object, one might give a reading that highlights the waste product, the object *a*, the piece of filth. The dream's meaning thus stumbles up against Freud's own object: the lost object.

Theoretical apathy?

I have argued that Freud's desire for truth is motivated by his obstinate quest for a real to which he is bound as though by a "diabolical force" and which is fundamentally comparable to the lost object. His manner of theorizing follows from his desire to reveal something that ought to remain hidden. The discoveries concerning the unconscious are of the order of the *Unheimlich*, the uncanny. Freud's style—his obstinate search for the event—does not escape the laws of unconscious discourse; annulment, retraction, and negation frequently figure in his statements (see *Beyond the Pleasure Principle*).

When, for example, in order to account for the paradoxes of "repetition", Freud puts forward his hypothesis of the death drive, he declares that "We should consequently feel relieved if the whole structure of our argument turned out to be mistaken" (*Beyond the Pleasure Principle*, p. 44).

This confession could lead us to believe that Freud's attitude was that of sceptical relativism towards theory. This is what several authors, in various ways, have claimed.[2]

I have preferred, however, to situate the problem rather in terms of Freud's passions of epistemology, and shall argue that Freud searches resolutely for certitude, even if he employs means that do not conform to a scientific ideal of rigour. It was, indeed, only through these means that he was able to save the truth. I shall also show, however, how he frees himself from the arbitrariness of interpretation and the danger of suggestion; in short, we shall see what kind of desire for scientific status leads him forward.

Let us suppose, for argument's sake, that Freud's discourse does not adhere to the sort of demonstrative rhetoric that entails conviction and persuasion. This is the opinion of Jean-François Lyotard, according to whom, "Conviction is the affect corresponding to the closing of the investigation, to making one's conclusions" ("*De l'apathie théorique*", p. 18).[3]

If Freud does not subscribe to a "rhetoric of learned discourse" (*discours savant*), Lyotard attributes this to the nature of his object: the ambivalent structure of the drive, to which neither a + or a − sign can be attributed, and which consequently belongs to the dimension of both Eros and Thanatos ("*De l'apathie théorique*", p. 18). This dualism of the drives objects to the principle of contradiction and would thus prohibit any conviction, "since it is impossible to argue for a cause here, for the latter is a stable and established relation between an effect and an agency" (p. 21). Lyotard attempts thus to show the impossibility of reaching any form of causal certitude in psychoanalysis, since the drives in question escape from the principle of contradiction. The meaning of Dora's symptoms—for example, her breathing—cannot be deciphered if we consider them from the perspective of this new theory of the drives: "It cannot be decided whether the symptom results from one or the other principles of the functioning of the drives. Her throat infection, her losing of her voice, her hoarseness, her asthma signify both life and death" (p. 21). Lyotard's analysis, which is more Jungian than Freudian, confuses the living (*le vital*) and the sexual. As for the death drive, it is not the seat of ambivalence, but the limit of sexual meaning.

Certitude, nonetheless, is the guiding principle of Freud's theory, and it is precisely the phenomena of repetition that are the least conducive to the theoretical ambivalence that Lyotard calls "theoretical apathy". Although Freud does not consider belief to be a safe bet, this does not mean that certitude is impossible. In confusing conviction and certainty, one confuses two different theories of theory, one of which is good and the other bad. Freud's "fiction-theory", as it is understood by epistemologists, is nothing less than a theoretical apathy that stifles the desire for certitude, in spite of what they say. I would argue, on the contrary, that this theory leads us to certitude, along paths that are precisely those taken by the analysand's speech: free association. Lyotard confuses a symptom with a postulate for research.[4]

What Freud does give up is a conception of truth as exactitude, a conception that is potentially delusional. He does so, as I have argued, in order to better circumscribe a real, a kernel of certainty that fictions are able to speak about but never grasp (see Cottet, "*Constructions et métapsychologie de l'analyse*").

The fact that a symptom is over-determined and has a number of causes does not, however, prevent one from attaining a certainty about the series they form, and indeed Freud always keenly seeks to establish the historical order of their appearance (*Dora*, pp. 24–25). In fact, the process that he called "soldering" (*Verlötung*) involves an analysis that divides into two parts elements that, in experience, are combined homogeneously. He argues that there are two heterogeneous elements, which belong to different periods in which sexual jouissance expressed itself in different ways: masturbation and the phantasy, the latter of which covers over the real of jouissance in the family romance (see Freud, "Hysterical Phantasies").

In "Analysis Terminable and Interminable", Freud also distinguishes the over-determination of the symptom from the fusion of the death and life drives. Far from ruling out any form of causal determination, this fusion, on the contrary, fuels Freud's determination to seek out the "little piece of reality": the trauma, the lost object.

For these reasons, the categories of the cause and the object-cause of desire cannot be dispensed with under the pretext that Freud's new theory of drive dualism makes it impossible to determine a single causal principle. The theory of the death drive does not entail the death of certitude.

Lyotard further claims that "the epistemological uncertainty that reigns there is nothing other than the undecidability of the effects on the 'body' in general" (p. 24). According to him, absence of conviction leads to an attitude of impassioned apathy. Theory is qualified as fiction and characterized by the particular affect of composure, rather than conviction.

The source of this thesis is a confusion of theory and truth. When one overlooks Freud's desire for certitude, one fails to see that his passion for certainty about dates is perfectly compatible with his extremely casual attitude to reconstituting facts (see Freud, *The Wolf Man*, and Lacan, *Seminar I*, pp. 12–14). It is a fiction only in relation to a truth that always remains linked to Freud's desire. In Lacan's opinion, "The truth is perhaps simply one thing, namely, the desire of Freud himself, the fact that something, in Freud, was never analyzed" (Lacan, *Seminar XI*, p. 12).

Freudian myths, like truth, are constituted by a semblance. Yet exactitude is what provides the signifying chain with the symbolic matter that engenders the truth that has been spun together, a truth that itself, is imaginary. In discussing the Rat Man, Lacan observes that "Freud goes so far as to take liberties with the exactness of the facts when it is a question of getting at the subject's truth" (*Écrits*, p. 249).

The scientific basis of psychoanalysis thus cannot be evaluated according to its adequation to "reality". As Lacan argues, "The major term, in fact, is not truth. It is *Gewissheit*, certainty. Freud's method is Cartesian—in the sense that he sets out from the basis of the subject of certainty. The question is—of what can one be certain?" (*Seminar XI*, p. 35).[5]

There is no criterion of truth other than what leads the subject—the desiring subject—to a sense of certitude, providing that what is in question is the desiring subject. The subject of certitude, like the desire of Descartes, with which Lacan compares it, is motivated by desire, a term that Lacan stresses: "I had always had an extreme desire to learn to distinguish true from false in order to see clearly into my own actions and to walk with safety in this life" (Descartes, p. 33).

These abstract considerations are a necessary preliminary if we wish to introduce what can and what cannot, in analytic experience, be inscribed in philosophical categories. Analogies aside however, there is a fundamental dissymmetry between Descartes and Freud, one that only the relation to the Other enables us to bring out; this relation is the one that takes deception as its axis. Psychoanalysis highlights the subject's relation not to truth but rather to certitude, a certitude for which hesitation, and especially doubt, are the indices. Each moment in the account of a dream is characterized by a particular syncope that marks the way in which the dream is communicated: "I doubt." Freud's reversal consists in stating that doubt is a cover for certitude, and is thus a sign of resistance. In analysis, the elements that should be privileged are precisely those that cause the subject to hesitate, or to say that she "doesn't know", as Freud's hysterics in his *Studies* respond when he tries to force them to admit a secret. This doubt, because it is a sign of resistance, becomes "the support of [Freud's] certainty" (Lacan, *Seminar XI*, p. 35).[6]

This inherent division in theory is homogeneous with the division of every subject, precisely because he speaks. This is the origin of the close relation between Freud's desire and the constitution of the psychoanalytic field. Lacan states:

> The very constitution of the field of the unconscious is based on the *Wiederkehr*. It is there that Freud bases his certainty. But it is quite obvious that it is not from there that it comes to him. It comes to him from the fact that he recognises the law of his own desire. He would not have been able to advance with this bet of certainty if he had not been guided in it, as his writings show, by his self-analysis. And what is his self analysis, if not the brilliant mapping of the law of desire suspended in the Name-of-the-father. Freud

advances, sustained by a certain relation to his desire, and by his own achievement, namely, the constitution of psycho-analysis. (*Seminar XI*, p. 48)

It is therefore impossible to suture the subject of certitude with truth. This is why Lacan calls science an "ideology of the suppression of the subject" (*Radiophonie*, p. 437). Reintroducing the question of the desire of science and of "the savant" is not a sign of subjectivism on our part. This question, which has been repressed by the savant, is, moreover, the very condition of his knowledge.

The Freudian real

Despite what one might think about Freud's quest to discover the truth and reveal secrets, his passion, according to Lacan, is oriented towards the real. "No praxis is more orientated towards that which, at the heart of experience, is the kernel of the real than psycho-analysis" (*Seminar XI*, p. 53).

The fact that the real escapes him—which Freud expresses in a number of ways, including his conception of the navel of the dream, trauma, and the enigma of woman's desire—further justifies his recourse to myths.

The primacy of the real in Freud's work has often been covered up through the emphasis given to the role of fate in, for example, the infernal machine of the Oedipus complex, in which a misdeed is transmitted from one generation to the next. These tragic accents are certainly not absent from Freud's work, since the Oedipus myth contributes to its organization and its various reconceptualizations. One ought, however, to understand the precise function of myths and their structure.

I would like to put forward the hypothesis that the Freudian real is not to "be unmasked" since it exceeds the imaginary and is not continuous with itself.[7] Indeed, it has more in common with nothingness, which a vain hope for something beyond leads us inevitably to encounter. It is this relation with a lack rather than with plenitude or with anything of a concrete or empirical nature that motivates Lacan's use of it. Lacan thereby pays homage to science and even to philosophy, which use x as a variable that stands in, not for what is unknown, but for what is unrepresentable; it marks the place of what eludes representation and exceeds the imaginary. It may be this dimension beyond representation, a dimension that cannot be attained by any signifier, that constitutes the stumbling-block to Freud's desire. This dimension resides beyond the pleasure principle:

> The real is beyond the *automaton*, the return, the coming-back, the insistence of the signs, by which we see ourselves governed by the pleasure principle. The real is that which always lies behind the automaton, and it is quite obvious, throughout Freud's research, that it is this that is the object of his concern. (*Seminar XI*, pp. 53–54)

In order to throw light on this problem, one can postulate that there is an opposition between the real and reality.

It might seem that phantasies rely on dreams and daydreaming rather than on the real. Yet it should be noted that not everything in a dream is an imaginative vision and that when Freud speaks of the dream's navel, he is designating a real that is beyond representation, and which the dream tries to reach (*The Interpretation of Dreams (II)*, p. 525). Furthermore, dreams ought not to be opposed to reality since, at least in the dream that serves as the paradigm for Freud's arguments—that of the burning child—what occurs within it is very close to what is happening in reality (see *Seminar XI*, p. 57).

This dream can serve as our guide in situating Freud's analytic act, since the structure of repetition, which is governed by the real, is well suited to the very invention of psychoanalysis. As we have already seen, Freud's "thirst for truth" proved to be inadequate to what was being played out in the repetition that constitutes his analytic act, which was his passion (*Seminar XI*, p. 33). The real ought therefore to be circumscribed in terms of the category of the Freudian cause, which cannot be done independently of the symbolic. This is what Freud wagered, in radical contrast to Jung, who assured him that the real was not *behind* the symptom or the dream, or that the symbolic was a mask or image that is analogous to other images. The real, instead, is nothing other than a failure of symbolization which the imaginary seeks to fill up and which bodily orifices—so many scraps of the real—attempt to stand in for.

> Impediment, failure, split. In a spoken or written sentence something stumbles. Freud is attracted by these phenomena, and it is there that he seeks the unconscious. There, something other

demands to be realised—which appears as intentional, of course, but of a strange temporality. (*Seminar XI*, p. 25)

If there is therefore a cause only when something fails, it is hardly surprising that Freud grants full power to speech, whose stumbling efforts allowed him to point out to the subject the signifiers that have alienated him and made him suffer. Lacan assimilates this gap to the navel of the dream, the hole evoked by a spoken or written word. This hole has no more signification than to say the alpha and the omega of the sexual relation.

Freud's decision to open up this gap carried with it a risk that he would only grasp later, in the light of the hostility aroused by psychoanalysis: the risk of the plague. This gap has every chance of closing up again, as the history of psychoanalysis shows us and recent events bear out. In 1964, Lacan had already stated that a sense of *transgression* was attached to the discovery of psychoanalysis; we can see this transgressive character in retrospect, since all of analytic culture has tried, ever since, to "suture" it. This shows the extent to which Freud's analytic act subverts the entire cultural edifice governed by the values of the good, beauty, the true, order, etc. Even psychoanalysis has followed suit in attempting to force the unconscious to keep in line. Concerning this gap Lacan tells us, "Believe me, I myself never re-open it without great care" (*Seminar XI*, p. 23).

Notes

1. See Melman, *"Enfants de la Psychanalyse"*, p. 65. Is the metaphor used by Melman suitable for Freud? This is what we are questioning here.
2. For example, see Lyotard (1977), Roustang (1982), and M. Mannoni (1979). Despite the diversity in their inspiration, these works confuse theory and truth. For Lacan, only truth has a structure of fiction.
3. "It may be asked whether and how far I am myself convinced of the truth of the hypotheses that have been set out in these pages" writes Freud on the dualism of the life and death drives (*Beyond the Pleasure Principle*, p. 59).
4. "If the hypothesis of the two drive-principles cannot produce belief in Freud himself, this is because it manifestly contradicts an essential axiom of the discourse of knowledge, at least as Freud imagines it: that of the decidability of causes" (Lyotard, p. 21).

5. We can add with Freud that truth can be deduced out of lies and out of the derailment of speech. This is the furthest from the scholastic definition of "*Adequatio rei et intellectus*". On the other hand, the desire to be scientific is based on "the knife-edge of chronological certainties alone" and not on lived facts (see Lacan, *Écrits*, p. 213).

6. Jones rightly opposes truth and certainty, but does so in order to transform certainty into a religious ideal, while only truth would be scientific. Lacan does the exact opposite. Nevertheless, we always reach a division which for Lacan resides in the signifier itself (see Lacan, *Seminar XI*, p. 47).

7. The real, like truth, is constructed (see chapter III). In *Démasquer le réel*, Leclaire seeks to construct the phantasy of the analyst, which refers to a real beyond discourse. My own orientation goes against this interpretation. On this issue, also see Leclaire, "*À propos d'un fantasme de Freud*", p. 31.

CHAPTER SEVEN

Truth and certitude

Freudian fictions

It is, of course, the case of the Rat Man that provides the surest basis
for Freud's certitude, as well as the guarantee best founded on experience for his theory that the law of desire depends on the law of the
father. Who else could have brought better proof to this hypothesis than
the Rat Man, whose repressed hatred for his father was as completely
imperceptible to himself as it was obvious to others? In this respect,
one sentence, however, is rather enigmatic: "Little by little, in this
school of suffering, the patient won the sense of conviction which he
had lacked—though to any disinterested mind the truth would have
been almost self-evident": the truth of the unconscious existence of his
hatred for his father (*The Rat Man*, p. 209).[1]

Freud, who was still faithful at the time to his restricted theory of
the Oedipus complex, considered that once the barrier of repression has
been lifted, he had done enough: he had enabled his patient to attain the
intellectual conviction that a drive for revenge persisted in his unconscious. Indeed, Freud claims that this certitude can be universalized.
One could wonder, indeed, who are the "disinterested mind[s]" for
whom every aspect of the Rat Man's neurosis would be as obvious as

the nose on his face (p. 209). In these conditions, one is left with an alternative. Perhaps Freud did not discover anything that everyone else did not already know, apart from the Rat Man himself, of course, whose neurosis was precisely a result of repressing this truth. Perhaps, on the other hand, Freud discovered something completely different, but whose implications he did not realize at the time: the foundation for the Rat Man's hatred persisted, after his father's death, in his symptom, determining both his "pathological mourning" and suicide compulsion (*The Rat Man*, p. 186). Perhaps this conviction is not obvious to readers today. Freud himself seems not to have realized the implications of his discovery. Although mortification is undeniably a symptom of an impossible revenge (for how can one take revenge on a dead man?) Freud persists in arguing that the Rat Man's feeling of guilt is justified. However disproportionate his remorse in relation to its cause, it is nonetheless perfectly adapted to an underlying offence, since the cause always depends on circumstances. For example, among the series of real events that gave rise to the Rat Man's feelings of guilt—his acts of cruelty towards his cousin, his insults to his father at the age of three or four, and his remorse at arriving too late at his father's deathbed—none justifies his feeling of being a criminal (*The Rat Man*, p. 176). This was not only his reassuring friend's point of view and the reasonable point of view, but also the opinion of everyone around him. Freud, however, contrary to the lay observer, is absolutely certain that the Rat Man's remorse was justified:

> When there is a *mésalliance*, [...] between an affect and its ideational content (in this instance, between the intensity of the self-reproach and the occasion for it), a layman will say that the affect is too great for the occasion—that it is exaggerated—and that consequently the inference following from the self-reproach (the inference that the patient is a criminal) is false. On the contrary, the physician says: "No, the affect is justified. The sense of guilt is not in itself open to further criticism. But it belongs to some other content, which is unknown (*unconscious*), and which requires to be looked for."
> (*The Rat Man*, pp. 175–176)

Freud's theory of false connections, which he discusses in his chapter on displacement in *The Interpretation of Dreams* is extended here to the field of clinical experience. The principle in question is that every affect that seems to have no cause, or whose cause is out of proportion with its effect, has its cause in the unconscious. In other words, the unconscious is ex-centric to its effects. This form of reasoning is somewhat Cartesian; it resembles the reasoning of Descartes's third meditation, where he argues that infinity is a proof of the existence of God. Freud's argument renders debatable his claim that it ought to have been obvious to everyone not only that the Rat Man unconsciously reproaches himself for his father's death, but also that his feelings of rage did not disappear, but instead grew, after the latter died.

There is, however, a point at which Freud's perspective differs from that of the lay observer. This is found in his statement that "The sense of guilt is not in itself open to further criticism" (*The Rat Man*, pp. 175–176). He fully supports his patient on the point where the latter remains convinced. The thesis that psychoanalysis should aim at removing guilt is incorrect. Here, a distinction needs to be made, one to which Lacan's teaching has made us sensitive, between removing anxiety and removing guilt; guilt, unlike anxiety, points to a repressed desire (see *Seminar XI*, p. 158). Yet, in Freud's theoretical explanations, and especially in the difficulties inherent in the doctrine that he presents to the Rat Man, two different certainties encounter each other:

> I concluded by admitting that this new way of looking at the matter gave immediate rise to some hard problems; for how could he admit that his self-reproach of being a criminal towards his father was justified, when he must know that as a matter of fact he had never committed any crime against him? (*The Rat Man*, p. 176)

In short, the Rat Man knows and his doubt protects him against his certainty. His unconscious knowledge comes to coincide with Freud's certitude and the aim of treatment becomes that of making the two identical: of leading the patient, through the long process of *Durcharbeitung*, to the point where the physician already is.[2] "A sense of conviction is only attained after the patient has himself worked over the reclaimed material, and so long as he is not fully convinced the material must be considered as unexhausted" (*The Rat Man*, p. 181, note 1).

These circumstances lead to a displacement of Freud's desire: he stops desiring to convince his patient. On a number of previous occasions, Freud had made it clear that he considered the question of the origin of obsessional neurosis as already settled. His letters to Fliess and the *K* and *H Manuscripts* had shed sufficient light on the specific mechanisms of obsession: the fact that early sexual activity is followed by reproach and that the latter is then displaced onto substitutes of the reprehensible action. Therefore, in *The Rat Man*, he does not make any major new discoveries on this subject. His main preoccupation shifts and now lies in centring obsession on the structure of the family romance. This re-centring on the Oedipus complex is enriched by his earlier discoveries, as well as by the Rat Man's own revelations, which he often greets with a certain show of surprise, as well as satisfaction. When the Rat Man confides that in his childhood his sensual impulses had been much stronger than during his puberty, Freud, who has not had such high expectations, admits that "He had now produced the answer we were waiting for." This use of "we" is worth noting. He goes on to specify that "I then got him to agree that I had not led him on to the subject either of childhood or of sex, but that he had raised them both of his own free will" (*The Rat Man*, p. 182).

This pleasant harmony enshrines the complete correspondence between the Rat Man's account and the structure involved.

Freud's construction, however, depends on very few elements. It would be more accurate to say that Freud gives these elements to his patient as a kind of prompt so that they will fit in with his Oedipal myth. They clearly receive a semblance of confirmation in his patient's rather atypical version of events. What can be seen at this precise point in the treatment, then, is an encounter between Freud's own wishes and the confirming material offered by his patient, the effect of which is Freud's surprise. He acknowledges to his patient his "construction" (and not "hypothesis" as it is has been translated into French) which is basically a summary of his own theory of infantile sexuality, as it is presented in his *Three Essays*:

> ... when he was a child of under six he had been guilty of some sexual misdemeanour connected with masturbation and had been soundly castigated for it by his father. This punishment, according to my hypothesis, had, it was true, put an end to his masturbating, but on the other hand it had left behind it an ineradicable grudge against his father and had established him for all time in his role of an interferer with the patient's sexual enjoyment. (*The Rat Man*, p. 205)

Freud's construction is based, on the one hand, on the fact that the Rat Man's amnesia started when he was six, and on the other, by Freud's own myth of a castrating and prohibiting father (*The Rat Man*, p. 161). More important, however, is Freud's reaction: "To my great astonishment the patient then informed me that his mother had repeatedly described to him an occurrence of this kind which dated from his earliest childhood and had evidently escaped being forgotten by her on account of its remarkable consequences" (*The Rat Man*, p. 205).

Unless Freud's conception of the real has been elucidated, this remark might seem strange. Freud never tells us what the real is as such, but instead constructs it on the basis of different versions of a particular event, a process that he himself assimilates to the structure of epic poems. The logic behind the deformation of memories emerges when one takes as a guiding principle the Rat Man's intention to conceal the act that motivated his father's reproach or prohibition: masturbation (*The Rat Man*, pp. 204–205).[3] Freud's surprise probably indicates his satisfaction at seeing his construction confirmed in this way, a construction that—whatever Freud himself may claim about it—clearly depends more on his Oedipal myth than on the elements provided by his patient. It is also a typical illustration of how he uses the Oedipus complex and of the "constructive" effect, as he calls it, of his own enunciation, which are also apparent in the case of Little Hans. If we enumerate the elements Freud refers to in order to point out the ineradicable character of the Rat Man's hatred for his father, we obtain the following series, whose demonstrative capacity is somewhat dubious:

- his father's interference when he was a child;
- his father's hostility to his marriage;
- his own ambivalence;
- his pathological mourning.

One cannot always be certain either about the reality or the currency of the components of this series. As Lacan has pointed out, Freud, in reconstituting the history of the illness, has a rather casual attitude towards the accuracy of the information he was given and takes certain liberties in his account of what his patient has said. For instance, the connection between the Rat Man's younger sister's death and his father's punishment of him at the same time remains unknown, but this does not prevent Freud from claiming that "a quantity of material information which had hitherto been withheld became available, and so made possible a reconstruction of the whole concatenation of events" (*The Rat Man*, pp. 209–210).

Freud's standard for reconstructing the history of the Rat Man's illness is clearly not that of real events alone. As Lacan has emphasized, it is not the latter's anger at his father's prohibition that reveals to Freud one of the crucial aspects of the analysis: the way in which the father's sin connects the Rat Man's destiny with an infinite and impossible debt. In other words, one must take into account what is real, symbolic, and imaginary in this observation in order to distinguish between exactitude and truth (Lacan, *Écrits*, p. 249). One can only be struck, indeed, by the imbalance between these two approaches of Freud's. On the one hand, he highlights the typical character of the Rat Man's illness or history, but on the other, he detects the very specific, indeed unique, symbolic element—the unary trait—that swallows up the subject's destiny. The latter is thus not reduced to a series of lived events but consists in a myth that has been transmitted by his parents' history and which concerns his father's debt (*Écrits*, p. 249).

The Rat Man should be read in the light of *Totem and Taboo* and *Constructions in Analysis*. Both of these texts illustrate Lacan's thesis of a hypothetical unconscious—one that is constructed on the basis of a repetition of signifiers and depends on the analysand's reconstruction of his personal history. A reconstruction can be made whether or not the analysand's memories are reliable; it is independent of his sense of having "lived through" the events.[4]

Thus, retroactively, one can better understand how Freud could play fast and loose with the facts involved, since a subject's lived experience is dominated by his relation to certain key signifiers. Freud's "forcing" of "solutions" onto his patient should be considered in this context.

Thus, for example, the Rat Man never actually remembered his "rage against his father", nor does he ever re-experience it (*The Rat Man*, p. 301). All that he can ever know about it comes from another excessive rage, which he expresses, in his transference, against Freud. These insults prove his paternal transference. It is only, however, through a process of "deduction" that he is able "little by little" to attain a conviction that is primarily Freud's: "It was only along the painful road of transference that he was able to reach a conviction that his relation to his father really necessitated the postulation of this unconscious complement" (*The Rat Man*, p. 209).

Freud's 1914 article "Remembering, Repeating and Working Through" enlightens us about this passage to the act, in which the element of "resistance" in his transference is revealed in the abuse that the Rat Man heaps upon him (pp. 145–156). In the absence of actual revelations, only the "transference-work" produces a sense of conviction. Does this mean that Freud has set up a particular operation that is capable of transmitting this conviction to his patient?

The Rat Man's hostility towards Freud is not merely a "shadow of the past"; it does not simply reproduce his rage against his father. It cannot be said that the transference is independent of interpretation; instead, transference is its motor. We know that the Oedipal schema that Freud uses during this period reduces various problems to the hatred of—or at least ambivalence towards—the father; it does not yet take into account the narcissistic aggressiveness that is the basis of obsessional neurosis. This is why Freud takes such liberties with the actual events of the Rat Man's history. If psychic reality is more important than material reality, it is because the former determines the latter (*Écrits*, p. 241).

It has been incorrectly suggested that Freud eliminates the causal character of events. In my opinion, it would be more accurate to say that Freud's preoccupation, at the time, is with how events have acquired their historical importance. They could only take on such importance within the context provided by the Oedipus complex.

The structure of truth

As we have seen, the Rat Man's history is reconstructed on the basis of an act of which he himself has absolutely no recollection. The very existence of the family legend surrounding this offence —which was committed when he was six—was enough to allow Freud to confer a sexual meaning upon it; nevertheless, its sexual character is not explicitly established. For Freud, the introduction of the prohibiting father into the narrative was sufficient to explain the whole range of his symptoms that had been motivated by hatred:

> The source from which his hostility to his father derived its indestructibility was evidently something in the nature of *sensual desires*, and in that connection he must have felt his father as in some way or other an *interference*. A conflict of this kind, I added, between sensuality and childish love was entirely typical. (*The Rat Man*, p. 182)

It is astonishing that Freud, who is otherwise so intent on establishing a detailed history of this case, refers the complexity of these events back to a "typical" schema. His desire to confirm this implicit structure in no way, however, eliminates his capacity to be "surprised". Freud allows himself be surprised, thus following the technical suggestions that he would provide later: "It is not a good thing to work on a case scientifically while treatment is still proceeding—to piece together its structure, to try to foretell its further progress, and to get a picture from time to time of the current state of affairs, as scientific interest would demand" ("Recommendations to Physicians", p. 114).

Freud's will to knowledge is, in fact, counterbalanced by the following advice: "The most successful cases are those in which one proceeds, as it were, without any purpose in view, allows oneself to be taken by surprise by any new turn in them, and always meets them with an open mind, free from any presuppositions" ("Recommendations to Physicians", p. 114). Such words correct any image we might have of Freud's "suggesting" to his patient that his history should coincide with a particular schema. In the treatment, this schema plays the role of a fiction that is intended to modify the transferential relation.

This claim can be backed up by examining a "second" situation, the Rat Man's marriage, which is analogous to the earlier occurrence (*The Rat Man*, p. 182). Indeed, Freud hypothesizes once again that there has been a paternal prohibition, which this time concerns the Rat Man's plans to marry his cousin. It is clearly, however, the Rat Man's mother and not his father who, in reality, has played this interfering role, since she is the one who made plans for him to marry another woman (*The Rat Man*, p. 198). Lacan has shown us that Freud's historical reconstruction is "factually inexact", but it could then be suggested that since his intention was to attain the "subject's truth", his procedure was not fundamentally wrong (*Écrits*, p. 249). This means that, whatever the actual facts motivating the Rat Man's rage towards his father, the latter inspired this hatred only to the extent that he was a "prohibiter", even if this status may not coincide with historical reality.

The castrating father who, for Lacan, is the real father, is not the Rat Man's actual father. The father to whom he is responding is, rather, a dead father, the symbolic father: "The father's castrating activity—which Freud affirms here with an insistence that might be believed systematic—played only a secondary role in this case" (*Écrits*, p. 249).

Thus, in examining Freud's indoctrination of the Rat Man, Lacan treats it as a "forcing" of the situation, but situates it on a symbolic level; it sought to bring out the truth. This is in contrast to a widespread tendency to see it as a rash manifestation of his own "counter-transference" (for example, see Ribeiro Hawelka, pp. 251–252, 255–257). In reality, it should be seen as compensating for a doctrine of narcissism, which had not yet been formulated, and without which he was unable to account for the destruction waged upon the unconscious by mortified symbols.

In his article "The Neurotic's Individual Myth", Lacan shows how the Rat Man can be interpreted in terms of Freud's theory of narcissistic alienation. Although during this period, Freud considers the Oedipal framework to be an actual fact of experience, which is reproduced in treatment, it should be considered as having a merely operative role. We can retroactively consider the effects of the narcissistic structure to be far more real; this structure, which combines idealization and aggressiveness, accounts for the Rat Man's substitution of Freud for his friend during treatment. "And very quickly, aggressive fantasies are unleashed. They are not related uniquely—far from it—to the substitution of Freud for the father, as Freud's own interpretation persistently tends to show, but, as in the fantasy, to the substitution of the figure called the rich woman for the friend" ("The Neurotic's Individual Myth", p. 415).

It is thus by means of a complete misunderstanding that the treatment advances, and this treatment is far removed from any possible conception of "unconscious-to-unconscious communication".[5] It seems, instead, that it was only the effect of truth produced by Freud's interpretation of his hatred for his father that enabled the Rat Man to shed his narcissistic ties; indeed, it triggered the decisive lifting of the mortifying symbols that oppressed him. Freud had not yet formulated the theory that corresponded to his practice and it is clear that his haste to conclude the treatment prematurely points to a desire to convince that was not yet tempered by doubts as to whether he really understood the nature of obsessional neurosis.[6] It is, however, in full consciousness of the opposition between material or historical truth, on the one hand, and psychic truth—or, as I have called it, the truth-effect—on the other, that he pursues his quest for an origin.

As we have seen, it is possible for truth and exactitude not to coincide. Freud, in probing further into the structure of the Oedipus complex, gradually becomes more aware of its mythical dimension.

In *Totem and Taboo*, the father-son relation is no longer presented as tragic. It was now in the "epic" that Freud seeks the "fiction" that will allow a recognition of a real that invariably escapes interpretation. Here, as in *The Rat Man*, Freud is haunted by the *act*. Thus, what will orient his search from now on will be the beginning, rather than the origin.[7] Now, the act by which history begins can only have a sexual nature: it must be a crime or a form of jouissance that concerns the father's sexual act. Freud's passion for this inaugural act of a particular destiny becomes linked with the question of the real father. The father who disturbs and prohibits sexual life is raised to the level of reality. Yet if the reality principle depends on this paternal function, then so too must "psychic reality" (see Falzeder, p. 482).

Notes

1. Unlike the Standard Edition, the French translation of *The Rat Man* which the author cites includes the last clause of this sentence in the quotation. See *Cinq psychanalyses*, p. 235 (translator's note).
2. See Lacan, *Seminar I*, p. 45: "Because the subject doubts, one must be certain."
3. However, Freud proposes several versions of a scenario which always ends up with a violent reaction against the father, including a case of an ordinary misdeed "of a non-sexual nature" (*The Rat Man*, p. 207, note).
4. *Totem and Taboo* situates the act at the root of thoughts whereas in "Constructions in Analysis" the treatment depends on the analytic act: on constructions. Note that the use of the term "construction" always has an historical connotation in Freud. The use of the term *"hypothèse"* (hypothesis) in certain French translations, such as that of the case history of the Rat Man, allows the dimension of the act—which is always the origin of a history—to escape (see "Constructions in Analysis").
5. It is true that Lacan asserts that it is precisely because of his "personal experience" that Freud has "the flash of insight" that allows him to discover the triggering role of the marriage proposition, which was arranged by his mother. Nevertheless, his theoretical tools remain dependent on the Oedipal concept of the castrating father.
6. In 1926 the mechanism of obsessional neurosis was still enigmatic. See Freud's *Inhibitions, Symptoms and Anxiety*.
7. See *Totem and Taboo*, p. 161: "In the beginning was the Deed" or, in German, *"die Tat"* (G. W.: IX, p. 194).

CHAPTER EIGHT

Reaching the real through constructions

In *Beyond the Pleasure Principle*, Freud abandons his aim of instilling meaning into symptoms, thus heralding a second period in psychoanalytic technique, one in which construction prevails over interpretation (p. 18). When some years later, in 1937, in his major article on constructions, he accounts for the activity of the analyst, he once again uses his customary metaphor of archaeology; this time, however, his intention is to accentuate the difference between patient and analyst (see "Constructions in Analysis"). Since the latter "neither experience[s] nor repress[es]" what the patient tells him, Freud thinks he should not therefore attempt to understand but rather, like the unconscious, simply set to work.

Thus, "The work of analysis consists of two quite different portions [and] it is carried out on two separate localities" ("Constructions in Analysis", p. 258). While one party splutters on, inspired by a passion for meaning, the other constructs the neurotic patient's family romance. Without presuming to predict the outcome of such a game, we can nevertheless measure the risk involved: that of creating the autistic tandem that Lacan warned us against in his seminar. Such a tandem could reproduce the situation illustrated in Kant's famous parable from his *Critique of Pure Reason*: there are two friends, one of whom "milks a he-goat, while the other holds a sieve underneath" (*Le séminaire XXIV*, p. 13). Does the passion for origins, however, lead inevitably to such an extreme consequence?

The consequence of inviting the analyst to form his own personal "delusion" incites Freud not only not to lose sight of the insistence of the real, but to subordinate his constructions entirely to a search for a fragment of lost reality. This leads to several questions. What would be the characteristics of an analytic procedure that is purely determined by speech and which leaves the real permanently in suspense? Second, if there are no indices of reality in the unconscious, what enables a construction to be transmitted? Finally, how can the psychic apparatus be modified so that the end of analysis leads to a "link between the two portions of the work of analysis, between [the analyst's] own part and that of the patient" ("Constructions in Analysis", p. 259)?

With reference to Freud's metapsychology, our aim in this chapter is to reveal that the process of treatment and the theory of the psychic apparatus have the same structure.

A two-person delusion

In what context does the notion of "construction" first appear and to what necessity in analytic treatment is it a response?

Freud thinks that the work of construction borrows its structure from psychotic delusions: "The delusions of patients appear to me to be the equivalents of the constructions which we build up in the course of an analytic treatment" ("Constructions in Analysis", p. 268).

From where does Freud take the notion of the structuring function of psychotic delusion? It first appears in his analysis of Schreber, where the term "reconstruction" is contrasted with the notion of defence; unlike the latter, a reconstruction is an attempt to return to reality. The term "reality" is again employed in this sense in Freud's 1924 article, "The Loss of Reality in Neurosis and Psychosis".

Freud's schema for treatment thus consists in a two-person delusional formation, yet this is only on condition that we remember that a true delusion—one formed following a loss of "reality"—is the least pathological element in psychosis, since it actually constitutes a means of escaping from the latter. "The delusional formation, which we take to be the pathological product, is in reality an attempt at recovery, a process of reconstruction" (*Schreber*, p. 71).

Let us note in passing that Freud never strayed from his ideal of recovering the original real kernel, the element of historical truth that was missing from his patient's discourse; on the contrary, he sought to recover it through a process of exchange that triggered a new articulation by the patient.

What exactly then constitutes the inherent kernel of truth, which is confused with the piece of disavowed historical reality (*Verleugnung*), thus ensuring the effectiveness of delusional constructions ("Constructions in Analysis", p. 268)? This is a crucial question since it orients Freud's technique towards the path that is illustrated in *Moses*, where the analyst creates a *fiction* that will compensate for irretrievably lost memories (*Moses and Monotheism*, pp. 129–130).

Freud is well aware that origins are invariably mythical and fictional and never immediately available to us.[1] Yet he also considers that it was only by penetrating the individual's prehistory and returning to his earliest years that an analysis can be brought to its end. Analytic experience thus sets both the conditions and the limits of the necessity for *constructing* the patient's history or prehistory. Freud's recourse to the process of construction is nothing new in itself; what is interesting, instead, is the use that he puts it to and his reasons for using it. In "Constructions in Analysis" he gives the following definition of a construction:

> ... it is a "construction" when one lays before the subject of the analysis a piece of his early history that he has forgotten, in some such way as this: "Up to your *n*th year you regarded yourself as the sole and unlimited possessor of your mother; then came another baby and brought you great disillusionment. Your mother left you for some time, and even after her reappearance she was never again devoted to you exclusively. Your feelings towards your mother became ambivalent, your father gained a new importance for you," ... and so on. (p. 261)

Whenever he needs to demonstrate the structure of a mythical history or a phantasy, Freud introduces a construction. Yet in the text of a phantasy, lacunae and distortions provide the indices that a construction needs to be made: something is missing from its intelligibility and continuity. Numerous examples of constructions can be found in texts that employ this notion, from Freud's *Leonardo* until his *Moses*. I would like now to clarify how he uses constructions, in order to show how they can be credited with determining the dynamics of the treatment.

Is psychoanalysis a form of idealism?

A construction is an auxiliary element that compensates for the absence of a real.[2] It is called for when a fragment of historical reality has been lost. Here, Freud's epistemological conventionalism asserts itself once again. In his *The Interpretation of Dreams* he claims, we remember, that: "We must always be prepared to drop our conceptual scaffolding if we feel that we are in a position to replace it by something that approximates more closely to the *unknown reality (Wirklichkeit)*" (p. 610, emphasis added). In this sense, chapter seven of *The Interpretation of Dreams* is itself a huge construction.

Yet how can one construction be chosen over another in analysis? I shall argue that our criterion for a construction's validity is the effect that it produces on the material provided by the patient. "Our construction is only effective because it recovers a fragment of lost experience," says Freud in "Constructions in Analysis" (p. 268). Once again, this is only an unveiling of an element of reality that has been hidden behind the imaginary.

This gives us the occasion to specify, as best we can, the connection between two imperatives, which ultimately amount to the same thing: recovering a missing piece of reality and reconstructing the patient's history. In this respect, Freud's venture has not always been considered either legitimate or comprehensible. Octave Mannoni, for instance, suggests that it was superfluous, even naïve, and that Freud was led astray in searching for a fragment of archaic reality ("*L'athéisme de Freud*", p. 31). In my opinion, however, Freud's obstinacy in this matter was not only justifiable but absolutely necessary in order to avoid the pitfall of idealism.

The real has not yet been distinguished from truth. One must remember that if truth is connected to the patient's history—since it is truth that is constructed by resorting to a text that compensates for the flaws and distortions in a history—reality, in the sense of psychic reality, is something that remains to be discovered. How, then, can the phantasy be distinguished from the real? What exactly is real in psychic reality? It is important to emphasize that, according to Freud, the phantasy is neither purely imaginary nor reduced to the play of signifiers; it consists, instead, in an activity of fragmenting the real ("bits of real"³). When an event itself is missing, *traces* of it remain in the present. What, for Freud, is the value of these traces or clues to the real? In *The Interpretation of Dreams* and the letters to Fliess, these clues are reduced to things that have been seen and heard. The latter are then refashioned, tinkered with, and re-employed at different periods of time and are thus made up of non-synchronous pieces. Flattened out onto a single scene—which is staged in the phantasy—they can only be experienced in terms of a feeling of reality (*Wirklichgefühl*), and it is on the basis of the latter that Freud establishes the *Wirklichkeit* of dreams (*The Wolf Man*, p. 33, *G.W. XII*, p. 59). The enunciation is thus, from the very start, the place of the Other and snatches the dreamer's identity from his own hands. In *The Interpretation of Dreams*, Freud had already explained that he considers each word and sentence not as the dreamer's creation but as things that had been said the day before (*The Interpretation of Dreams (II)*, p. 510).

Another criterion of the real is, as Freud reminds us in *The Wolf Man*, immobility, or sustained attention. The immobility of the wolves represents the sustained attention of the uprooted or banished (*gebannt*)⁴ subject, who has been abandoned to jouissance and rooted to the spot. The real, in this case, is in the place of something that is impossible—the impossibility of bearing internal excitations—and the drive is in the position of *Wirklichkeit*. It is not surprising that in his "Constructions in Analysis", Freud refers back to *The Wolf Man* both as an example of a feeling of certitude in relation to a kernel of lost reality, and also in relation to a second criterion: the quality of being *überdeutlich* (ultra-clear).⁵ With regard to the therapeutic effectiveness of a construction, Freud explains that "[it] achieves the same therapeutic result as a recaptured memory" ("Constructions in Analysis", p. 266).

What, then, are the elements that provide us with clues about the real? They are not actual events, but rather remains or photographic negatives that have later been transformed into images (*Moses and Monotheism*, p. 126). Earlier (in Chapter One), we considered the question of Freud's conception of reality in terms of his quest for a fragment of reality around which the different psychic layers become encysted (see "Constructions in Analysis", p. 266). Now it is necessary to highlight the function of retroaction in constituting reality. For Freud, psychic reality is always an encounter between an event, which is of no particular importance in itself, and a signifier. If the real is traumatic, it is only by means of an encounter with language. So long as the event is not understood (in *The Wolf Man*, Freud uses the word *versteht*), it will have no effect. As soon, however, as it becomes a signifier of reality—that of sexual difference—it takes on the value of reality for the subject, as a sign of the latter's division.

The phantasy and constructions

The analyst's construction is also a deconstruction or dismembering of the phantasy, which itself has been constructed from diverse elements. A true harlequin's cloak, the phantasy, rather than masking reality, compensates for the lack that has brought it about. Seen from this perspective, it too is a "construction". Freud does not use this word in his *Leonardo da Vinci* when he contrasts phantasies and memories, but the mistake that appears in the French translation can be used to our advantage: "The scene with the vulture would not be a memory of Leonardo's but a phantasy, which he *constructed* at a later date and transposed to his childhood" (*Leonardo da Vinci*, p. 82).[6]

The phantasy is thus a construction, but an unconscious one. The real that is included in it resides at the very limit of nothingness, as is suggested by the enigmatic German expression, "real nothing" (*reale Nichtigkeit*) (*Leonardo da Vinci*, p. 83, G. W., VIII, p. 151).[7] As a consequence, a construction in analysis follows on the trace of the phantasmatic construction that is to be dissolved and it is therefore homogeneous with the latter. The elaborating of the phantasy therefore provides analytic work with a schema that will become more and more important in Freud's work. Indeed, if the objective is to construct that which has been forgotten on the basis of traces left by that very process of forgetting, then what we are dealing with is a palimpsest. Each text covers over another one, which was apparently written during a different period.

Freud's approach reaches its full potential in *Moses and Monotheism*. Although it is a sort of historical novel, a work of fiction, Freud's reconstruction never sinks to the level of religious delusion.[8] The coherence of his construction can be attributed to the element of truth contained in the legend of Moses: the traces of his murder were eradicated. Just as the event only acquires consistency after a certain lapse of time, so too does the lacunary and truncated text produced by a patient only acquire "historical truth" as a construct. It is the present that needs to be constituted; the symbolic meaning that is attributed to the real by the neurotic, and which reveals traces of repression, is interpreted as a return of the past in the present. Freud observes in his *Leonardo* that "[S]ome remains of the past were given a wrong interpretation in order to fit in with contemporary ideas" (*Leonardo da Vinci*, p. 83).

This implicit warning against the history of historians (see, for example, Michel de Certeau's *L'écriture de l'Histoire*) is particularly relevant in the case of psychic reality, which, more clearly than anything else, testifies to the persistent trace of the past in the present (see Freud, *Civilization and its Discontents*, pp. 71–72, G. W., XIV, p. 427). Hence also the limits of the metaphor of archaeology from which Freud takes his notion of construction. It can be shown, however, that the notion of construction refers to a stratified conception of the psychic apparatus that is derived from the metaphor of writing or inscription.

Stratification and transference

This leads us to try to connect two fields: those of the dynamics of treatment and the value of constructions, since there is no other guarantee for the latter than the experience of treatment. Treatment is established in the transference, which transforms a neurosis into a transference neurosis (see S. Freud, *Introductory Lectures*, pp. 413–447). Early on, in *Dora*, Freud had already referred to this transformation, which "gives a new meaning to the symptom", as a revised edition or transcription of a particular text (*Dora*, p. 116).

Once the analyst has been "introduce[d] [...] into one of the psychical 'series', which the patient has already formed", what takes place in the transference becomes a revised edition of an initial conflict ("The Dynamics of Transference", p. 100). The model for the dynamics of treatment then becomes the moments that have constituted the structure of the subject: the moments that have formed the psychic apparatus itself. We can thus show how Freud conceives of the dynamics of transference—its impetus, scansion and limits—in terms of the model of the psychic apparatus provided in his *Project*.

The notion of "successive epochs of life" and their various modes of inscription in the psychic apparatus first appears in a letter to Fliess: "The material present in the form of memory traces being subjected from time to time to a *rearrangement* in accordance with fresh circumstances—to a *retranscription*. [...] I should like to emphasize the fact that the successive registrations represent the psychic achievement of successive epochs of life" (Masson, pp. 207–208).

It is, indeed, a matter of layers, the arrangement of which controls the technique of historical construction. This is confirmed by Freud's observation about Elisabeth von R, which has been cited by Pierre Kaufmann (*Psychanalyse et théorie de la culture*, p. 97): "Thus it came about that in this, the first full-length analysis of a hysteria undertaken by me, I arrived at a procedure which I later developed into a regular method and employed deliberately. This procedure was one of clearing away the pathogenic psychical material layer by layer [*Schichtung*]" (*Studies on Hysteria*, p. 139).

It was this concept that led Freud to compare psychoanalysis with archaeology in his *Studies on Hysteria*, a comparison that motivates Kaufmann's attempt to connect the theory of culture to that of analytic experience (*Studies on Hysteria*, pp. 287–289). It also explains our present attempt to look for the law governing the analyst's action, place, and desire in the very functioning of the psychic apparatus. A certain number of texts on transference that deal with the problem of technique have proved helpful in this undertaking.

My aim is now to show how Freud arranges his constructions: into what "series" they are integrated, and by what means, in the transference. In the same text, the *Studies on Hysteria*, Freud uses the metaphor of a kernel to illustrate the processes both of treatment and, in particular, of resistance, in which the signifier twists and turns like the knight in a game of chess. It thus appears that the process of writing—of constructing a patient's history—is completely consistent with the structure of the psychic apparatus. In Lacan's words, "The complete reconstitution of the subject's history—is the element that is essential, constitutive and structural for analytic progress" (*Seminar I*, p. 12). This was Freud's conviction right up to his "Constructions in Analysis". The two following questions spring to mind concerning this scheme:

1. What impact can the different stages of treatment have on the constitution and arrangement of the psychic strata? (see Masson, pp. 221–223).
2. In what way does transference neurosis, which remodels these strata into concentric layers around the analyst—considered as a kernel—consist in a new, intermediary, and symbolic version of them?

The result is that the field of Freudian treatment should be conceived of in terms of a topology that is isomorphic with the psychic apparatus. The analyst, who has always occupied centre stage in the treatment, is also gradually integrated into the centre of the patient's neurosis.

This is what is shown by Freud's orientation, an orientation that begins with the *Traumdeutung* and extends to his "Introductory Lectures on Psycho-analysis", in which the concept of transference, which had been enriched by Ferenczi's elaborations, is conceived of as an introjection, in the sense of a catalyzing action (see Ferenczi, "Introjection and Transference"). This is the meaning of the notion of "integration into one of the psychic series", which implies that this place has existed from the beginning. There is, nevertheless, a discontinuity within the process of treatment, which leads one to pass, at a given moment, from one epoch to another. The analyst is then integrated, under the aegis of a construction, as a symbolic introjection. Yet how should we conceive of the new meaning that the introjection of the analyst gives to the symptom, a meaning that ultimately leads to transference neurosis (see S. Freud, "Introductory Lectures", p. 299)? The latter is an intermediary space and a production whose aberrant nature is indicated in Freud's customary gardening metaphors: it is like the "cambium layer in a tree between the wood and the bark" ("Introductory Lectures", p. 444). He argues that:

> We are no longer concerned with the patient's earlier illness but with a newly created and transformed neurosis which has taken the former's place. We have followed this new edition of the old disorder from its start, we have observed its origin and growth, and we are especially well able to find our way about in it since, as its object, we are situated at its very centre. ("Introductory Lectures", p. 444)

This formula is identical to the metaphors Freud uses to describe the formation of concentric layers around a repressed kernel, layers that correspond to the different periods of a subject's experience. Freud himself considers it possible to locate the "exact points" at which repression occurs ("Introductory Lectures", p. 438).

The patient's relation to the analyst, in these conditions, can no longer be conceived of in terms of influence or suggestion, since the value of the construction is now thought to receive its confirmation, not from the real, but from what the patient adds to this construction in order to complete it and from the use he makes of it in reconstructing his individual myth:

> The analyst finishes a piece of construction and communicates it to the subject of the analysis so that it may work upon him; he then constructs a further piece out of the fresh material pouring in upon him, deals with it in the same way and proceeds in this alternating fashion until the end. ("Constructions in Analysis", p. 260)

On the interpretation of dreams

The study of dreams provides Freud with a solution to the problem of the analyst's influence on the patient. There he shows that transmission or communication between preconscious and latent thoughts is subjected to a mechanism that excludes any form of psychological interpretation. The general question of the physician's influence on the material provided by the patient can be compared with the specific case of the relation between the day's residues and unconscious desire.

Once Freud has established the role played by the preconscious and the day's residues in elaborating the dream thoughts, the question remains: how is this model used within the analytic relation? In 1925, in "Some Additional Notes on Dream-Interpretation as a Whole", Freud once again takes up his theories from *The Interpretation of Dreams*, without altering his principle of an opposition between dreams and the waking state, an opposition that he pins down by using two signifiers: "usefulness" and "pleasure" (*Lustgewinn*) (p. 127). He then concludes that if dreams respond only to a desire to sleep rather than to a desire to solve the previous day's problems—a task that is left to the preconscious—then they are consequently unable to communicate anything to anyone (*Mitteilung an einem anderen*). Thus, the dream processes themselves provide Freud with the reason why an analyst is unable to induce a patient to dream. The very structure of dreaming—*der Traümen*—makes it impossible for another person to suggest, not their professed purpose—their manifest thoughts—but their mechanisms. This is what Freud demonstrates in his other 1923 article, "Remarks on the Theory and Practice of Dream-Interpretation" (p. 109). A sentence in chapter seven of this article explicitly connects the problems of the analyst's influence on both dreams and analysis: "if we replace the dream by the dream-thoughts which it contains, the question of how far one can suggest dreams 4 with the more general question of how far a patient in analysis is accessible to suggestion" ("Remarks on the Theory and Practice of Dream-Interpretation", p. 114). Soon afterwards, Freud claims that "On the mechanism of dream-formation itself, on the dream-work in the strict sense of the word, one never exercises any influence: of that one may be quite sure" (p. 114).

This remark leads us to consider more precisely the question of how the analyst intervenes and how her constructions are integrated in the work of the treatment.

Conviction and rejection

According to this perspective, analytic constructions are homogeneous with the constitutive pieces of personal history that a patient provides. They consist of the series of signifiers that have determined a patient's history, and which, a fragment at a time and through a mechanism of interlocking—rather like the pieces of a jigsaw puzzle—work towards reconstructing the events that have woven his destiny and have contributed to his sense of existence ("Remarks on the Theory and Practice of Dream-Interpretation", p. 116).

Here, Freud provides a model for the end of analysis that evokes the image of a hole or gap that is filled in by two separate teams, which are originally from different psychic locations but which have succeeded in coming together. This may be a dangerous metaphor, however, as it suggests that primal repression can be covered up completely. Yet since the effect of a construction is to create some order in the set of the subject's signifiers, it is no longer a question of re-experiencing forgotten memories or of rediscovering a kernel of lost reality; instead, the task of analysis is to bring about a feeling of conviction in the patient. From a therapeutic point of view, this feeling of conviction has "the same therapeutic result as a recaptured memory" ("Constructions in Analysis", p. 266). So how exactly does the latter come about?

Freud tells us that the truth-value of a conviction depends on whether it is confirmed or rejected (*Bestätigung oder Verwerfung*) ("Constructions in Analysis", p. 265). Yet it seems that an analyst can never lose at this game of heads or tails.[9] If she makes a false construction, it does no harm unless she makes a habit of it and ends up losing her patient's trust. It cannot be inferred from this, however, that the unconscious is invariably truthful. This is because if a construction reaches something that is unconscious, then it will always be slightly off the mark, and will be related to a connected point; the patient's response thus has a metonymic character. The patient's confirmation always occurs indirectly and allusively in relation to details that "fit in" in general with the content of the construction.

In reality, there is never any genuine confirmation of the analyst's constructions, only effects that resemble dream hallucination or that trigger a sense of reality, as described in the *Project*. These effects can be attributed to transference, which can be compared with the displacement of the intensity of a representation onto an indifferent element, or with a detail's capacity to attract what has been repressed. Freud, however, never confuses truth with reality. Truth, which has been repressed, returns either in the form of an hallucination or at least as something that is *Uberdeutlich* (ultra-clear).[10] Freud, having had the audacity to put hallucinations and the real on the same level, was convinced, ever since *The Interpretation of Dreams*, that the feeling of reality (*Wirklichgefühl*) is a sign of the repressed.

A construction therefore constitutes a "reality test" for the subject, and the way in which the latter responds to a construction recalls the vicissitudes of the drive; this drive is either accepted or rejected (*verworfen*) once it has been "submit[ted] … to examination by the highest agencies of our mind" (Freud, "My contact with Josef Popper-Lynkeus", p. 221). Again, it is the modality of transference that plays the decisive role.[11]

Just as a construction brings into play a logic of material implication, it also testifies that, as Lacan tells us in *Television*, "The unconscious impl[ies] that it be listened to" (p. 14). Thus, the analyst provides modest glosses on an unconscious of which she herself constitutes a part, neither takes control over this truth nor lays any claims to having any "authority for it", or any authority to construct it ("Constructions in Analysis", p. 265). Instead, she relies on the time for understanding, rather like Nestroy, whose answer to any question was invariably, "It will all become clear in the course of future developments" (p. 265).

Notes

1. "The determination of the original state of things thus invariably remains a matter of construction" (Freud, *Totem and Taboo*, p. 103, note).
2. See S. Freud, *A Child is Being Beaten*. A censored statement must be introduced into the composition of the phantasy: "My father is beating me" is a construction.

3. Lacan uses the term "bits of real" ("*bouts de réel*") in *Seminar XXIII* (p. 123).

4. In German, *gebannt* means "fascinated" and "banned". See *G. W.: XII,* p. 135.

5. Concerning the history of this concept, see J. Strachey's translator's footnote to "Constructions in Analysis", p. 266, and Granoff, p. 368.

6. The translation from the Standard Edition has been altered in order to reproduce the faulty element that the author notes in the French translation. Strachey's translation actually uses "formed", rather than "constructed" (translator's note).

7. In the Standard Edition, Freud's term here, *reale Nichtigkeit*, is translated as "a real event of no importance" (*S. E., 11,* p. 83); the "enigmatic" French translation to which Cottet refers is "*riens réels*" (translator's note).

8. "We too believe that the pious solution contains the truth—but the *historical* truth and not the *material* truth" (*Moses and Monotheism,* p. 129). Concerning this point, see Clément's *Le Pouvoir des mots,* which rightly sets up an opposition between construction and hermeneutics (p. 67).

9. Freud makes a (Karl) Popperian objection to himself: the psychoanalyst is irrefutable—heads I win, tails you lose. The article goes on to solve this aporia with a proof "by its effects".

10. "They have had lively recollections called up in them—which they themselves have described as 'ultra-clear'—but what they have recollected has not been the event that was the subject of the construction but details relating to that subject" ("Constructions in Analysis", p. 266). See also note 42.

11. Alexander anticipates this point by conceiving of the treatment as the equivalent of reality-testing when it is judgement, rather than repression, that decides the fate of the drive; this supposes that the superego's interference has ceased (see Alexander, "A Metapsychological Description of the Process of Cure", p. 13).

CHAPTER NINE

Freud's excavations and the archaeologist's desire

As we have seen, Freud's search for an "archaic" element is a protective measure against suggestion: a guarantee of the Other Scene that the analytic scene seeks to attain through speech. Two conceptions of the real involved in treatment can therefore be proposed:

- Either there is no "reality" other than that of the transference, and the goal of treatment is to encourage the latter to emerge. The transference thus becomes the truth of everything the patient has said and the only referent of psychoanalysis.
- Or else, the efficacy of the transference depends solely on the signifier; in other words, it is a result of interpretation. Transference is therefore an effect of theory and a product of the signifier, and, as such, it is not external to discourse.

The first hypothesis, put forward by Octave Mannoni in *Un commencement qui n'en finit pas: transfert, interprétation, théorie*, leads to a conception in which psychoanalytic discourse must perpetually miss its object. This hypothesis suggests that Freud's archaeological desire was founded on a question that he constantly avoided: what is the place from which the analyst speaks? The unsaid in psychoanalytic investigation would therefore be both the condition for discovery and the primally repressed material that characterizes psychoanalysis (Mannoni, *Clefs pour l'imaginaire*, pp. 115–130).

Mannoni's argument, which I shall be contesting in this chapter, is that transference and theory are incompatible. More precisely, transference is the indigestible object of theory, and as such reveals both the extent of the latter's error and the limit that it cannot admit into its field: "Theory cannot theorise its relation to transference. [...] Theory is deployed around transference, like the image of the world around the *punctum caecum*. It would be even better to say that theory serves as a defence—and often very usefully—against transference" (*"Un commencement qui n'en finit pas"*, p. 44).

Thus, according to Mannoni, theories are fictions that are organized around the thing-in-itself: the transference. Applied to Freud, this conception provides the key to his desire: look for the transference that underlies each new stage of his theory. Mannoni's prime example is Freud's transference to Fliess, which, he argues, had to be dissolved before Freud's theory of paranoia could emerge (*Clefs pour l'imaginaire*, p. 115).

The consequence of Mannoni's interpretation is that there can be no possible theory of transference itself. He tells us that "The pathological element of theory is not error," and leaves us to conclude that it is, instead, the theoretician's transference (*"Un commencement qui n'en finit pas"*, p. 45). In these conditions, transference takes on the character of a shadowy irrationality; theory becomes the place of an illusion of mastery that compensates for the loss suffered by the ego. In Mannoni's opinion, "Transference does not pose this kind of problem, for it is already the very essence of the pathological, an essence that is necessary for us" (p. 45).

The real of psychoanalysis becomes the *diabolus in psychanalytica*. Thus, Freud's transference to Jung contains the truth of his desire in the Wolf Man case. The analytical situation consists not in a dual but in a three-person relation. Theory is a part of what is at stake in the treatment, and Freud's love of theory is determined by his relation with a third party, with whom he is settling his theoretical accounts. Mannoni meanwhile claims that historical truth cannot be established on the basis of the signifier alone and contrasts Freud's situation with that of Heinrich Schliemann, the archaeologist who "founded historical *truth* on the *realities* that he had dug up in Asia Minor" ("*Un commencement qui n'en finit pas*", p. 44, emphasis added). He nevertheless concludes that Schliemann's approach is unsuited to psychoanalysis, since the only reality of any consequence in treatment is transference.

> In analysis, the *reality of the past* cannot function as evidence, for it cannot prove a memory's truth; outside the memory, this reality has no existence. Freud had already made this unfortunate choice during the Wolf Man's analysis. The tenacity of this attitude says a lot about the importance of transference to him. (p. 44, emphasis added)

Several remarks can be made about this question. As we have seen, Freud distinguishes clearly between historical or reconstructed truth and material truth (*Moses and Monotheism*, p. 129). This is why he allows for several different versions of the primal scene. It is always a matter, as Lacan says, of giving "an epic form" to structure: "Even if the memories of familial suppression weren't true, they would have to be invented, and that is certainly done. That's what myth is, the attempt to give an epic form to what is operative through the structure" (*Television*, p. 30). If there is a Freudian epistemology, it is oriented by the principle that the truth-effects produced by an interpretation have the same nature as theory itself. What provides the vectors of Freud's desire and sometimes makes his style of interpretation seem wild is the character of truth: the "carp of truth" can be caught with "our bait of falsehood" (Freud, "Constructions in Analysis", p. 262).

Truth, in other words, depends on being half-said. In this sense, truth and psychic reality have the same nature; truth in this context is defined as the limit of what the psychic apparatus can tolerate: "The psychical apparatus is intolerant of unpleasure; it has to fend it off at all costs, and if the perception of reality entails unpleasure, that perception—that is, the truth—must be sacrificed" ("Analysis Terminable and Interminable", p. 237).

Truth cannot be disassociated from fiction.[1] One cannot treat truth and theory in terms of an opposition between that which is absolute versus that which is relative; Freud's criterion for a good theory is that it should produce truth-effects during treatment. It is only on the condition that theory contains an element of myth that there can be any saying (*dire*) of truth. Far from opposing theory and transference in terms of a semblance versus a real, Lacan maintains that the transference is "nothing real in the subject" but signals a stagnation, or even a symptom. This dialectic between transference and interpretation invalidates any conception of transference in terms of a relation to an actual person. Even trust, which is only a part of transference, largely depends on the truth-effect produced by a construction. According to Freud, such effects are far more important than any possible "concordance" with the real.[2] This is because what truth fills up is not an imaginary lacuna—a memory—but a symbolic lacuna, which can only be produced by speech.

This is why Freud thinks it essential to distinguish between the analyst's "phantasy" and the reality that is involved in the patient's phantasy (*The Wolf Man*, p. 52). This distinction concerns the scientific status of analysis. Indeed, Freud seeks in the real, whether or not it is traumatic, the grounds of repetition. In *The Wolf Man*, for instance, Freud tells us that "either the analysis based on the neurosis in his childhood is all a piece of nonsense from start to finish, or everything took place just as I have described it above" (*The Wolf Man*, p. 56). We have seen, however, that Freud's aim is to establish not historical truth, but rather certitude. As a comparison of *The Wolf Man* and "Constructions in Analysis" shows, he gives the same value to constructions as to memories. This equivalence, which he justifies by means of the therapeutic effect obtained, supports his—and therefore his patient's—certitude that psychic and material reality cannot be treated in terms of an opposition between imaginary and real. There is something of the real in dreams. In *The Wolf Man*, Freud explains that "It is this recurrence in dreams that [he regards] as the explanation of the fact that the patients themselves gradually acquire a profound conviction of the reality of these primal scenes, a conviction which is in no respect inferior to one based on recollection" (*The Wolf Man*, p. 51).

Many of Freud's commentators, the first of whom was Jung, have seized upon this point. Even Freud himself wonders, in 1925, whether, before he discovered the Oedipus complex, he had not suggested his patients' phantasies to them ("An Autobiographical Study", p. 34). On the other hand, he never ceases to believe in the element of truth in his theory of seduction. He also, in *The Wolf Man*, tries very seriously to make sure of the "reality" of the primal scene, and does so with a determination that affects the development of the treatment. Lacan even hypothesizes that there is a direct causal relation between Freud's obstinate search and the turn taken in the Wolf Man's analysis in 1925. He also notes that Freud is unable to describe the function of the phantasy without resorting to the category of the real (*Seminar XI*, p. 41):

> We feel that throughout this analysis, this real brings with it the subject, almost by force, so directing the research that, after all, we can today ask ourselves whether this fever, this presence, this desire of Freud is not that which, in his patient, might have conditioned the belated accident of his psychosis. (*Seminar XI*, p. 54)[3]

For Freud, the primal scene has the same effect of seducing the patient and activating his symptoms as the trauma had in hysteria. The retroactive effect of this scene shows the extent to which this schema from hysteria endures, despite all Freud's subsequent theoretical reformulations. The scene acts, he says, "like a second seduction" (*The Wolf Man*, p. 47).

Far from being condemned to disappear, the principle of seduction is preserved and enriched by Freud's theories of civilization and collective myths. The myth of *Totem and Taboo* had just provided a cultural basis for the individual primal scene: the *Urszene*—the primal father's sexual act. Whereas in the individual myth, the father enjoys only the mother, in the group myth, he is now considered to enjoy all women. We note in passing that the father's jouissance is implicated in all the so-called "primal" phantasies: castration, the primal scene, and seduction.

Freud thus does not abandon his primal scene in *The Wolf Man*. Indeed, he in fact considers it no less "benign" than before. Furthermore, it concerns nothing less than the very origin of civilization. Originally depicted as a private scene, it now attains the status of a collective scene witnessed by all. As such, it inaugurates a new order that Freud calls "civilization" and which Lacan, in the context of structuralism, calls the symbolic order. Schliemann can be mentioned once again, since, beneath the various phantasies, the real of the father's jouissance can be found. *Totem and Taboo* restores the *Urszene* of the murder of the father, which Freud conceived of as real: "It is as if Schliemann had once more excavated Troy, which had hitherto been deemed a fable" (Masson, pp. 391–392).

In a well-known article, "Fantasy and the Origins of Sexuality", Laplanche and Pontalis bring out the importance of these primal phantasies and attempt to identify Freud's theoretical paradigm with his desire. They observe that, having undergone a first reversal in favour of the search for "an ultimate truth", "the same schema is used once more, the dialectic of the two successive historical events, the same disappointment—as if Freud had learned nothing—as the ultimate event, the 'scene', disappears over the horizon" (p. 121). What takes the role of the ultimate bedrock, however, has been displaced from an individual to a collective level. According to Freud, these are primal phantasies, *Urphantasie*, which constitute the stage on which the inaugural drama of society is played out, a stage which had been set by the murder of the *Urvater*:

> In the concept of original fantasy, there is a continuation of what we might call Freud's desire to reach the bedrock of the event (and if this disappears by refraction or reduction, then one must look further back still), and the need to establish the structure of the fantasy itself by something other than the event. (Laplanche & Pontalis, p. 121)

In relation to this statement, a passage at the end of *The Wolf Man* becomes relevant. Freud tells us:

> Wherever experiences fail to fit in with the hereditary schema, they become remodelled in the imagination a process which might very profitably be followed out in detail. It is precisely such cases that are calculated to convince us of the independent existence of the schema. We are often able to see the schema triumphing over the experience of the individual; as when in our present case the boy's father became the castrator and the menace of his infantile sexuality in spite of what was in other respects an inverted Oedipus complex. (p. 119)

It is thus essential to distinguish between structure and event. Freud is no longer attempting to unveil an event but rather to construct a real, and this disrupts his whole theory of construction. His aim is no longer to disclose to the patient the Oedipal myth—the encounter between psychic reality and paternal interdiction, a conjunction that, as he tells us in *The Rat Man*, surprised him enormously. On the contrary, he now believes that psychic reality is founded on a material reality that is independent of the contingencies of history and chance encounters.

This real, which we are all forced to confront, is the sexual act (*Totem and Taboo*, pp. 69–70).

Events that had been experienced, such as childhood impressions, played a far less important role in Freud's work after *The Wolf Man*, primarily because they have been lost to memory, and secondly because reconstructing them "achieves the same therapeutic result as a recaptured memory" ("Constructions in Analysis", p. 266). When Freud, to his surprise, discovers that memories and constructions are equivalent from a therapeutic point of view, his recourse to primal phantasies provides the necessary means to account for this paradox. This appeal to the real—the invocation of Ananke—indeed constitutes a last effort on the part of psychoanalysis to dispel the myth that the all-mighty castration is universal and even the analyst is subjected to it. In letting his patients know this in a number of different ways, Freud was able to avoid occupying the place of God. It cannot be claimed that he ever abandoned his quest for a primal scene. It is important, however, to distinguish between the "reality" of the scene itself and the real that it covers over: the castration of the Other. That this real can only be apprehended by following the path of myths confirms Freud's theory that psychic reality is subordinated to the symbolic.

Notes

1. Maud Mannoni, because she does not distinguish truth from theory, ends up mistaking theory for fiction. See M. Mannoni, *La Théorie comme fiction: Freud, Groddeck, Winnicott, Lacan*.

2. This is why Freud places Gradiva as an ideal model or rather as Norbert Hanold's object *a*: both cause and object of desire. In the analytic relation, on the other hand, transference is the obstacle that turns the analyst into a signifier that does not respond to love. See Freud, *Delusions and Dreams in Jensen's Gradiva*.

3. Freud's intervention "in the real" has aroused very different reactions. In his article on the Wolf Man, Serge Leclaire claims that at this moment, Freud abandons the place of the symbolic father in order to institute an imaginary mode of "anal exchange", thus creating the conditions for his patient's entry into psychosis (see "*À propos de l'épisode psychotique que présenta 'L'homme aux loups'*", p. 83.) Just as it can be doubted that the Wolf Man ever had a psychotic episode, so also can one doubt that Freud's desire drove him mad. What is certain is that the place of symbolic father is not the best one to occupy if the analyst wishes to avoid

the worst. Lacan diminished the analyst in order, in the end, to put him in the place of the object, rather than of the symbolic father; this can remind us of the ravages that the latter position can involve. Freud, in his own way, had enough intuition to refuse the place of saviour, preferring—not, it is true, without a certain awkwardness—scientific "curiosity". Since then, there has been worse; I have explored this in *"Profession: homme aux loups"*.

CHAPTER TEN

Successful paranoia

The psychoanalytic process tends occasionally to veer towards interpretative delusion. We shall take it for granted that this was not Freud's orientation. According to him, this delusion is, instead, the realm of philosophy, which as a *Weltanschauung*, reduces all the problems of our existence to "a single principle", which can be characterized as an interpretative delusion (*New Introductory Lectures*, p. 52).

It is nevertheless currently fashionable to claim that theory and delusion have the same character. Indeed, according to some authors, psychoanalysis undermines all attempts to discriminate between theory and madness (see Mannoni, 1980, and Fédida, 1978). They borrow Freud's argument that psychoanalysis resorts constantly to fiction, phantasy, and the imaginary.[1] Rather than pursuing this debate along epistemological lines, I would prefer to consider the reasons why Freud holds psychoanalysis to be something other than a delusion. The difference between psychoanalysis and paranoiac delusions will shed new light on the nature of his desire.

In a letter to Ferenczi, Freud claims to have overcome his own personal paranoia:

> You not only noticed, but also understood, that I *no longer* have any need to uncover my personality completely, and you correctly traced this back to the traumatic reason for it. Since Fliess's case, with the overcoming of which you recently saw me occupied, that need has been extinguished. A part of homosexual cathexis has been withdrawn and made use of to enlarge my own ego. I have succeeded where the paranoiac fails. (Jones, 1955, p. 92)

Does this necessarily mean that psychoanalysis is a successful paranoia? The question of the treatment can also be asked in Lacan's terms, for in "Aggressiveness in Psychoanalysis", he speaks of a "guided paranoia" (*Écrits*, p. 89). It is important to emphasize this notion of guidance, however, in order to differentiate properly between a real delusion and the aim of the psychoanalyst, which is to encourage the subject to recognize what tempts him: the acceptance of the repressed drive. In other words, it is not so much the psychoanalyst who takes the paranoiac as his model but rather the patient who, in the course of treatment, inevitably experiences a negative transference. In this context, the persecuting figure of the Other can appear in the place of his bad object or fundamental *kakon*. If the latter is repressed, hatred comes to dominate the transference, as is clearly illustrated in *The Rat Man*.

Is it not, then, precisely Freud's desire that prevents psychoanalysis from being a delusion? This is possible since the paranoiac's desire is to be represented by all the signifiers in the world, and it is thus systematically opposed to Freud's desire to renounce all visions of the world. It is true that this trait would not, in itself, be enough to distinguish psychoanalysis from delusion, since philosophy can also, in this respect, be assimilated to paranoia (see Assoun, pp. 103–105). If philosophy can be considered the "prototype" of a *Weltanschauung*, it is because the underlying principle of the former, like that of paranoia, is narcissism. Freud, who argues that philosophy was a form of animism, defines it as "an intellectual system that describes the totality of the world as a single set that starts off at one point" (Assoun, p. 103). Indeed, it was ultimately as a reaction against this narcissistic pride that he rejects philosophy, and the reassuring efforts of its proponents to control existence. To the latter, he opposes a "need for certitude" that transforms the psychoanalyst's desire into an *x* that is correlated to the desire that characterizes science (Freud, *Inhibitions, Symptoms and Anxiety*, p. 96).

Psychoanalytic objectivity does not seek refuge in verification: its objectivity is strictly linked to the analytic situation. Since the latter cannot be verified by a third party, it is invalidated as a science and can respond only by means of the structure of the imaginary. This is what Lacan means when he defines psychoanalysis as "the science of mirages that arise within this field" (*Écrits*, p. 339).

This is why Freud's letter to Ferenczi, which he wrote shortly after his account of Schreber, ought to be considered in the context of the passage in which he highlights the "striking conformity" between Schreber's delusions and his own theory:

> Schreber's "rays of God", which are made up of a condensation of the sun's rays, of nerve-fibres, and of spermatozoa, are in reality nothing other than a concrete representation and projection outwards of libidinal cathexes; and thus they lend his delusions a striking conformity with our theory. His belief that the world must come to an end because his ego was attracting all the rays to itself, his anxious concern at a later period, during the process of reconstruction, lest God should sever His ray-connection with him, these and many other details of Schreber's delusional structure sound almost like endopsychic perceptions of the processes whose existence I have assumed in these pages as the basis of our explanation of paranoia. (Freud, *Schreber*, pp. 78–79)

Freud wishes to claim this discovery for himself, however, asserting that he had developed his theory of paranoia before he "became acquainted with the contents of Schreber's book" (*Schreber*, p. 79). It is therefore to his correspondence with Jung that we should turn in relation to this initial discovery. Since, however, I am specifically concerned with the relation between psychoanalysis and delusion, and since Freud tells us that he has been able to escape the avatar of a homosexual relation, my aim is to establish the process that makes psychoanalysis into a successful paranoia. If what psychoanalysis shares with paranoiac delusion is the theory of the libido, this is because paranoia highlights a structure of desire: one in which narcissism prevails and in which the relation with the other excludes a symbolic relation with the Other.

There may even be a closer connection between them. Octave Mannoni, for example, writes that:

> There is no doubt that the first therapeutic analysis, which was also the first training analysis, was also the first treatment that prevented an outbreak of paranoia. This is not without its importance. There is also a certain relation between paranoiac understanding [*connaissance*] and the knowledge [*savoir*] founded on unconscious desire. (*Clefs pour l'imaginaire*, p. 118)

In my opinion, however, Mannoni's conclusion misses the point, which is that paranoia—like psychoanalysis—is a theory of the sexual relation. In his attempt to found a science of sexual desire—in seeking a mathematical "proportion" between men and women—Freud accords great importance to Fliess, whose aim was to give mathematical expression to this relation. It is extremely important, however, to distinguish clearly between Fliess and Freud. If we consider Fliess's theory of periods to be paranoiac, we disqualify its claim to scientific status; this does not, however, mean that it necessarily contradicts observation.

What gives this esoteric aspect to Fliess's periodicity is that the real of the body is harmonized with the movement of the heavens: the female cycle is seen to correspond to cosmic rhythm, and the celestial bodies—the clocks of our world—accord with feminine periods. According to both Schreber and Fliess, feminine and masculine elements are ultimately inscribed in numbers, the woman's number being twenty-eight and the man's twenty-three. Fliess's delusional theory of the anatomical analogy between the nose and the genital organs circumvents sexual difference by not assigning it a symbolic inscription. His theory of bisexuality reduces the difference between man and woman to a purely quantitative difference, thus justifying his mathematical flights of fancy. His clever combinations of the two numbers simply compensate for the impossibility of writing a symbol that could account for the relation between man and woman. It is precisely on this point that Freud, putting forward his lack of mathematical knowledge as an excuse, differs from Fliess (Masson, p. 450).

Freud's reticence to side with Fliess in this matter paradoxically reveals the proximity of his desire with that of the mathematician, who is precisely not led astray by the jouissance of meaning *(sens)*. Fliess, on the other hand, believes that he can attribute sexual meaning to a mathematical proportion. The very universe resounds to the note of mathematical difference that he invariably discovers in all his calculations. It seems that introducing sexual difference into a complicated calculation is thus only a short step away from linking men and women through a simple arithmetical operation. Only by abandoning his own efforts to establish the correct proportion between masculinity and femininity is Freud ultimately able to use Fliess's delusional theory of bisexuality constructively.

It was not without irony that Freud remarks to Fliess that:

> Today several very strange things occurred to me, which I do not yet properly understand at all. As far as I am concerned, there is no question of deliberation. This method of working moves along by fits and starts. God alone knows the date of the next thrust, unless you have figured out my formula. (Masson, p. 379)

Freud's formula suggests that, in his own case, the particular vicissitude of the sexual drive in question in paranoia—homosexuality—has, instead of regressing to narcissism, been sublimated. The expansion of the ego in this case suggests that one of the avatars of paranoia could lead to psychoanalysis. Rather than two discourses, one of which would be the obverse of the other, we are dealing with the paradoxical outcome of a question that concerns both science and madness. Freud's reference to a "formula" refers to his past relations with Fliess, who was led to formulate his delusional theory precisely because his homosexuality had not been sublimated. It remains to be shown, however, that the result of this failure is precisely his doctrine of biological bisexuality, in which all signs of masculinity or femininity are transferred to the real and to the entire universe. Indeed, a delusional theory of the division between men and women is also present in ordinary ideology, with the difference that it has not been formulated as a doctrine, as Fliess has done. Fliess sought to express desire in terms of a formula; he wanted to represent the sexual relation in terms of knowledge about the cycles that determined its course. Since this cycle is inherently mechanical and subjected to cosmic laws, Freud's revolution lies in renouncing this imaginary model of astral revolution, despite the fact that, in his references to Copernicus, he uses this revolution as a model for psychoanalysis.

Freud's ironic remarks might thus serve as a theoretical illustration of the inherent opposition between a paranoiac conception of sexuality, according to which the foreseeable nature of desire is a result of a prior encryption (*chiffrage*), and his own conception of sexuality, which postulates that there is a constant "pushing" of the drive. This latter principle, which marks a theoretical *coup d'état*, subsequently guides his entire doctrine of sublimation. The premise of this doctrine is a theory that libido is a form of energy that can be transformed, but about which one can know nothing—since libido is a myth—except that it is a constant, and therefore makes desire indestructible.

One can thus see how psychoanalysis is related to science; this relation is not, however, to be found in any similarity with theories that are analogous to paranoiac delusions. What would a "science" be if it remained unaware of the impossibility of a sexual relation and, under the cover of a specific knowledge about difference, kept alive the hope of reducing it to a single principle?[2]

It is a miracle that Freud, who never abandoned the scientistic ideals inspired by his teacher Brücke, did not transform psychoanalysis into a paranoiac delusion. The safeguard against this turns out to have been Fliess's delusion itself. Fliess's failure, which Freud attributes to a homosexual drive that has not been sublimated, proved to be highly instructive.

We might wonder what it was that especially seduced Freud before he read Schreber's *Memoirs* on Jung's recommendation. Dreaming of giving a scientific status to psychoanalysis, he may have turned to Fliess, until he was forced to confront an impossibility. Science is the phantasy of an impossible mastery of the real, and Freud now begins to present the real of sexuality in terms of the enigma of femininity: of the absolute Other that cannot be formalized.

Notes

1. In "Constructions in Analysis", Freud admits that he is tempted to succumb to the attraction of an analogy between theory and delusion given the "kernel of truth" included in the latter (p. 268).
2. Freud once again highlighted this danger in 1917, in reference to Groddeck's work: "I am afraid that you are a philosopher as well" (E. L. Freud, p. 318).

CHAPTER ELEVEN

The Freudian myth

A change of couch

In 1925, Freud confides to his disciple Kardiner that his patients no longer interest him unless they contribute to his own theories (see *My Analysis with Freud*, pp. 68–69). His enthusiasm for therapy, in any case, was never so great as to lead him to sacrifice his taste for pure speculation to it. In 1928, for example, he writes to Pfister that "I have often said that I hold that the purely medical importance of analysis is outweighed by its importance to science as a whole, and that its general influence by means of clarification and the exposure of error exceeds its therapeutic value to the individual" (Meng & Freud, p. 120).

It is clear, however, that if there was a change in Freud's attitude towards clinical practice, it was caused by the clinic itself and by the real that it had brought to light. His loss of interest is in part caused by his discovery of his patients' "negative therapeutic reaction", which, to his great surprise, emerges as the ultimate source of resistance (Freud, *The Ego and the Id*, pp. 49–50). His inability to heal and the patients' inability to be cured are not to be the limits of a doctrine that differs from others by being able to go back to the sources of desire, in the death drive.

If nothing can be done about what is impossible, he can, nevertheless, analyse the real which constitutes a symptom in civilization.

Freud thus compensates for his lack of interest in his patients after 1925 by defending the Freudian cause. Unable to lead them to a point that they could locate as the cause of their desire, he identifies himself with the alternative cause of propagating analysis and extending its implications to civilization. This is what he does in *Civilization and its Discontents*. It is not civilization itself that Freud indicts, but rather repression, which accounts for the symptom constituted by civilization. Lacan tells us that as Freud "progressed there, he leaned more toward the idea that repression was primary. That, on the whole, is what tipped the scales toward the second topography. The greediness by which he characterizes the superego is structural, not an effect of civilization, but 'discontent (symptom) in civilization'" (*Television*, p. 28).

Freud's primary patient from then on was humanity itself: "It was no small thing to have the whole human race as one's patient" (Freud, "Resistances to Psycho-Analysis", p. 221). Just as the analyst's "constructions" are intended to capture forgotten memories—and if necessary produce their symbolic equivalent—so too, in seeking to go back to the sources of the discontents in civilization—it is necessary to invent "Just so Stories" (*Group Psychology*, p. 122). Such stories locate, at the very birth of civilization, the act that inaugurated a fatal history. It is most certainly in his texts on the father—and, in particular, on his death and the myths relating to his murder—that Freud's desire can find a light to guide its path.

An indication of the latter had already appeared in the famous example of forgetting the name "Signorelli" in the opening chapter of the *Psychopathology of Everyday Life*. In his remarks on this example, Lacan explains that what is *unterdrückt* evokes the absolute Master, or death. Indeed, Freud's work has, from the very start, been oriented towards this myth, in which death is linked to the father's murder. For this reason, Lacan asks, "Do we not see, behind this, the emergence of that which forced Freud to find in the myths of the death of the father the regulation of his desire?" (*Seminar XI*, p. 27).

Lacan's use of the term "regulation" suggests that myths are necessary to legitimize sexual desire. This is the way, as we have seen, that Freud himself uses the Oedipus myth with Little Hans, in order to lift the small boy's repression of his aggressiveness towards his father.

Just as strange phantasmatic scenarios can only be deciphered by introducing the signifiers that have been censored, so also the bizarre construction of Freud's own myth refers back to a truth that remains veiled in his text. The work of censorship confers an appearance of hidden depth and obscure mystery on an otherwise straightforward text; we can conclude from this that Freud's own myths are similarly founded on repression. It is, indeed, the very multiplication of these different versions of his myth of the father's murder that puts us on the trail of its repressed signification. Each new version, instead of adding a new meaning that has been hidden by the others, shows how the same structure keeps emerging. These myths are so many "Just so Stories", all of which point to the same stumbling block: their attempt to avoid the father's castration. The father is not castrated. This could be the repressed truth at the heart of the mythical edifice of the Oedipus complex, which is also related to Nietzsche's myth of the death of God. In Lacan's opinion: "Perhaps this myth is simply a shelter against the threat of castration" (*Seminar XI*, p. 27).

Freud does not seem very far from the myth of Oedipus when he constructs the figure of the *Urvater* of the horde. There is a difference, however, between the ideology of the Oedipus complex, in which murdering the father leads to liberation, and that of the myth of the horde, where the father's murder is neither a message of good tidings nor a sign of hope.

Having them all

If, as Lacan says, the Oedipus complex was only a dream on Freud's part, we can draw the two following conclusions:

1. It can be deciphered like a symptom, for it has a latent content that can be brought to light.
2. The dream is a realization of a desire, and therefore either Freud's invention contains the grounds of his desire or it can point us in the right direction.

We thus have a way to look for Freud's "individual myth", to use Lacan's expression (see Lacan, "The Neurotic's Individual Myth"). The latter, however, raises a certain number of paradoxes, since it contradicts the ethnological definition of a myth, which says that a myth is a fiction that relates a whole community to its origin, thus ensuring it an historical continuity.

The collective character of a myth distinguishes it, for example—as Georges Dumézil liked to say—from a novel. This character, according to Freud, accounts for the predominance of individual novels over myths in modern societies, the very societies that generate neuroses. The neurotic, with his individual family story, is thus a poet without a name. Yet the poet, thanks to his talent, can use his neurosis to create a social fabric by communicating what is universal in his story, thus giving an epic form to his Oedipus complex. "[O]ur actual enjoyment of an imaginative work proceeds from a liberation of tensions in our minds. It may even be that not a little of this effect is due to the writer's enabling us thenceforward to enjoy our own day-dreams without self-reproach or shame" ("Creative Writers and Day-Dreaming", p. 153). To the ego's individual story, Freud thus opposes the literary genre of myths, legends and tales containing "the *secular dreams* of youthful humanity" (p. 152).

So what exactly should we make of Freud's own myths, and in particular, his favourite, *Totem and Taboo*? It is precisely this text that enables Lacan to identify what he calls Freud's neurosis, after having already often pointed to its symptomatic status in Freud's work:

> It is curious that I have had to wait this long for it to be pos-
> sible to make a similar assertion, namely that *Totem and Taboo* is
> a neurotic product, without also throwing doubt on the truth of its
> construction. This is even why it testifies to the truth. One does not
> psychoanalyze a work, and still less Freud's own. One critiques it.
> (*Seminar XVIII*, p. 161)

What exactly does Lacan mean when he defines the Oedipus myth as a product of neurosis? What remains censored and veiled in this myth emerges more clearly in *Totem and Taboo* (pp. 140–142) and *Moses* (pp. 81–82). Neither of these texts considers the prohibition of incest. Instead, *all* women are forbidden to the sons and only the father has access to jouissance. Yet in the earlier Oedipus myth, no mention is made either of the royal bed or of the father's jouissance. Moreover, if it is the father's death that enables the son to have access to jouissance, Oedipus remains totally unaware of this. In fact, in the Sophoclean version of the Oedipus myth, what is described is not really an Oedipal murder, for the Oedipal father is the one who recognizes his son, rather than being the one who is killed. It also cannot be said that jouissance is made possible by transgression. Nothing is forbidden since there is no law; the law prohibiting incest is absent in this version of the myth. The only law of any importance is that of Jocasta's desire. In its later version, however, relations are reversed. Not only is the father deliberately and collectively killed, but this action does not lead to sexual liberation. His murder is motivated by rivalry and sexual jealousy aroused by his gluttonous appetites. It is clear that his pure jouissance cannot be shared, but no law forbids it to the sons. The prohibition bears on all women, rather than on any particular woman. Lacan's conclusion is that according to Freud, the father's jouissance is not barred. The primal father who possesses all women is thus an epic representation of Lacan's formula of universal castration—$\forall x. \Phi x$—with the exception of the father: $\exists x. \overline{\Phi x}$ (*Seminar XX*, p. 79). In *Moses and Monotheism*, Freud defines the father of the horde as follows: "The strong male was lord and father of the entire horde and unrestricted in his power, which he exercised with violence. All the females were his property—wives and daughters of his own horde and some, perhaps, robbed from other hordes" (p. 81).

Freud's myth, however, dresses up what we might call a logical impossibility as a *de facto* incapacity. Sexual relations are prohibited because the father keeps all women for himself. The foundation for the prohibition of jouissance is not the myth of the father's supreme power and the consequences of his murder are not what might have been expected. There is even less jouissance afterwards. Indeed, it is the sons who subsequently prohibit women to themselves so that the sexual rivalry that has not ceased after the father's death will not entail the disappearance of the whole species:

> ... the brothers disputed with one another for their father's heritage, which each of them wanted for himself alone. [They realized] the dangers and uselessness of these struggles [...]. The first form of a social organization came about with a *renunciation of instinct*, a recognition of mutual *obligations*, the introduction of definite *institutions*, pronounced inviolable (holy) that is to say, the beginnings of morality and justice. Each individual renounced his ideal of acquiring his father's position for himself and of possessing his mother and sisters. Thus the *taboo on incest* and the injunction to *exogamy* came about. (*Moses and Monotheism*, p. 82)

This particularly Darwinian version of the myth does not, however, account for the bond of love that binds the sons to the father. It is only because they love him that they take him as a model. If each of them aspired to take his place, their number alone would threaten the existence of this place. They therefore abandon their attempts to occupy this place out of respect for the father. As Freud notes in a striking short cut, "The primal father had prevented his sons from satisfying their directly sexual impulsions; he forced them into abstinence and consequently into the emotional ties with him and with one another which could arise out of those of their impulsions that were inhibited in their sexual aim" (*Group Psychology*, p. 124).

The idea that renunciation depends on love for the despot was supported by Freud's new theory that the inhibition of the drive (*Zielhemmung*) is the source of affection and love. Freud, as we know, generally claims that while renouncing the sexual object and direct jouissance of it leads to idealization and affectionate feelings for it, the prohibiting figure, on the other hand, arouses hatred (*The Rat Man*, pp. 204–205). The father who appears at this point is therefore a new one: a figure who inspires love precisely by prohibiting jouissance. In a letter addressed to the "Committee" in 1924 following the publication of Rank's and Ferenczi's works, Freud reiterates his theory of paternal interdiction as follows: "In analysis we shall always come upon the father as the bearer of the prohibition" (Falzeder, p. 482).

There is no reason, however, to equate this father of the law with the unrepentant father. On the other hand, in the myth of the horde, there is no other law than that of the father's blind jouissance.

According to Lacan, this explains why guilt can only be understood in the context of a love relation ex-sisting between father and son:

> The bo-knot only translates something that I was reminded of last night: that love, and, to top it all off, the love that can be called eternal, is related to the function of the father since the father is the bearer of castration. It is insofar as the sons are deprived of women that they love the father—an incredible thing, which is confirmed only by Freud's intuition. (*Le séminaire XXIII*, p. 150)

In *Moses and Monotheism*, this new articulation between narcissistic satisfaction and the renunciation of jouissance offers us a glimpse of Freud's desire to save the father. Whereas *Civilization and its Discontents* is concerned with the cost of this renunciation—the revenge taken by the superego—in *Moses and Monotheism*, the phenomenology of renunciation is different. The superego becomes a model to which the subject must conform:

> Whereas instinctual renunciation, when it is for external reasons, is *only* unpleasurable, when it is for internal reasons, in obedience to the super-ego, it has a different economic effect. In addition to the inevitable unpleasurable consequences it also brings the ego a yield of pleasure—a substitutive satisfaction, as it were. [...] When the ego has brought the super-ego the sacrifice of an instinctual renunciation, it expects to be rewarded by receiving more love from it. (pp. 116–117)

The father is thus radically different in these two constructions. In *Moses and Monotheism*, the appeal to the law fundamentally disavows the murder of Moses, the "substitute for the father", a murder that repeats the murder of the *Urvater* (pp. 116–117). These laws, as Lacan shows us, can be reduced to the law of love required by the Father of religion (*Seminar VII*, pp. 167–178). The prohibition of incest, which is veiled by the ten commandments, points to the secret connection between this Father of religion and the jouissance of the father of the horde. It is, indeed, only because Freud succeeded in maintaining this relation between the symbolic father of *Totem and Taboo* and the imaginary Father of religion, that he was able to prevent psychoanalysis from slipping towards the latter. This also explains why Lacan says that Freud, with his "e-Mo(ses)tional character [*emmoïsation*]", may have been a dupe, but was nevertheless "the right kind of dupe, the kind who does not wander [*qui n'erre pas*]" (*Le séminaire XXII*, pp. 103–104).

Freud constructs this "exalted father" in the period between 1925 and 1930 with an intuition that there would be discontents in psychoanalysis (*The Future of an Illusion*, p. 22).[1] The nostalgia—which belongs specifically to childhood—for a father who actually amounted to something, would indeed place the analyst in a position where his responsibility grows, and where his act becomes subordinated to an ethic.

Note

1. On Freud's subjective position in relation to nostalgia for the father, see Conrad Stein's classic article "*Le père mortel et le père immortel*".

PART III

FREUDIAN ETHICS

I have tracked down a symptomatic action in myself. While I am analyzing and am waiting for the patient's reply, I often cast a quick glance at the picture of my parents. I know now that I always do this when I am following up the infantile transference in the patient. The glance is always accompanied by a particular guilt feeling: what will they think of me?

—Karl Abraham, *Letter to Freud*, 7 April 1909.*

*Falzeder, *The Complete Correspondence of Sigmund Freud and Karl Abraham 1907–1925*, p. 88.

CHAPTER TWELVE

The ethics of desire

According to Lacan, "An ethics must be formulated that integrates Freud's conquests concerning desire: one that would place at the forefront the question of the analyst's desire" (*Écrits*, p. 514).

Freud's discovery of repression and its effects in symptoms leads to a form of treatment in which the psychoanalyst is not entirely neutral. The psychoanalyst wants something—to lift repression ("Five Lectures", p. 39). Consequently her interventions, technique and interpretations all imply that she has taken a position on the question that philosophers have always asked: whether or not one should give up one's desires. Moralists, on the whole, are adamant. As Lacan says, "It has always been the political secret of moralists to incite the subject to remove [*dégager*] something—his stakes from the game of desire" (*Écrits*, p. 573).

Freud clearly does not agree. His entire work consists in an attempt to bring to light the ravages caused by "renouncing" the drives. According to him, it is precisely the discontents of desire that lead to the discontents in civilization. There is a special difficulty in being a desiring person in a society that on principle reduces all its activities to the level of utility, thereby putting a check on what is useless: sexual jouissance.

All moralities are moralities of repression since they consider that suspending desire—renouncing the drives—is always meritorious. Freud tries to give a "metapsychological" foundation for this belief in his analysis of the superego.

An entire facet of Freud's work is devoted to showing that renunciation is not a virtue but rather a form of cowardice. This is not in order to advocate a reversal of morality—which would be just as arbitrary in its principles as what it condemns—but for structural reasons concerning psychic reality.

Freud reverses the values attributed by moralists to guilt: one is guilty less because of forbidden desires than because one has been forbidden to satisfy them. He brings to the foreground the difference between two kinds of renunciation: that which is imposed by civilization, and the kind that the subject imposes upon himself. The latter is the *Versagung*.[1] In contrast to the theory that the criterion for normality is adapting to reality, he notes that individuals fall ill and become neurotic when they attempt to renounce a certain type of phantasized satisfaction in exchange for an object that ensures "a step forward from the point of view of real life" ("Types of Onset of Neurosis", p. 234). He provides three examples, three types of subjects, who are prey to desires that they prefer to renounce in order to comply with the ideals of civilization: first, the man who decides to stops masturbating in order to "choose a real object"; second, a young woman who wishes to transfer her affection for her father onto the young man who is courting her; third, a woman who, despite her phantasies of prostitution, aspires to found a family.

In all three cases, the desired displacement is impossible and the three subjects fall ill as a result of their renunciation. The conflict between reality and desire thus ends in a failure to adapt to reality:

> The change which the patients strive after, but bring about only imperfectly or not at all, invariably has the value of a step forward from the point of view of real life. It is otherwise if we apply ethical standards: we see people falling ill just as often when they discard an ideal as when they seek to attain it. (*Types of Onset of Neurosis*, p. 234)

Freud's conclusion, which lends justification to the analyst's prudent reticence, now brings us onto the subject of neutrality.

The meaning of neutrality

Since the analyst's so-called "benevolent neutrality" is not in fact a Freudian concept, I shall begin by clarifying what is generally meant by the term "neutrality", for while analysis clearly rules out the use of suggestion, this does not mean that the analyst is indifferent nor that her interventions cannot, on occasion, be active.[2] Freud certainly rules out the pride of the educator:

> We refused most emphatically to turn a patient who puts himself into our hands in search of help into our private property, to decide his fate for him, to force our own ideals upon him, and with the pride of a Creator to form him in our own image and see that it is good. ("Lines of Advance in Psycho-Analytic Therapy", p. 164)

In 1918, however, following the Budapest congress and under Ferenczi's influence, he begins to envision a more active technique, having until then bracketed off the question of the practical consequences of an analysis before its conclusion. I therefore propose to consider both the implications and the limits of the psychoanalyst's "abstinence" which clearly does not imply abstaining from desire.

"Neutrality", in the strictest sense of the term, means "neither one nor the other". In either Freud's use of it in his technical papers or in his discussion of transference love, its only possible meaning is that the analyst should not favour one element in an unconscious conflict over another (see "Analysis Terminable and Interminable", pp. 216–253, and *An Outline of Psycho-Analysis*, pp. 172–173). It is, indeed, the very structure of the subject of the unconscious—the concept of a divided subject—that obliges the analyst to suspend her judgement, a suspension that has an ethical character: it seeks not to suture the psychic conflict through an imposed interpretation, which would only be either a form of suggestion or educational training. In both of these cases, it is always posited that one force—for example, instinct—must be domesticated by another. It cannot be denied that Freud himself, on occasion, resorts to the concept of mastery, yet even his well-known idea of the ego's capacity to "dominate" the id, which subsequently led to the ideology of the strong ego, should not be considered in too dynamic a sense.

What Freud means, instead, is that an analyst should not presume to choose between two opposed agencies—contradictory signifiers—which govern the subject's unconscious and push it in contradictory ways. When he writes to Ferenczi that "A man should not strive to eliminate his complexes but to get into accord with them," he is evidently alluding to a form of division illustrated by the conflict of the drives (see Jones, 1955, p. 188).

From 1917 onwards, Freud places more and more of an accent on the conflict of the drives (*Triebkonflict*), describing the ego as their arbitrator, or even their victim, rather than as one of the terms figuring in the conflict.

> A recommendation to the patient to "live a full life" sexually could not possibly play a part in analytic therapy—if only because we ourselves have declared that an obstinate conflict is taking place in him between a libidinal impulse and sexual repression, between a sensual and an ascetic trend. This conflict would not be solved by our helping one of these trends to victory over its opponent. ("Introductory Lectures", pp. 432–433)

He is thus clearly opposed to a sexological interpretation of the analytic ethic such as the one proposed by Wilhelm Reich. Unlike Reich, Freud believes that the analyst's role in directing the treatment is not that of a mentor. According to him, "There is nothing [the analyst] would rather bring about than that the patient should make his decisions for himself" ("Introductory Lectures", p. 433).

If such decisions were inspired by a triumphant ascetic ideal, then the analyst would have nothing to say against them, provided that it is the conflict itself that is pathogenic, and not the values that the individual adopts in order to fit in with those of civilization. If psychoanalysis, on the other hand, is believed to be "inimical to culture", this is because it considers that the price paid by the individual in this case is far too high ("The Resistances to Psycho-Analysis", p. 220). The resulting paradox, however, is that one "cannot explain the therapeutic effect of psychoanalysis by its permitting a full sexual life" ("Introductory Lectures", p. 435).

In his "Introductory Lectures on Psycho-Analysis" Freud appears to choose a middle path between sexual asceticism and debauchery. Having denounced the sexual hypocrisy of civilization, whose moral code, in his opinion, "calls for a bigger sacrifice than it is worth", Freud prefers to appeal directly to his patients' critical judgement:

> ... if, having grown independent after the completion of their treatment, they decide on their own judgement in favour of some

midway position between living a full life and absolute asceticism, we feel our conscience clear whatever their choice. We tell ourselves that anyone who has succeeded *in educating himself to truth about himself* is permanently defended against the danger of immorality, even though his standard of morality may differ in some respect from that which is customary in society. (p. 434, emphasis added)

Freud certainly considers that the neurotic's moral conflict implicated in neurosis should be respected. He does not believe that this conflict is simply a symptom that must be eradicated. What is pathological is the repression of this conflict. Civilization's discontents require some other form of sedative.

Impossible harmony

Freud's theory thus provides neither an ethics of jouissance nor an invitation to a sexual activism that might ensure "phallic happiness". He brings neither good tidings, nor hope of reconciliation between conflicting psychic agencies. Nevertheless, his conception of how to direct the treatment implies an encounter between the subject and his unconscious desire. In Freud's opinion, there can be no solution to this conflict as long as it continues to remain unconscious: as long as the "adversaries" in question are unaware of each other and are unable to confront each other. According to Freud, "A true decision can only be reached when they both meet on the same ground. To make this possible is, I think, the sole task of our therapy" ("Introductory Lectures", p. 433).

While this apparent suspension of desire or apathy on Freud's part might seem suspect, I do not consider that it is of crucial importance. For if an analyst intends the goal of analysis to be an "encounter" between the subject and his repressed desire, she cannot possibly imagine that she is able to remove her own stakes from the game. What testifies to this is the negative transference that results if the analyst comes either to incarnate this object or to mime the real. Everything happens as if, on the contrary, the cards have already been dealt before repression has been lifted. In the encounter with his object *a*, the subject can only recognize his fundamental alienation and accept the destiny conferred on him by his unconscious. Now, as Freud himself admitted, if desire is indestructible, a new repression is impossible and the subject can now only be the dupe of his desire.

Freud does not, however, consider the possibility that the analyst could herself be this object, or that the encounter with the real could be mimicked by the analytic session itself. This was Lacan's subsequent contribution. It is important to note, however, that for Lacan, such an encounter is always missed (see Miller, *"Réveil"*, p. 49).

It would be tempting to imagine that psychoanalysis could offer us wise advice, a new guide to living. Yet beyond its inability to bring us any good news, it also confronts us with the fact that the requirements that a subject of language submits to are contradictory. Freud says:

> We are warned by a proverb against serving two masters at the same time. The poor ego has things even worse: it serves three severe masters and does what it can to bring their claims and demands into harmony with one another. These claims are always divergent and often seem incompatible. No wonder that the ego so often fails in its task. Its three tyrannical masters are the external world, the super-ego and the id. ("New Introductory Lectures", p. 77)

Perhaps the ego's "weakness" in failing to ensure an impossible harmony would justify the analyst's attempt to establish a "contract" with it. Yet what possible guarantee of success can an analyst, even helped by the Other, really expect? If the ego fails in its attempt at reconciliation, how can an analyst possibly be justified in attempting to "reinforce" it? To what extent, indeed, is this formula, which has become a recipe for analysis, and has known great popularity as such, originally Freud's idea? If it was Freud's idea, is it consistent with his fundamental discovery? Wouldn't it be unreasonable to try to provide a foundation for a practice in which the psychoanalyst tries to aid an ego that is fundamentally stupid, "dislocated and restricted" ("Analysis Terminable and Interminable", p. 221)?

The analyst therefore has two strategies to choose between, strategies that raise an ethical problem. Either she should reinforce the ego, in keeping with the ideology of mastery, or she should decide not to take a position regarding libido: she should choose neither to free nor to control it.

Betting on the hope of controlling the libido is a contradiction in terms, since Freud describes it as "daemonic": it is driven by a constant pressure, never rests, and therefore resists any effort to cut or lessen it

("The Dynamics of Transference", p. 99; *Beyond the Pleasure Principle*, p. 21). The second option, which is clearly more in keeping with the "New Introductory Lectures", to which we are referring, consists in a better distribution of libido, which is plastic and can have new cathexes; the analyst would be the master-builder of this new distribution, by means of the transference of which she is the object. Since mastery is impossible, this new displacement of libido will be brought about in conformity to the vicissitudes of the drives, in particular that of sublimation.

Freud does not, however, consider the analytic treatment to be comparable to the process of sublimation. Encouraging a patient to sublimate, in his opinion, pointed purely to the kind of self-glorifying therapeutic motives that he so severely criticizes in 1912: "It must further be borne in mind that many people fall ill precisely from an attempt to sublimate their instincts beyond the degree permitted by their organization" ("Recommendations to Physicians", p. 119).

Furthermore, sublimation, according to Freud, gives free rein to the death drives, as if desexualizing the libido means "a liberation of the aggressive instincts in the super-ego" (*The Ego and the Id*, p. 56). For the analyst, becoming the master of desire would be the equivalent of acceding to the demand of the neurotic, whose anguish of not desiring in conformity to the superego creates his suffering.

Notes

1. Freud sometimes writes *Liebesversagung*; see G. W.: *XII*, p. 324.
2. Freud uses the expression *gleichschwebende Aufmerksamkeit* which means "attention at an equal level" and which we translate as "attention paid as much to the signifier as to the signification".

CHAPTER THIRTEEN

Strategy and tactics

In *An Outline of Psycho-Analysis*, Freud explains that the analyst plays an active part in the patient's psychic conflict.[1] Through the transference a "pact" is made, according to which the patient agrees to say everything that comes to his mind in return for the analyst's help. It seems, however, that once Freud had gained his patients' trust, he did not hesitate to use his power for what—somewhat surprisingly—appears to be educational purposes. Did Freud seek to be the object *a* of the phantasy or the master?

My aim in this chapter is to define the analyst's role in the transference, and thus Freud's strategy in his analyses. I shall show that Freud's desire ultimately emerges beyond the educational tone of his discourse.

The analyst's place in the phantasy and in the real

It is generally thought that Freud took on the role of a father in his analyses, as he indeed explicitly suggests in a number of texts, for example, *The Rat Man*.[2] More often, however, he thinks of the analysand/analyst relationship as a form of tutelage, whereby the latter becomes a model or master to the former. These are the terms he uses in "Analysis Terminable and Interminable" (pp. 219–224). It is primarily the active character of these terms that strikes us, before we even begin to consider how they affect his tactics and strategy. In this context, one must ask whether Freud considers that the term "model" relates to the analyst's person *per se*—his real talents—or whether, on the contrary, it is precisely its fictional character that allows an analysis to be successfully concluded.[3]

In his last work on analytic technique, *An Outline of Psycho-Analysis*, Freud discusses the analyst's relation to his patient in terms of the symbolic or even legal mediation provided by a contract. The power struggles that arise in analysis are immediately situated in the dimension of semblance. The treatment finds its metaphorical basis in military strategy. The terms "strong" and "weak" ego and his occasional references to the "strengthening" of the ego, became, as we know, so popular that they inspired a whole branch of psychoanalysis to adopt the re-education of the ego as its credo: "The ego is weakened by the internal conflict and we must go to its help. The position is like that in a civil war which has to be decided by the assistance of an ally from outside" (p. 173).

This ally is the analyst, but does this suggest that her role is to reinflate a subject who has already found refuge in his narcissistic fortress? Does this not, however, undermine Freud's ethical imperative: "*Wo es war, soll Ich werden*" (Where id was, there ego shall be) ("New Introductory Lectures", p. 80)?

Freud goes on to say explicitly that "We serve the patient in various functions, as an authority and a substitute for his parents, as a teacher and educator" (*An Outline of Psycho-Analysis*, p. 181). Does the ideal of the analyst rejoin that of the master? Is the analyst supposed to glue the dispersed pieces of the personality back together, and thus to ally herself with the so-called "healthy part of the ego"?

Let us examine more carefully Freud's use of military and political metaphors when describing the analyst's actions. In order to shake up a neurotic ego, the analyst—serving as the ego's crutch or prosthesis—intervenes, as Freud tells us, and this enables it to regain power over an area over which it has lost control. What is really at stake in these texts is to rearrange the patient's intra-psychic equilibrium in a way that is advantageous to the ego. If she represents the patient's ego, the power struggle must first tip over to her side. Freud is not quite so conclusive, however, regarding the final outcome of this combat:

> ... the final outcome of the struggle we have engaged in depends on *quantitative* relations—on the quota of energy we are able to mobilize in the patient to our advantage as compared with the sum of energy of the powers working against us. Here once again God is on the side of the big battalions. (*An Outline of Psycho-Analysis*, pp. 181–182)

Yet is it really a question of allowing the ego to reconquer what it has lost? In an ironic comment on the fate of ego psychology, Lacan explains that the "community to which [Freud] bequeathed this remedial task has proclaimed the synthesis of a strong ego as a watchword, at the heart of a technique in which the practitioner believes that he obtains results by incarnating this ideal himself" (*Écrits*, p. 677). The result, unfortunately, is that "the pre-Socratic tone of Freud's precept, 'Wo es war, soll Ich werden', [is replaced by] the croaking strains of—'the ego (the analyst's, no doubt) must dislodge the id' (the patient's, of course)" (*Écrits*, p. 714).

It is certain that a number of Freud's expressions have led to a degree of confusion, or at least to interpretations suggesting that the analyst's role is to re-establish or reinforce the ego. This is particularly true, as we have seen, of his *An Outline of Psycho-Analysis*.

The reason why Freud makes the ego the analyst's partner is to be sought in the model of construction in analysis, which bridges the gap between the ego's judging activity and the construction proposed by the analyst. Sometimes Freud, faithful to his theories of the ego in the *Project*, detaches the activity of judging from the pleasure principle; at other times, he makes the ego the reservoir of narcissism. It is always a matter, indeed, of finding the symptom's password, of interposing signifiers: "The function of the pleasure principle is to lead the subject from signifier to signifier, by generating as many signifiers as are required to maintain at as low a level as possible the tension that regulates the whole functioning of the psychic apparatus" (*Seminar VII*, p. 119).

This programme conforms to the reality principle, the task of which is to make alterations, corrections, or detours, in order to call us back to order. Now, the constructive role of the ego, according to the *Outline*, "consists in interpolating, between the demand made by a drive and the action that satisfies it, the activity of thought" (*An Outline of Psycho-Analysis*, p. 199).

Freud's theory of the ego is thus the key to understanding the ideal that the analyst creates for herself and her purposes for doing so. His description of the ego's powers in *An Outline of Psycho-Analysis* does not differ greatly from his earlier version in the *Project*. The ego always has an inhibiting function; it prevents the free circulation of excitation and lowers the level of pleasure. Lacan says that behind the *Project*, there is an ethical experience, and the same can be said about *The Ego and the Id* and *Inhibitions, Symptoms and Anxiety*. In the latter works, however, Freud also introduces a new character: the psychoanalyst.

A certain number of analogies can be drawn between the ego's activity and that of the analyst, whose task is to represent reality. This confers a properly metapsychological status on what Freud, in his technical writings, simply terms the analyst's "attitude". Freud specifies, for instance, that the analyst's "reserve" is more precisely a "reserve of quantities". There is, he tells us, "a group of neurones which retains a constant cathexis and which thus constitutes the vehicle for the store of quantity required by the secondary function". A bit later, he adds that "Where, then, an ego exists, it is bound to inhibit psychical processes" ("Project for a Scientific Psychology", pp. 384–385).

The ego thus builds, creates reserves, and inhibits. These texts on the ego also shed a great deal of light on the psychoanalyst's position, despite the fact that they seem to exclude it as such.

Is not the rule of abstinence the counterpart of free association in an analysis? Such an association would confer a metapsychological status on the pact between the analyst and the patient. The analyst comes to represent the psychic apparatus, since she serves the secondary process, while the patient, in following the fundamental rule, is effectively subjected to the primary process.

The ego, in *An Outline of Psycho-Analysis*, seems to obey the command to be prudent, a quality that becomes related to the reality principle. The ego, for instance, decides whether it is advisable to postpone a particular undertaking or whether:

> ... it may not be necessary for the demand by the instinct to be suppressed altogether as being dangerous. (Here we have the *reality principle*.) Just as the id is directed exclusively to obtaining pleasure, so the ego is governed by considerations of safety. The ego has set

itself the task of self-preservation, which the id appears to neglect. (*An Outline of Psycho-Analysis*, p. 199)

A closer examination of this text, however, leads us to conclude that, far from seeking to contradict the pleasure principle, the ego simply institutes reality-testing, which is precisely what it is no longer able to do in neurosis ("Loss of Reality in Neurosis and Psychosis", pp. 183–187). The ego's effort to moderate primary activity is therefore less a means of erecting a rampart against excitation than of providing representations—signifiers—by means of which reality-testing in relation to previous satisfactions becomes possible.

The duplicity of the analyst

A metaphor drawn from the inexhaustible field of political and military strategy in *The Ego and the Id* not only gives us another conception of the weakness of the ego, but also clearly reveals the ethical dimension of psychoanalytic experience. Having first reminded us that "Psychoanalysis is an instrument to enable the ego to achieve a progressive conquest of the id," Freud goes on to explain that:

> As a frontier-creature, the ego tries to mediate between the world and the id, to make the id pliable to the world and, by means of its muscular activity, to make the world fall in with the wishes of the id. In point of fact it behaves like the physician during an analytic treatment: it offers itself, with the attention it pays to the real world, as a libidinal object to the id, and aims at attaching the id's libido to itself. It is not only a helper to the id; it is also a submissive slave who courts his master's love. Whenever possible, it tries to remain on good terms with the id; it clothes the id's *Ucs.* commands with its *Pcs.* rationalisations; it pretends that the id is showing obedience to the admonitions of reality, even when in fact it is remaining obstinate and unyielding; it disguises the id's conflicts with reality and, if possible, its conflicts with the super-ego too. In its position midway between the id and reality, it only too often yields to the temptation to become sycophantic, opportunist and lying, like a politician who sees the truth but wants to keep his place in popular favour. (p. 56)

With the introduction of the second topography, the weakness of the ego should be understood not as a sign of cowardice or impotence, but as a simple indication that it is weak enough to submit to the id in order to avoid anxiety. Freud's references to narcissism and the anxiety of losing love throw light on this "function" of the ego, where anxiety is produced as a signal. Compromise, self-betrayal, and lying are all ethical considerations that point by their contrast to the ethical position of the analyst who substitutes herself, as Freud tells us, for the threatened ego. The neurotic is a divided subject in quest of a partner with whom he can make himself loved. Freud, in this context, uses the analytic relation as a *model of the patient's psychic activity and not the other way round* the relation between analysand and analyst becomes simply a way of staging the neurotic's scenario. The ego attempts to create a transference that will ensure it is loved by the id. It is striking to see Freud, considering his knowledge of the real, credit the ego with having the qualities of a psychoanalyst. This is precisely his mistake, since the id itself clearly has no such consideration for the real. The ego, indeed, makes itself the instrument of the death drive:

> Towards the two classes of instincts the ego's attitude is not impartial. Through its work of identification and sublimation it gives the death instincts in the id assistance in gaining control over the libido, but in so doing it runs the risk of becoming the object of the death instincts and of itself perishing. In order to be able to help in this way it has had itself to become filled with libido; it thus itself becomes the representative of Eros and thenceforward desires to live and to be loved. (*The Ego and the Id*, p. 56)

The conflict thus appears to have been displaced. It is no longer on the terrain of the ego and the id, but, instead, within the id itself that the battle between Eros and Thanatos rages, while the ego looks on in the role of an umpire. The ego signs its own death warrant, however, in taking a position against the libido in the process of repression, since, as Freud points out, it thereby effectively liberates the death drives.

Identification with the father does not have a pacifying effect in this respect. While winning the father's love admittedly signals the end of the Oedipus complex, this process nevertheless results in a splitting between aggression and libido (a disassociation of the drives). Aggression is thus freed, with the result that the ideal is itself split between the ego ideal, on the one hand, and, on the other, the cruel superego, which directs the aggressive drive back against the subject.

Freud thus concludes that narcissism is not a defence against the death drives. The libido detaches itself from external objects in order to fix onto the ego, which thereby comes to represent Eros and becomes the reservoir of the libido; thus the ego itself is put at risk in the ensuing combat: "[T]he ego, by sublimating some of the libido for itself and its purposes, assists the id in its work of mastering the tensions" (*The Ego and the Id*, p. 47). Here is a true chiasmus, a paradox, and a nightmare. The stronger the ego is, in the sense that it has become bloated with love, the weaker it is in the face of the death drives, which have been separated from the object libido (and vice versa). Freud expresses this paradox in the following comparison: "In suffering under the attacks of the super-ego or perhaps even succumbing to them, the ego is meeting with a fate like that of the protista which are destroyed by the products of decomposition that they themselves have created" (*The Ego and the Id*, pp. 56–57).

The effect of repression is thus to liberate the death drive. In *Civilization and its Discontents*, Freud explicitly states that the more one renounces jouissance, the more exacting the superego becomes. If this is true, it becomes rather comic to claim that the aim of analysis is to harmonize relations between the ego and the other psychic agencies. The ego makes compromises and syntheses, but the goal of analytic therapy is certainly not to permit the ego to do so, even if it has always spent its time doing this. There is a clear alternative between analysis and synthesis; there must be either an analysis of the symptom or nothing at all. Lacan has shown that Freud, in his second topography, portrays the ego as a function of misrecognition. This implies that the ego, which is unreadable to itself, has the structure of a symptom: it is an enigma to itself.

The psychoanalyst, entering the conflict and becoming one of its protagonists, thus constitutes a new psychic agency. Why would her desire be to fortify the ego if the latter is a symptom? It is structured as a symptom and is a function of misrecognition. These two characteristics, indeed, amount to the same thing, since it is by making compromises with the drive that the ego is able to assimilate it, and this reconciliation can only take place at the cost of the ego's misrecognition of the drives. This is particularly clear in chapter III of *Inhibitions, Symptoms and Anxiety*. In discussing the ego's resistance, Freud evokes the notion of an illness's secondary benefits. After having remarked that there is no natural hostility between the ego and the id, and that there is therefore no need to install a barrier between them, Freud insists that if there is an inherent contradiction, it is to be found within the ego itself: "In this [...] defensive struggle [against the drive] the ego presents two faces with contradictory expressions" (p. 98). Since the ego aspires to making connections, to unifying, and to synthesizing, it tries to incorporate the symptom. In other words, repression creates the symptom, which is a compromise between a satisfaction and a defence. The ego, by its nature, seeks to assimilate the symptom and therefore makes a compromise, but in doing so, it misapprehends the repressed twice over. Symptoms, indeed, satisfy the requirements of the superego—considered here as an agency of repression within the ego— but are also the expression of the return of the repressed. According to Freud, symptoms are frontier posts that are occupied by two countries:

> In this way the symptom gradually comes to be the representative of important interests; it is found to be useful in asserting the position of the self and becomes more and more closely merged with the ego and more and more indispensable to it. It is only very rarely that the physical process of "healing" round a foreign body follows such a course as this. (p. 99)

Resistance to analysis thus merges with the benefit that the ego derives from an alliance with the repressed. This does not make the analyst's task any easier, especially if we consider that the foreign body that the ego is attempting to assimilate is the analyst herself. It is in this sense that the transference can be said to be a resistance, but not a defence. Instead, resistance and defence appear as two contradictory processes, one of which seeks synthesis and compromise, while the other acts as an agent of repression. Freud states: "When the analyst tries subsequently to help the ego in its struggle against the symptom, he finds that these conciliatory bonds between ego and symptom operate on the side of the resistances and that they are not easy to loosen" (p. 100).

The symptom, however, is only a negation of the repressed drive, and also represents it: it plays the drive's role. The repetition compulsion constitutes the limit of this compromise since the drive relentlessly requires satisfaction. Nothing can stifle or silence it. Any attempt to do so simply "obliges the ego in its turn to give the signal of unpleasure and put itself in a posture of defence" (p. 100). How can the analyst "help the ego" in such contradictory conditions, if the latter is structured like a symptom (p. 100)? Is not the division of the subject what the analyst must finally desire if, in her surgical function as separator, she must disjoin the ego from its untenable coalescence with the symptom?

A supplementary difficulty arises in this context: how can she possibly succeed in doing this if she herself has become a part of the patient's phantasy, if—thanks to the transference—she has herself become the object *a*, the foreign body that the neurotic is attempting to "introject" (see Ferenczi, "Introjection and Transference")?

Freud explains that the neurotic is able to let go of his symptoms out of love for his analyst in the transference, but this change does not improve the situation. The analyst herself has become a new symptom that needs to be analysed: a new foreign body that the ego is attempting to assimilate. Should the analyst really lend herself to this cannibalism? Her desire is the function that counters identification in favour of an absolute difference: the object *a*, which opposes the ego. These formulations, it is true, are Lacan's own and nothing in Freud's work indicates that he himself wanted to occupy the place of an object in his analyses. This is nevertheless the place that is necessary if we are to have any hope of situating his act.

Notes

1. "The analytic physician and the patient's weakened ego, basing themselves on the real external world, have to band themselves together into a party against the enemies, the instinctual demands of the id and the conscientious demands of the super-ego. We form a pact with each other" (*An Outline of Psycho-Analysis*, p. 173).
2. Freud himself confided as such to Kardiner: "I have several handicaps that disqualify me as a great analyst. One of them is that I am too much the father" (Kardiner, p. 69).
3. "What we desire, on the contrary, is that the ego, emboldened by the certainty of our help, shall dare to take the offensive in order to reconquer what has been lost" (*An Outline of Psycho-Analysis*, p. 178).

CHAPTER FOURTEEN

The analyst's ideals

Freud certainly does not consider that forming an ideal—which necessarily implies overestimating the object and is always a cause of tension—can possibly serve as a guarantee for the end of analysis. Ordinary people, he tells us, are less subject to this kind of conflictual tension since their ego ideals are not the measure of the legitimacy of their desires. In these conditions, repression will not take place, since the ideal is the agent that brings it about ("On Narcissism", pp. 94–95).

By following Lacan's commentary in *Seminar XI* we can deduce that since analysis is the opposite of hypnosis—and therefore of idealization—the analyst is not the Ideal, but the little *a*. Little *a* and the capital I are indeed as far removed from each other as they possibly can be (p. 273). In other words, far from trying to ease the tension between them, the psychoanalyst's desire aims at accentuating the radical difference between the ideal and the object of desire.

As I have stated, if the ideal imposes repression and the analyst wants to lift it, she cannot indefinitely maintain the balance between what Freud, in his *Introductory Lectures on Psycho-Analysis*, calls the individual's sensual and ascetic sides. Analysis should, instead, aim to disclose the underlying connections between the object of desire and the object of identification, a task that is elaborated in detail in the second topography.

"Not wanting to cure or to be cured"

Freud's conception of "neutrality" consists, as we know, of precisely *not* seeking to suture the patient's unconscious conflict but, on the contrary, of trying to maintain a distance between ego and object libidos, without dreaming of any reparative harmony.

Freud's prudence in relation to therapy—which led him to conclude that a cure is simply an "added bonus"[1] of the treatment—is part of an ethical perspective that allows the subject to choose which path she will take. This prudence should be understood as an attempt not to fall into the thaumaturgical ideology that is part of the analytic process. Freud recalls this again in 1925: "There was something positively seductive in working with hypnotism. For the first time there was a sense of having overcome one's helplessness; and it was highly flattering to enjoy the reputation of being a miracle-worker" ("An Autobiographical Study", p. 17).

Freud, on the contrary, attributes therapeutic results neither to his own personal talent nor to the desire to heal as such. Indeed, without consequently undermining the value of his own act, he did not hesitate to appeal to God—that is, the subject—for help. This is why he appropriates Ambroise Paré's dictum: "I dressed his wounds, God cured him" ("Recommendations to Physicians", p. 115).[2]

The analyst's "surgical" action serves as a metaphor not for theoretical apathy, and even less for the analyst's "benevolence" but, on the contrary, for the safeguard against therapeutic pride. The psychoanalyst does not accomplish therapeutic "feats" as such. While Freud's modesty could be interpreted as a sign of apathy—the proof of a lack of desire on his part—I find it clear that Freud is indicating the analyst's inability to cure; however much he may want to do so, this wish may not receive his patients' consent.

Besides having no particular calling for charitable work,[3] Freud explicitly emphasizes the danger of having a therapeutic ideal in a letter to Jung in 1909: "Just give up wanting to cure; learn and make money, those are the most plausible conscious aims" (McGuire, p. 203).

Further, he points out that not only are an analyst's therapeutic aspirations always thwarted, but there is also a certain baseness in requiring these as a reward for his efforts:

> … you [haven't] yet acquired the necessary objectivity in your practice, [...] you still get involved, giving a good deal of [yourself] and expecting the patient to give something in return. Permit me, speaking as the venerable old master, to say that this technique is invariably ill-advised and that it is best to remain reserved and purely receptive. We must never let our poor neurotics drive us crazy. (McGuire, pp. 212–213)

Freud later becomes even more distrustful of the therapeutic effects of analysis when he discovers, in the 1920s, that his patients' resistance to recovery points to an unconscious desire, on their part, for punishment.[4]

Orienting his desire once again on that of the subject, Freud warned his disciples against an invasive desire to cure, one that would not take the subject's unconscious desire into account. In 1917, before discovering the negative therapeutic reaction, Freud had already emphasized a clinical phenomenon that was clearly related to the physician's desire: his patients' manifest "unwillingness to burden [themselves] for the second time in [their] life with a load of gratitude" ("Introductory Lectures", p. 290). He thus recommends a certain therapeutic apathy to his disciple, Weiss: "The patient with whom you were here to see me will probably not give in as long as she can guess how much her recovery means to you" (Weiss, p. 75).

The fact that Weiss's patient "knows exactly what special importance her recovery has for your cause" is a hindrance to treatment (Weiss, p. 76). In the same letter, Freud also points out that a patient's desire to "spoil the physician's triumph" clearly implies a negative transference for which the analyst is not innocent (Weiss, p. 76). "It is often enough to praise them for their behaviour in the treatment or to say a few hopeful words about the progress of the analysis in order to bring about an unmistakable worsening of their condition" ("New Introductory Lectures", p. 110).

Thus, in the absence of a "desire to cure", what can the analyst possibly want that does not have the effect of arousing the patient's hostility and "the aggressive repercussions of charity" (Lacan, *Écrits*, p. 87)?

In *The Ego and the Id*, Freud explains that the patient's "resistance to recovery" cannot be described without reference to the physician's desire, which is provoked by its "defiant" character (p. 49).

Freud, as we have said, attributes the subject's need for punishment to his refusal "to give up the punishment of suffering" a form of resistance in which he discerns a "moral factor", one that can unfortunately, on occasion, tempt the analyst to "play the part of prophet, saviour and redeemer to the patient" (*The Ego and the Id*, pp. 49, 50).

The patient's attitude of "defiance" nevertheless requires the analyst to take responsibility for this "aggressiveness" in order to disclose its symbolic character. If the mediation of the Other is clear here and if there is also an obvious appeal to the desire of the Other, is there really any need to hypothesize that the refusal to be cured is caused by a "need for punishment", a primary masochism?

In "Aggressiveness in Psychoanalysis", Lacan tries to explain the negative therapeutic reaction by emphasizing the intertwining of the patient's narcissism or "self-esteem" with his desire for death:

> What appears here as the arrogant affirmation of one's suffering
> will show its face—and sometimes at a moment decisive enough to
> give rise to the kind of "negative therapeutic reaction" that attracted
> Freud's attention—in the form of the resistance of *amour-propre*, to
> use the term in all the depth given it by La Rochefoucauld, which
> is often expressed thus: "I can't bear the thought of being freed by
> anyone but myself." (*Écrits*, p. 87)

Abandoning the *furor sanandi* for another battle, Freud undertakes, with the patient, a "struggle" (*Kampf*) on the field of the transference, the outcome of which is uncertain: "This struggle between the doctor and the patient, between intellect and instinctual life, between understanding and seeking to act, is played out almost exclusively in the phenomena of transference" ("Observations on Transference-Love", p. 171; "The Dynamics of Transference", p. 108).

It is the ethical dimension of this fight that we now wish to consider (*Écrits*, p. 323).

The psychoanalyst's push-to-jouissance

Freud's readers have occasionally been surprised by his advice to psychoanalysts who try "to make everything as pleasant as possible for the patient" ("Lines of Advance in Psycho-Analytic Therapy", p. 164). His technique, on the other hand, clearly did not allow his patients to simply sit back and indulge their symptoms: "A condition of privation is to be kept up during the treatment" (p. 164).

Far from implying that a patient should renounce jouissance in the name of an ascetic ideal, this rule brings about the sort of compromise that characterizes the symptom. Symptoms are merely deceptive "substitutive satisfactions" that spare the subject from seeking a "real" object ("Lines of Advance", p. 164; "Introductory Lectures", p. 453). They are, however, according to Freud, not nearly as bad as replacement satisfactions. The analyst should never be in a hurry to cure symptoms, since the pain that they contain is precisely the real of forbidden jouissance.

The patient's frustration in analysis thus serves to mimic the real, since the latter prohibits jouissance. Physicians who prefer to indulge their patients, on the other hand, "make no attempt to give [them] more strength for facing life and more capacity for carrying out [their] actual tasks in it" ("Lines of Advance", p. 164).

The psychoanalyst therefore imposes the rule of abstinence in order to counter the impulses of his "good heart".

It is this real that substitute satisfactions, by appearing in the "place" of symptoms, attempt to circumvent; in taking this place, however, they also take on its "accursed share": the prohibition and punishment that result from it. There is a truth in the symptom that is muzzled by curing the analysand, for the symptom's double signification—the condensation of pleasure and punishment—disappears as a consequence. The subject uses replacement solutions, but it is the symptom itself that is replaced by pleasures, interests, and habits: these are so many diversions that had once been covered over by the symptom. This "liberation" of the libido that has been imprisoned in the symptom is, however, purely illusory. The object of desire, conquered in analysis, becomes a symptom in its turn. If, for example, the love-object takes the place of a symptom, it carries with it a punishment that is disguised as success.

What replaces guilt will now, for example, be an unhappy marriage ("Lines of Advance", p. 164). Object choice is once again alienated in the form of self-punishment or organic illness. The fundamental rule thus derives its "cruelty" only from its goal, which is certainly not the subject's "comfort". Freud indeed explicitly states that:

> Cruel though it may sound, we must see to it that the patient's suffering, to a degree that is in some way or other effective, does

not come to an end prematurely. If, owing to the symptoms
having been taken apart and having lost their value, his suffering
becomes mitigated, we must re-instate it elsewhere in the form
of some appreciable privation; otherwise we run the danger of
never achieving any improvements except quite insignificant and
transitory ones. (p. 163)

A choice therefore has to be made between replacing the symptom and
obtaining the object. One must remember, however, that when a symptom is abandoned, another appears in its place, producing exactly the
same guilt.

It is significant that, for Freud, a symptom can be identical with a
situation in which a man "prematurely [attaches] himself to a woman",
a comparison that throws light on Freud's ethical position" (p. 163).
A love choice is determined by the repetition compulsion. In "The
Theme of the Three Caskets", he explains that if a woman is a symptom
for a man, it is because of an inevitability that pushes him to choose
someone who will destroy him: Atropos, the Inexorable or Terrible.
"A choice is made where in reality there is obedience to a compulsion;
and what is chosen is not a figure of terror, but the fairest and most
desirable of women" (p. 299).

The strategy, which Freud elaborates in his "Lines of Advance",
is based on the dialectic that would be illustrated later in *The Ego
and the Id*: the symptom is nourished by guilt, and the superego is
both its agent and the prosecutor. Freud thereby not only puts the
psychoanalyst's "indulgence" on a par with the neurotic's "distractions", but also posits that the rule of abstinence is the equivalent of the
harsh reality of life.

Freud does not, however, advocate adapting to the demands of
civilization, which require the subject to give up desire and renounce
not the symptom but jouissance, in favour of substitute satisfactions.
Freud's answer to this prudent morality was, as we have seen, precisely
to renounce the renunciation and to take a radical position on the object
of desire. What, fundamentally, is Freud's thesis? It is certainly not that
one satisfaction is as good as another. An analytic technique could have
been promoted in which, by virtue of the signifier and the displacement
and detours—or "turning[s] away"—imposed by the lost object, might
have led to a certain form of liberalism ("Formulations on the Two Principles of Mental Functioning", p. 18). According to Freud, however, the

displacement of satisfaction, as a substitution, is both good and bad. "Replacement" satisfactions in themselves simply postpone "true" satisfaction, since the neurotic is incapable of either acting or experiencing jouissance ("Introductory Lectures", pp. 453–454).

Freud derives a number of both technical and moral consequences from this situation, consequences that throw light on how his own desire was oriented regarding sexual relations:

> It is the analyst's task to detect these divergent paths and to require him every time to abandon them, however harmless the activity which leads to satisfaction may be in itself. The half-recovered patient may also enter on less harmless paths—as when, for instance, if he is a man, he seeks prematurely to attach himself to a woman. ("Lines of Advance", p. 163)

What Freud uses to oppose civilization's effort to sedate the real of the symptom is a "surgical" technique, a metaphor that refers to the reopening of the unconscious, which had been sealed off by the pleasure principle. This is the meaning to be given to his statement that psychoanalysis is "inimical to culture" ("The Resistances to Psycho-Analysis", p. 220). Indeed, in opposing the claims and demands (*revendications*) of the individual to civilization, Freud was not setting up an opposition between the real—as the "order of the universe"—and the individual's search for "free love" (*jouissance sans entraves*). Instead, he was emphasizing the profound connection between the person's well-being and the social organization of the libido. Society's distractions, it seems, do not in the least affect the common order of pleasures (*Civilization and its Discontents*, p. 76).

What divides the individual is not civilization, but is, instead, the price he has to pay for his well-being: his renunciation of jouissance, which incontestably contains an element of pain, and which the pleasure principle attempts to transform. "The task of avoiding suffering pushes that of obtaining pleasure into the background" (p. 77).

Civilization and its Discontents further elucidates the strict connection between Freud's criticism of civilization and his rule of abstinence, which aims to awaken the subject to his desire. The neurotic forms a secret pact with civilization in exchange for the sedatives and "auxiliary constructions" (*Hilfskonstruktionen*) it can offer (p. 75). Since it attempts to relieve suffering, this programme is not opposed to the pleasure principle. Substitute satisfactions, drugs, art, and religion are all, in this sense, part of the same programme: that of helping us to "bear life" and to anaesthetize us; they are, as such, merely "illusions in contrast with reality" (p. 75). These tempting humbugs are directly opposed to Freud's ethical imperative, which is founded precisely on the insistence of the drive. Civilization and psychoanalysis thus have completely opposing views on the role of illusion: "We must not forget that the analytic relationship is based on a love of truth—that is, on a recognition of reality—and that it precludes any kind of sham or deceit" ("Analysis Terminable and Interminable", p. 248).

Freud himself was most surprised to learn in 1904 that his doctrine could be reduced to a mere sexology, a theory that "regard[s] sexual privation as the ultimate cause of the neuroses" ("On Psychotherapy", p. 267). Not only does such a notion completely undermine the whole concept of psychoanalytic practice, it also neglects to take into account what is the *sine qua non* of neurosis: "the neurotic's aversion from sexuality, his incapacity for loving, that feature of the mind which I have called 'repression'" ("On Psychotherapy", p. 267; also see "'Wild' Psychoanalysis", p. 223).

This text shows the moral quality that Freud attaches to this concept of repression, and it thus anticipates his "Constructions in Psychoanalysis", in which he associates the neurotic's guilt with his inability to love.

It is, unquestionably, the inhibition of sexuality in the largest sense of the term—including the inhibition of love by hate in *The Rat Man*, the different forms of impotence, and especially, the neuroses of destiny—that draw Freud's attention to the difficulty of desire. He invariably sought the solution to these neurotic conflicts in a detachment of libido from the objects to which it has been linked, rather than by forcing desire onto the object of the phantasy. His encouragement of his patients—under the influence of Ferenczi's active therapy—to remain abstinent should thus be understood as a renunciation of the pleasure principle, which is a condition for reaching a real jouissance. The following anecdote provides us with an example of this.

Freud's Italian disciple, Weiss, came to him to ask for supervision for a case of an impotent patient. The patient's problem had first arisen after his wife's suicide. In order to calm Weiss's therapeutic ardour, Freud begins by insisting that he take his time. The root of the conflict turns out to be the subject's relation to his father for whom, it seems, his wife is a substitute. According to Freud, the patient's impotence is a consequence of his "fixed renunciation of women" (Weiss, p. 35). Faced with a subject who cannot connect with woman, Freud advises Weiss to discourage this patient from resorting to substitute satisfactions in the form of masturbation or prostitutes. There should be "no attempt to burden him with our more liberal opinions about sexual intercourse" (p. 36). In fact, Freud sees in this man a problem that is not sexual, but, instead, "moral", since the symptom is linked to remorse and repentance. Since nothing can be done *in absentia* or *in effigie*, this state of tension should be maintained in order to be able to analyse it.

The accent here has been displaced from the Oedipal conflict to a conflict with the superego. Weiss's impotent patient is not described according to the precepts of Freud's 1910 text, "Contributions to the Psychology of Love", in which a woman, as a representative of the mother in the unconscious, short-circuits desire, instead of being its object (see Freud, "A Special Type of Choice of Object"). It would thus be the barrier of incest that renders desire impotent. In Weiss's case, it is, instead, the subject's inability to consider woman as anything other than a Name-of-the-Father that bars the way to desire. Inhibition is no longer motivated by a fixation on the mother, but by an intense fixation on the father.

As in the cases mentioned earlier, Freud suggests that the subject is resigned to avoiding woman, and consequently invites him to confront the object of his desire.

Notes

1. The expression is Lacan's: it is justified by Freud's thesis that the analyst should abstain from making any synthesis. See, for instance, Freud's letter to Pfister dated 9 October 1918: "In the technique of psycho-analysis there is no need of any special synthetic work; the individual does that for himself better than we can" (Meng & Freud, p. 62).
2. Freud also tempers the therapeutic ardour of Smiley Blanton, an American in supervision in 1935: "You are perhaps too anxious about your patients." He adds that "You must let them drift. Let them work out their own salvation" (Blanton, p. 76).
3. Freud writes to Ferenczi: "I lack that passion for helping" (Jones, 1955, p. 496).
4. "The ego treats recovery itself as a new danger" ("Analysis Terminable and Interminable", p. 254).

CHAPTER FIFTEEN

Desire and its discontents

The ethic that can be deduced from *Civilization and its Discontents* has no foundation other than in the imperatives of the superego: in the subject's self-inflicted aggression and cruelty. Reinforcing the ego means nothing other than removing it from the pressure of the superego. Yet since the latter derives its energy from civilization's requirement of limiting aggressiveness, one can see the meaning of the formula that psychoanalysis is the "enemy of civilization" (p. 122). This is an ethical position taken in relation to the subject's cruelty to himself, and therefore Freud's final texts on the superego undertake a revision of the analytic ethic.

Freud's thought oscillates between the two following conceptions of psychoanalysis: a) it is a sort of post-education, which teaches renunciation (see Millot); b) it enables the analyst to help the subject cope with the overwhelming and voracious superego.

In this second sense, the conception of the strong ego is constructed on the basis of the sense of easing that follows the relaxation of the superego.

Freud's maxim, *Wo es war, soll Ich werden*, could thus be corrected on the basis of this discovery: it is the price to pay for renouncing the drives. If an ethic is defined as a "renunciation of the drives" (*Triebversicht*), it could be concluded that the analyst who—as has been stated earlier—represents "reality" and not the pleasure principle, is a new figure of the master (*Moses and Monotheism*, p. 116; *G. W., XVI*, p. 223).

The cruelty of the superego

The term "reality" in the expression *Erziehung nach Realität*—"education to reality"—which appears in *The Future of an Illusion*, masks what is actually involved in this process: an operation that aims specifically to introduce the subject to his desire (p. 49). The reality in question is the subject's desire. Contrary to what one might think, however, the analyst does not represent a "paternal authority" who would seek to provide the subject with a proper moral conscience. Once the inhibited aggression has been "introjected and interiorized", it "is ready to put into action against the ego the same harsh aggressiveness that the ego would have liked to satisfy upon other, extraneous individuals" (*Civilization and its Discontents*, p. 123).

This turning around of aggression upon the ego, far from having any moral value as such, merely confirms the all-powerful nature of the drives, which civilization is only able to tame through the intervention of a "superego", "by setting up an agency within [the individual] to watch over [his desire for aggression], like a garrison in a conquered city" (p. 123).

The result of this situation is the paradox of conscience: "The more virtuous a man is, the more severe and distrustful is its behaviour, so that ultimately it is precisely those people who have carried saintliness furthest who reproach themselves with the worst sinfulness" (pp. 125–126).

While the superego clearly has its roots in the aggressiveness that the subject directs at the prohibiter of jouissance, it does not disappear once jouissance has been renounced. Its power, on the contrary, increases in direct proportion to the subject's renunciation. It is a true Moloch, for the more one gives in to it, the more it demands; the drive, indeed, is a "constant" force, whose energy is indestructible. When it is repressed or inhibited, it only increases its demand for satisfaction.

The neurotic's self-inflicted cruelty has no other source than the subject's renunciation, which Freud considers to be a general feature of neurosis: "If we survey the whole situation we arrive at a simple formula for the origin of a neurosis: the ego has made an attempt to suppress certain portions of the id *in an inappropriate manner*, this attempt has failed and the id has taken its revenge" (*The Question of Lay Analysis*, p. 203).

It is, of course, repression that Freud qualifies as acting in "an inappropriate manner". What, then, would be the "right" way of dealing with the drive? Are there other forms of renunciation that are not subjected to the arbitrary law of the superego and which an analyst might actually *desire* to encourage? These questions clearly revolve around the central question of Freud's relation to the law.

It is, once again, *Civilization and its Discontents* that helps to shed some light on this question. The analyst does not, as we know, encourage the analysand to follow the paths of either sublimation or saintliness, for both continue to affirm the demands of the drive, which obliges the subject to resort to measures of defence. Since, however, conscience is by definition "strict and vigilant", nothing escapes it, not even the subject's thoughts (*Civilization and its Discontents*, p. 126). This evokes the infantile origin of the "Other who cannot be deceived", whose role in the unconscious is demonstrated in both culture and neurosis. If the Other, indeed, is aware of forbidden thoughts, what better definition can be given of the superego than Lacan's description of the psychoanalyst as a "subject supposed to know"? The subject who is supposed to know these prohibited thoughts is, in Freud's works, named the superego.

Indeed, "Nothing can be hidden from the super-ego, not even thoughts", and this is why the analyst cannot reduce guilt to a mere illusion (*Civilization and its Discontents*, p. 125). In obsessional neurosis, for example:

> The patient's ego rebels against the imputation of guilt and seeks the physician's support in repudiating it. It would be folly to acquiesce in this, for to do so would have no effect. Analysis eventually shows that the super-ego is being influenced by processes that have remained unknown to the ego. It is possible to discover the repressed impulses which are really at the bottom of the sense of guilt. Thus in this case the super-ego knew more than the ego about the unconscious id. (*The Ego and the Id*, p. 51)[1]

Thus the superego represents the pure jouissance that is found in the imperative: it "can be super-moral and then become as cruel as only the id can be" (*The Ego and the Id*, p. 54).

Freud, in *Civilization and its Discontents,* thus draws out the full consequences of the paradox of conscience, which he had originally highlighted in *The Ego and the Id*: "The more a man checks his aggressiveness towards the exterior the more severe—that is aggressive—he becomes in his ego ideal" (*The Ego and the Id*, p. 54).

The source of these ethical requirements is rooted in the overcoming of aggressiveness, which benefits neither civilization nor the subject.

This mechanism is not purely imaginary, however, so it cannot be reduced to a merely quantitative and energetic representation. The intrusion of the superego in the form of the Other's knowledge establishes a false authority that behaves violently, whatever the subject may do:

> Thus we know of two origins of the sense of guilt: one arising from fear of an authority, and the other, later on, arising from fear of the super-ego. The first insists upon a renunciation of instinctual satisfactions; the second, as well as doing this, presses for punishment, since the continuance of the forbidden wishes cannot be concealed from the super-ego. (*Civilization and its Discontents*, p. 127)

One of the main reasons for the failure of therapy is, as has been stated, the subject's unconscious need for punishment, which would lead Freud to consider the full implications of the negative therapeutic reaction (*The Ego and the Id*, p. 50).

Freud's conception of conscience as a symptom has proved to be "foreign to people's ordinary way of thinking". According to ordinary conceptions, conscience causes the subject to renounce the drives; it is considered to be an external spiritual principle to which the drives can be subjected (*Civilization and its Discontents*, p. 128). Freud, in contrast, suggests that if renunciation exacerbates guilt, it is because there is a direct causal relation between the two. Since guilt results from the conscience, the latter owes its form to renunciation itself. Freud's theory can be summarized as follows: just as the cause has the same nature as its effect, so too conscience must have the same nature as the drive that feeds it. They both spring from the same source: aggressiveness.

"Every renunciation of instinct now becomes a dynamic source of conscience and every fresh renunciation increases the latter's severity and intolerance" (p. 128). Since, in other words, "Conscience is the result of instinctual renunciation," it cannot be rooted in an autonomous spiritual principle (p. 129).

Freud does not, however, consider that it is *only* the aggressive drives that, once inhibited, find an outlet by being turned around and discharged against the ego. Indeed, he also remarks that moral conscience has another origin than the renunciation of the drives. What is fundamental, instead, is an aggression that is directed at the prohibition of any form of drive satisfaction, "whatever their kind" (p. 129).

The authority that has required any renunciation "now turns into his super-ego and enters in possession of all the aggressiveness which a child would have liked to exercise against it" (p. 129).

Indeed, when Freud recounts the genesis of aggressiveness, he tries to suppress any opposition between the internal—renunciation—and the external—rejection of authority. It is, once again, the Oedipus complex that fixes the outcome of the drives: "A considerable amount of aggressiveness must be developed in the child against the authority which prevents him from having his first, but none the less his most important, satisfactions" (p. 129).

The infernal character of guilt thus has its own particular logic, for it is actually increased "by every piece of aggressiveness that was suppressed and carried over to the super-ego" (p. 132).

Yet furthermore, civilization increases guilt in its attempt to counter individual aggressiveness. "Since civilization obeys an internal erotic impulsion which causes human beings to unite in closely-knit groups it can only achieve this aim through an ever-increasing reinforcement of the sense of guilt. What began in relation to the father is completed in relation to the group (p. 133).

Is the analyst's task, then, the obverse of the desire of civilization? Is draining the Zuider Zee compatible with the "conquest of the id" (*The Ego and the Id*, p. 58)? In the eternal quarrel between love and the desire for death, where is the desire of the analyst to be situated (*Civilization and its Discontents*, p. 133)?

"Don't give up on your desire"

Having examined Freud's theories in *Civilization and its Discontents*, Lacan summarizes the ethics of analysis with the following formula: "Don't give up on your desire."[2]

As we have already shown in a detailed study of chapter seven of *Civilization and its Discontents,* the result of renouncing the drives is to arouse anxiety in the face of the superego. "[A]n occasional satisfaction" of temptations, however, "causes them to diminish, at least for the time being" (p. 126). This might perhaps be interpreted as pointing to a certain ethical laxity on Freud's part or even, as he himself on occasion remarked, to certain "more liberal opinions about sexual intercourse" (Weiss, p. 36).

Psychoanalysis does not, however, advocate "free love" ("*jouissance sans entraves*"), since it is precisely the barrier to pleasure that provides the subject with access to jouissance. Yet the self-inflicted cruelty that results from this renunciation constitutes a paradox that, as we have seen, motivated both Freud and Lacan to turn their attention to the question of the ethic of desire.

Freud's conclusion regarding the outcome of repressed drives is that a clear distinction must be made between the consequences of "privation" and those of the "repression of aggression" (*Civilization and its Discontents*, p. 138). In contrast to the general tendency at that time, led by Jones, Isaacs, Klein, and then Reik and Alexander, Freud refused to see the strengthening of the sense of guilt as the consequence of "any thwarted instinctual satisfaction". There must, instead, be an earlier detour: aggressiveness must first be directed towards "the person who has interfered with the satisfaction". He adds that "It is after all only the aggressiveness which is transformed into a sense of guilt, by being suppressed and made over to the super-ego" (p. 138).

Freud thus clearly sets himself apart from his contemporaries, who had begun to conceive of oral and anal aggressiveness in terms not of the Oedipus complex, but of the pregenital drives. In a text that is entirely devoted to the question of group formations and the role in the latter of the symbolic father, Freud highlights, instead, the part played in the genesis of the superego by unconscious hatred of the father. He gives a simplified summary of the difference between two avatars of desire as follows: "When an instinctual trend undergoes repression, its libidinal elements are turned into symptoms, and its aggressive components into a sense of guilt" (p. 139).

This preoccupation with hatred and its repression in the context of culture helps to cast a new light on the formation of neuroses and the definition of conflict. The death drive is defined here, as certain authors have already pointed out, as a destructive drive, and not essentially as a tendency towards repetition. In *Civilization and its Discontents*, Freud places the two conflicting drives at the heart of a combat in which the psychoanalyst plays a role, while never allowing himself to forget that "God is on the side of the big battalions" (*An Outline of Psycho-Analysis*, p. 182).

The new theories of the drive, and particularly the self-destructive role accorded to the death drive suggest that, rather than being a component of Eros, it is an obstacle to the fulfilment of desire. It is this point that I now wish to examine.

Assuming that the analyst's desire is essentially an x—an obstacle that confronts the subject with the function of the law as a barrier against the mere homoeostasis of pleasure—then how far can the analyst hope to lead his patient in the process of lifting repression? The question of repression cannot be separated from hatred on the pretext that civilization is the antithesis of aggressiveness. The presence of the father's murder and the sons' guilt is a leitmotif in *Civilization and its Discontents*, to the point that this hatred for the creator, once transferred to the superego, nourishes the symptoms that are the most difficult to cure. Now, if a possible cure is "[treated] as a new danger", then this danger can only be that of castration ("Analysis Terminable and Interminable", p. 238). In this context, the analyst reveals himself to be a "substitute" for the father, and the refusal to be cured comes to mean a refusal to bow down before him. "The patient must not become well but must remain ill, for he deserves no better" (*An Outline of Psycho-Analysis*, p. 180).

In these conditions, the analyst's role, as Freud tells us, is to help the patient become conscious of this resistance and thereby to "bring about the slow demolition of the hostile super-ego" (p. 180). He specifies, on the other hand, that there also exists another type of resistance, "our means of combating which are specially inadequate"; the latter arises when, as a result of "far-reaching defusions of instinct", there occurs a "liberation of excessive quantities of the destructive instinct directed inwards" (p. 180).

Freud thus apparently questions the validity of the theory, which he had accepted until then, that every phase of a psychic conflict is intrinsically "linked" to the Oedipus complex. Thus, in chapter six of *Analysis Terminable and Interminable*, after having come up against an "independently-emerging tendency to conflict [that] can scarcely be attributed to anything but the intervention of an element of free aggressiveness", he goes so far as to state that resistance has a biological foundation that lies outside the realm of the Oedipus complex and the superego. "The question at once arises [...] whether all that we know about psychical conflict should not be revised from this new angle" (*Analysis Terminable and Interminable*, p. 244).

Does this mean that there is a form of aggressiveness that is not linked to the symbolic? Since the impasses of therapy can be reduced to this bedrock of aggressiveness, we come up against a paradox: either aggressiveness is linked to the Oedipus complex and castration, in which case there is an impassable limit, or else one accepts that there is a certain form of free aggression, which is not linked to the signifier of the dead and castrating father and which consequently has its origin in something else.

It seems to me that this dual origin of the death drive is what leads Lacan to distinguish between the imaginary and symbolic fathers. What is original about Lacan's thesis is that the superego does not derive from the relation with the castrating father but with the father of privation; the privation in question is not that of the mother but of being. This imaginary father, who has to be distinguished from God, is the figure whom the subject holds responsible for having "screwed him up".

If this is indeed the case, then the superego cannot be reduced to an internalization of law and, on the contrary, constitutes a "discordant statement" that points to a flaw in the subject's understanding of the law, which is consequently perceived as arbitrary and nonsensical (Lacan, *Seminar I*, pp. 197–198).

I shall therefore conclude by putting forward the following hypothesis: if hatred for the father—the creator—pushes back the boundaries that castration seems to have imposed, the horror of truth can be the extra step that is to be crossed. If there is indeed a dimension beyond castration, then there has to be another way of ending analysis. Freud missed this because of his desire to protect the father from castration. It would appear that a son can only punish himself for his own crimes, not for those of his father.

Notes

1. See also *Civilization and its Discontents*: the "omniscience of the superego" (p. 137).
2. "[T]he only thing one can be guilty of is giving ground relative to one's desire" (*Seminar VII*, p. 321).

PART IV

THE DESIRE OF THE OTHER

The psychoanalyst's desire is his enunciation ...

—Lacan, *Proposition of 9 October 1967.**

---

*Analysis 6 (1995), p. 7.

CHAPTER SIXTEEN

The psychoanalyst's action

Freud's own "case" is thus the invisible but crucial "other side" (*envers*) of psychoanalytic practice. The way of understanding the analyst's implication in his practice—the role that his *libido sciendi* takes in the treatment, in interpretation, and in the end of analysis— would later be transformed by Lacan. This is due to several factors.

According to Lacan's definition of desire, the psychoanalyst's desire is situated in the realm of the Other. Desire is, in other words, necessarily mediated by the Other. He proposes a number of variations of this formula: the subject's desire for recognition or his desire for the Other's desire, which are indeed simply variations on the same theme. As soon as there is a reciprocity of desire, it seems that the desire of the analyst can be deduced immediately by referring to the field of the Other. The desire of the one relates, in its essence, to the desire of the Other.

It is thus by bracketing off one's own personal desire that the function of desire as originating in the place of the Other becomes manifest. In other words, the more the analyst remains silent about his desire, the more obvious it becomes that the patient's desire is alienated in this place. The psychoanalyst's desire is therefore not an analyst's personal desire; instead, it is a function that is essential for the expression of desire, for this expression requires a recognition. From this, we can grasp the ataraxia of the psychoanalyst. If the result is a certain passivity on the analyst's part, it can only be justified theoretically by this detour through the desire of the Other.

The idea that the analyst supports the function of the Other as such implies that the analytic process will be dominated by the dialectics of recognition. It would be an error, however, to reduce Lacan's teaching to this single conception, which, as we shall see, leads to a number of impasses. It could, indeed, make us think that the symmetry of two desires would reduce the treatment to a dimension of intersubjectivity. If this were the case, then the role of the third term in the treatment would be eradicated by the return to a dual relation. This is what allows the so-called "countertransference" to be explained: it is a confusion between functions and persons. It is this movement that I shall now describe:

- The success of ego-psychology in the United States, due in part to Heinz Hartmann, oriented analysis in a direction that reduced the analytic situation to a dual relation. Lacan reacts to this by insisting on the function of the "symbolic" in the treatment, in order to destroy the illusions of dual reciprocity, of the communication between unconsciousnesses and of a "counter-transference" (*Écrits*, p. 276). The "false consistency of the notion of counter-transference" has led, in his opinion, to "deviations" that cause analysts to identify with their patients and thereby to shed any personal responsibility for their own actions (*Écrits*, p. 276). "The analyst thereby avoids considering the action that it is incumbent upon him to take in the production of truth" (*Écrits*, p. 276). In the years following the Rome Congress of 1953, Lacan devoted his efforts to criticizing this tendency to analyse "from *ego* to *ego*" (*Seminar I*, p. 32). One of his main reasons for radically distinguishing between little *a* and big A—the symbolic dimension of speech or the signifier—is to discredit the ideology of interpersonal communication.
- This rectification has several consequences. If the analyst's criterion is to strengthen the ego and its mastery over the drives, then he must himself reach this ideal of perfection and come to incarnate this model. Michael Balint even went so far as to say that the end of treatment consists in successful identification with the analyst (*Écrits*, p. 281). If the analyst's strategy is to ally himself with the healthy part of the ego, then the result will be compromises and moralizing

deviations: genital love, adaptation, maturity, and other ideals that characterize the American way of life.

For Lacan, because they did not question the analyst's desire or ask themselves about their own desire, post-Freudian analysts allowed the theory of transference and of the end of the treatment to take the place of a proper theorization. What these deviations have in common is not only an ignorance of, but also a scorn for Freud's theory of the ego, which it had been their aim to strengthen. It is also true, however, that this technique does prevail over the analysis of discourse in a certain number of Freud's works.[1] It is, in any case, pointless to ask what the analyst wants in theories that presuppose that the latter is a paragon of normality. What can he possibly want, other than to form his subjects in his own image?

The analyst's narcissism is thus an obstacle that prevents him from questioning his own desire, which is the effect of a resistance in the analytic sense of the term, since it is precisely the ego that resists. The theory of the ego is thus an alibi that allows the analyst to disengage and, under the cover of a false notion of apathy disguised as "benevolent neutrality", to avoid formulating an adequate theory of the end of analysis. Freud's verdict on this naïve hope is that "It cannot be disputed that analysts in their own personalities have not invariably come up to the standard of psychical normality to which they wish to educate their patients" ("Analysis Terminable and Interminable", p. 247).

The theory of the end of analysis has therefore precisely the same nature as the desire of the analyst who has produced it: incarnating an ideal, what Freud calls an *Ideal Fiktion*: a fiction or hypothesis has been transformed into an ideal or norm (p. 235). Why, then, would an analyst think that he could possibly incarnate such an ideal unless he himself has been exempted from being analysed? In this context, Lacan asks: "What must the analyst's ego thus be if it assumes the role of being the measure of truth for all of us and for each subject who puts himself in the analyst's hands?" (*Écrits*, p. 281).

The "service of goods" and the countertransference

For a long time, the notion of countertransference has provided the theoretical answer to this question, an answer that treats as secondary any question of the analyst's personal responsibility in conducting the treatment. One would seek in vain in Freud's work for any concepts that back up the various theories that, from the 1950s onwards, have come together under the notion of countertransference.[2]

Over the course of this period, a new image of the psychoanalyst has appeared. Unlike the theory of the analyst as an immobile plane mirror, this new tendency does not consider it unacceptable for an analyst to have feelings about a patient. The portrait of the analyst as having no memory, desire, or understanding is thus replaced by that of a desiring subject. This obvious fact began to appear in dictionaries of analytical concepts under the term of countertransference, a term defined in the following way:

- The effects produced by an analyst on a patient. This is clearly a result of Freud's warning to analysts, to the effect that the analyst's personal equation and his person emerge through his interpretations, and show whether his own analysis has been pushed far enough. These are commonsense remarks. Margaret Little, in particular, adheres to this school of thought (see her article "Counter-transference and the patient's response to it").
- Paula Heimann, on the other hand, chooses to emphasize the feelings that the patient activates in the analyst (see "On Counter-transference"). The term "countertransference" thus no longer applied to the feelings that the analyst inspires in the patient, but rather to those that he experiences himself. This reversal in perspective has little other effect than to create a great deal of confusion. Indeed, if the analysand can be the *cause* of a desire or passion in the analyst, one must wonder whether these feelings are the mark of analysis, and whether the analyst is undergoing an analysis with the analysand. If this is indeed the case, then what is in question here is merely a *transference*. The term of countertransference thus serves only to identify the analyst to himself, for the main question is the following: who exactly is in analysis with whom?

Roger Money-Kyrle, following Paula Heimann's tracks, shows that what is presented as feelings in the analyst are not his own doing and do not belong to him, but are, instead, an aspect of the patient's transference (see "Normal counter-transference and some of its deviations"). The analyst's feelings are no longer an obstacle to the analysand's transference, but are its displaced manifestation, extended onto the analyst. The analyst's feelings and thoughts anticipate elements that have been repressed in the analysand. One might more appropriately speak of a transference of the analysand's unconscious onto the analyst, as opposed to an interaction of their two unconsciousnesses, a formulation that would suggest an affective and quasi-sexualized "touchy-feeliness" (see Porge, "*Sur le désir de l'analyste*"). It is true that Heimann uses the concept of unconscious-to-unconscious communication, but she emphasizes its single and homogeneous quality rather than the reciprocal nature of the feelings involved; for her the countertransference is the patient's creation. Here is one way—Lacan's—of taking up and situating this approach to analytic treatment: "The transference is a phenomenon in which subject and analyst are both included. To divide it in terms of transference and counter-transference—however bold, however confident what is said on this theme may be—is never more than a way of avoiding the essence of the matter" (*Seminar XI*, p. 231).

Lacan himself only gives a negative meaning to countertransference. It is in relation to Freud himself that he used it in a critical way. It comes to refer to a particular way in which the analyst can drift away from his orientation: the enigma of feminine desire sent Freud scurrying back to the prejudices of his time. Indeed, Lacan's only definition of the countertransference was "the fact of being an idiot" (*Seminar I*, p. 228).

Lacan's criticism of the countertransference is thus directed at the analyst's failure to take into account the symbolic dimension, which, in his opinion, accounted for the success of the concept, far more than its emphasis on the "analyst's affects".[3] Freud himself uses the term to refer to the feelings of sympathy that a patient can arouse, and the technical problems that they raise are limited to a questioning of their manifestations in the analyst. Regarding the "problem of the counter-transference" raised by Binswanger in his correspondence with Freud, the latter responds in his letter of 20 February 1913 that:

> [It] is—technically—among the most intricate in psychoanalysis. Theoretically I believe it is much easier to solve. What we give to the patient should, however, be a spontaneous affect, but measured out consciously at all times, to a greater or lesser extent according to need. In certain circumstances a great deal, but never from one's own unconscious. I would look upon that as the formula. One must, therefore, always recognize one's counter-transference and overcome it, for not till then is one free oneself. To give someone too

little because one loves him too much is unfair to the patient and a
technical error. This is all far from easy, and perhaps one has to be
older for it, too. (Fichtner, p. 112)

It is clear that Freud establishes no relation between the countertransference and the analyst's unconscious. If, in this letter, he invites analysts
both to recognize and overcome their countertransferences, this merely
suggests that the latter are symptoms that can easily be dealt with. His
letter to Binswanger is, on the other hand, one of the few indications of
the interest that he took in his patients. It therefore tempers what can
sometimes sound like an aversion to therapy on his part,[4] and can help
qualify popular opinion regarding his attitude to difficult patients.

The popular view, largely fuelled by Paul Roazen—according to
whom Freud intensely disliked analysing his psychotic patients—is
not false (see *Brother Animal*, chapter VI) but should be understood
in the light of certain factors that are both theoretical and contingent.
It is perfectly true that Freud liked some of his patients and disliked
others, mainly for ethical reasons. He thus apparently refused to analyse "a scoundrel who was not worth [the] trouble", while, on the other
hand, he took a certain interest in a young American patient of whom he
grew to be relatively fond (Weiss, p. 36). The latter, known as A.B., was
indeed the object of correspondence between himself and Pfister, who
had originally referred him to Freud: "My belief as a physician that he
is on the verge of a paranoid dementia has increased. I was again very
near the point of giving him up but there is something touching about
him which deters me from doing so" (Meng & Freud, p. 101). Freud
later observes that "I feel a great deal of sympathy for him, and cannot
make up my mind to send him away and risk a disastrous outcome"
(p. 108). "A not inessential factor is the impression that his personality
is worth any amount of trouble" (p. 106).

These letters to Pfister are all the more remarkable in that they reveal
a rare level of affection in Freud, especially considering the person to
whom they are addressed. The Swiss pastor's naïvete and heart-breaking
optimism usually encouraged Freud to darken his picture of mankind
during the post-war years. Freud once writes to him, for example, that:

Ethics are remote from me, and you are a minister of religion. I do
not break my head very much about good and evil, but I have
found little that is "good" about human beings on the whole.

In my experience most of them are trash, no matter whether they
publicly subscribe to this or that ethical doctrine or to none at all.
(pp. 61–62)

Freud was far too aware of the aggressive motives underlying affection
to be taken in by the latter, even, and perhaps especially, when they
come from the analyst.[5] Indeed, Freud always condemns the counter-
transference for ethical rather than technical reasons:

> Since we demand strict truthfulness from our patients, we jeopardize
> our whole authority if we let ourselves be caught out by them in a
> departure from the truth. Besides, the experiment of letting oneself
> go a little way in tender feelings for the patient is not altogether with-
> out danger. Our control over ourselves is not so complete that we
> may not suddenly one day go further than we had intended. In my
> opinion, therefore, we ought not to give up the neutrality towards
> the patient, which we have acquired through keeping the counter-
> transference in check. ("Observations on Transference-Love", p. 164)

Freud's criticism of this concept is fundamentally motivated by his
desire for sincerity and rigour.

The analyst is not in the position of the real Other of demand and
so cannot be identified with a good mother.[6] Freud criticizes Ferenczi
precisely for identifying with a "tender mother" (Jones, 1957, p. 175);
for Freud, therapeutic activism and maternal identification have exactly
the same origin. In the obituary note on Ferenczi, he writes that "The
need to cure and to help had become paramount in him [übermächtig]"
(Freud, "Sándor Ferenczi", p. 229).

In this statement, Freud is taking aim at a technique that indulges
in the comforts of oblativity. By not revealing his feelings or making
fine speeches, Freud enables himself to be this form of nothingness, by
which the subject can reach the object of his desire.

Freud's moment to conclude

One cannot claim that the end of analysis is marked by an effect that is
as spontaneous as the initial triggering of the transference. In no other
aspect of treatment is the analyst's action so sought-after as it is in this
endgame. This is especially true because, as the title of Freud's article,

"Analysis Terminable and Interminable" indicates, a clear choice must be made between these two kinds of analysis. I would go so far as to say that the direction of the treatment cannot be approached by purely technical standards, and that here, especially, the analyst's responsibility is absolutely central. Lacan dramatically illustrates this in the following example:

> Is not the contribution that each individual, Freud apart, brings to the subject of the transference something in which his desire is perfectly legible? I could do an analysis of Abraham for you simply on the basis of his theory of part-objects. It is not only a question of what the analyst wants to do with his patient in the matter. It is also a question of what his patient wants to do with him. Abraham, we might say, wanted to be a complete mother. (*Seminar XI*, pp. 158–159)[7]

Freud did not encourage patients to produce a negative transference, for which Ferenczi reproached him, as he points out in the second chapter of "Analysis Terminable and Interminable". Yet since Freud does not propose a specific theory of the analyst's desire, one is left guessing what he desired his patients to do with him. On the other hand, Ferenczi had brought out the role of the psychoanalyst as "catalytic ferment" in 1909, and one certainly cannot think that Freud wanted his patients to make of him a total object, a complete mother, which seemed to be the ageing Ferenczi's tendency (p. 39). Did Freud desire to be a partial object? Although there is no theory in his work of the analyst as an object *a,* cause of desire, he was clearly far from occupying the role of the thing in itself, or of the absolute Other.

Freud's debate with Ferenczi on the subject of maternal transference indeed explicitly indicates that, rather than wanting to represent an ideal object, he wanted to be a cause, in the sense of a trigger that could modify the patient's intra-psychic power struggles ("Sándor Ferenczi", p. 229; "Analysis Terminable and Interminable", p. 247).

Thus, the "irresistible power of the quantitative factor" is Freud's name for the psychoanalyst's inability to detach the subject from the object of his sexual phantasy (p. 226). The correlate of the libido's fixation on the object is the impossibility of displacing the transference and thereby of metonymizing a desire that has been subverted by the phantasy; this is what he calls the "adhesiveness of the libido" (*Klebrigkeit der Libido*) (p. 241). Freud thus links the possibility of detaching the libido to that of displacement, but this displacement of desire in the treatment is necessarily symbolic, since it is organized by the possibility of substitution. This leads us to suppose that the impossibility of accepting a substitute for the father (*Vaterersatz*) and the "viscosity" of the libido are one and the same thing. Freud therefore makes the possibility of destabilizing the phantasy depend upon a purely symbolic phenomenon: the transference as a substitution of signifiers from the Other, leading to a modification of desire. Not every element of the phantasy, however, is a signifier. The object of the drive, since it exceeds symbolic reformulations, belongs to the category of the real. Freud qualifies the latter as an economic or "quantitative factor", in order to indicate that no substitution can cover up this deficit, this x, which symbolizes the object. That is why this object represents what comes to seal the $-\phi$. This phallic lack can accept any form of substitution—*ersatz*—except this particular residue, which cannot be absorbed, and which, for Freud, is *Penisneid* in women and castration anxiety in men. In both cases, the repudiation of femininity (*Ablehnung der Weiblichkeit*) becomes the stumbling block of desire, a stumbling block that receives an imaginary annulment in the phantasmatic scenario (p. 252).

If this quantitative factor is impervious both to interpretation and to constructions, is this not because it is heterogeneous to any symbolic control? As a consequence, this failure shows the mode of revelation that is provided by the imaginary, to which the phantasy's resistance owes its consistency. The subject's adherence to the phantasy is a fixation not on signifiers—which could be liberated from the chain—but rather on an object, on the real of the drive. This is precisely what makes the analyst's task so difficult, as Freud has shown in several ways. Fixation—the "viscosity" of the libido—imposes a limit on the signifier's effects on the subject. The subject, bound to his phantasy, is unable to "call out all [...] possible instinctual conflicts from the transference situation", because they do not belong to the dimension of the symbolic but to the real (p. 233). This is why, since they are not "currently active", they do not belong to the dimension of reality that the subject is struggling with, but to the "real": the real of castration that explains the psychoanalyst's impotence.[8] Let us say that this impotence stems from the impossibility of acting upon the "quantitative factor" only through the signifier. In thermodynamic terms, I might say that the conversion of psychic phenomena is never complete and that the libido invariably leaves behind a deficit or residue that is impossible to symbolize. According to Lacan, "Libido, in Freud's work, is an energy that can be subjected to a kind of quantification which is all the easier to introduce in theory as it is useless, since only certain *quanta* of constancy are recognized therein" (*Écrits*, p. 722).

Yet if psychic energy cannot be confused with the energy of the libido, it is because the latter is not essentially defined by psychic reality, but is related, instead, to the real of castration. This real, as Freud tells us, can neither be inscribed in language nor find any possibility of "attachment" (*Bindung*) ("Analysis Terminable and Interminable", p. 268). This "force", which does not enter into the calculations of the psychic apparatus and which is consequently not "psychically bound" to the ego, superego, or id, is thus an "unmistakable indication" of the death drive; in other words, it constitutes the limit of the signified, of phallic signification (p. 243). Freud calls this the "exhaustion of receptivity", an exhaustion that is "due to [...] a kind of psychical entropy" (p. 242). It was to this point of failure that Freud aspired to take his patients.

Notes

1. This is the case in "Analysis Terminable and Interminable" and in *An Outline of Psycho-Analysis*.
2. On the history of this concept, see the commentary by E. Ribeiro Hawelka, the French translator of Freud's journal of his analysis of the Rat Man, p. 255 ff.
3. On Freud's personal equation, see Roazen, *Freud and His Followers*, p. 168 ff.
4. For example, Freud writes in a letter to Max Schur that "I have no interest in these patients [psychotics]; they bore me and I find them too foreign to myself and to all that is human" (cited by M. Mannoni, p. 119).
5. We saw that Freud condemned therapeutic fanaticism, the *furor sanandi*, because of the pride that motivates it (see "Observations on Transference-Love", pp. 170–171).
6. As Freud confided to H.D., "I do *not* like to be the mother in transference" (*Tribute to Freud*, pp. 146–147).
7. On this topic, see Éric Laurent's article, "L'effet mère", which points to Karl Abraham's transferential object as "that of the good mother who watches the growth of the unambivalent object" (p. 30). Laurent makes a comparable analysis of Winnicott in "Une phobie moderne".
8. "The real, I will say, is the mystery of the speaking body, the mystery of the unconscious" (Lacan, *Seminar XX*, p. 131).

CHAPTER SEVENTEEN

Socrates's desire

L et us now examine the actual mechanism of the transference which, Lacan insists, is impossible to conceive of without supposing the existence of the psychoanalyst's desire: "It is ultimately the analyst's desire that operates in psychoanalysis" (*Écrits*, p. 724).

This formula implies a theory that clearly differs from Freud's. *On the one hand*, Lacan radically separates transference from repetition (*Seminar XI*, p. 33). Unlike repetition, which implies a failed encounter with the real, the transference cannot be defined in terms of the real, and it is relative to interpretation. As early as his discussion of Dora, Lacan indicates that "transference is nothing real in the subject", thereby emphasizing its artificial character (*Écrits*, p. 183). In other words, Lacan considers it to be an effect of the operation of the treatment and therefore it has a unique structure, which is to be distinguished from that of its spontaneous occurrence outside treatment. Indeed, in this case, it can be said that "As soon as the subject who is supposed to know exists somewhere there is transference" (*Seminar XI*, p. 232). *On the other hand*, Lacan specifies that transference is a resistance; it is a moment of closure as opposed to an opening of the unconscious, which distinguishes it again from repetition, which is characterized by the rhythm of eclipse

(*Seminar XI*, p. 143). Since this resistance essentially takes the form of love, transference love becomes the most characteristic way of showing the function of the supposed Other. The latter cannot, however, be defined entirely by the function of the subject supposed to know; there must, in addition, be a supposition that the analyst desires, and is not only "desired". The analyst is a "subject supposed to desire".[1]

The desire of the analyst must therefore be constructed by means of a conception of transference that includes this double definition of a subject who is supposed both to know and to desire. This is what Lacan does in his seminar: in 1960 in *Transference,* and then in 1964 in *The Four Fundamental Concepts of Psychoanalysis.* In these two seminars, his main point of reference is not Freud, however, but Plato's *Symposium*, in which Alcibiades declares his desire while Socrates conceals his own.

The subject supposed to desire

Lacan's reference to Socrates's desire is motivated by what has now become a famous analogy between the psychoanalyst and the father of philosophy. Socrates enables a new relation, not so much to truth, but to desire, to emerge; for the first time in Western history, the desire of the Other is considered as an object: "There is an entire thematic area concerning the status of the subject when Socrates declares that he does not place desire in a position of original subjectivity, but in the position of an object. Well! Freud, too, is concerned with desire as an object" (*Seminar XI*, p. 13).

The new object that Socrates distinguishes from all the other passions is not quite yet Lacan's object-cause of desire. The new object that Socrates isolates in the sphere of the passions is desire itself: the desiring, rather than the desirable object. If desire is precisely the desire for desire the desire—for the Other—then no one before Freud was better placed to show this than Socrates in the *Symposium*, who astonished Alcibiades by slipping away from his sexual advances. This slipping away is indeed all the more puzzling since, from the outset, he is described as having "expert knowledge of nothing but erotics" (Plato's *Symposium*, p. 7).[2] With Socrates, the lover substitutes himself for the beloved and desire gains the upper hand over desirability. The one who desires, the ἐραστής (*erastes*, the lover), takes the place of the ἐρώμενος (*eromenos*, the beloved) (Lacan, *Le séminaire VIII*, p. 70).

Socrates readily admits in the *Lysis* that in all domains other than love, he is "of mean ability, indeed useless, in respect to everything else, but this much has been given me—I don't know how—from god, the capacity to recognize quickly a lover and an object of love" (Plato's *Lysis*, p. 4).

It is therefore the desire, not of the person who is desirable, but of the one who desires, that justifies Lacan in taking Socrates as the reference for a conception of the analyst's desire that would go beyond Freud. Such an analogy is only possible, however, if Socrates is not only an expert on love, but is also the subject who is supposed to know what the object of desire is. Socrates's approach to love, indeed, differs radically from previous views by distinguishing love, which is a god, from desire, which implies a lack. Yet the essential point, which concerns a rapprochement with the analyst, revolves around three characters: Agathon, Socrates, and Alcibiades. The *Symposium* teaches us that where love is concerned, there are always three parties involved. Socrates is the mediator in the relation between Alcibiades and Agathon, a relation that Alcibiades does not understand. Other forms of mediation also play a role, the most famous of which are the αγάλματα (*agalmata*, glories or delights) contained in Socrates's body.

Lacan assimilates these marvellous objects or icons to the object of desire, which analytic theory had, until then, merely considered as a partial object. Plato's text, indeed, perfectly illustrates the Kleinian dialectic of good and bad internal objects that trigger desire. Alcibiades misunderstands this function of the object as cause of desire, and hence why he loves Socrates. Nevertheless, he is only able to declare his love in relation to the desire of Socrates—the *erastes*, the man who desires—who, through the call that generates knowledge about love, triggers this passion. This, as Lacan emphasizes, is the moment of the encounter between the patient's and the analyst's desire: "The subject, in so far as he is subjected to the desire of the analyst, desires to betray him for this subjection, by making the analyst love him, by offering of himself that essential duplicity that is love" (*Seminar XI*, p. 254).

While Socrates is perfectly aware of the deceitful character of love, he nevertheless plays the game for a time, in order to divert Alcibiades towards the object of his desire: Agathon. This is the transference-effect that can best foreground the analogy. Yet this deceitfulness exists only in relation to Socrates's knowledge, to his claim to know the truth about love: that it is not an exchangeable good.

Socrates responds to Alcibiades's declaration of love by proposing an unusual form of exchange, based on his claim that the truth about love that he possesses is incommensurate with love itself:

> Really, my dear Alcibiades, you're no sucker if what you say about me is really true and there is some power in me through which you could become better. You must see, you know, an impossible beauty in me, a beauty very different from the fairness of form in yourself. So, if, in observing my beauty, you are trying to get a share in it and to exchange beauty for beauty, you are intending to get far the better deal. For you are trying to acquire the truth of beautiful things in exchange for the seeming and opinion of beautiful things;[3] and you really have in mind to exchange "gold for bronze". (*Plato's Symposium*, p. 49)

Socrates is thus, to a certain extent, responsible for arousing Alcibiades's love since it is his claim to know the truth about love that commits the younger man to this deceptive contract. He plays the fool in order to get information and, beyond his ironic tone, openly admits that he is in the position of the subject supposed to know. In exchange for the deceitfulness of beauty, Socrates wants the truth. If truth were simply marketable, however, Socrates, whose desire is elsewhere—beyond beauty and the *agalmata*—would be the first to lose out:

> But who knows better than Socrates that he holds only the meaning he engenders in retaining this nothing, which enables him to refer Alcibiades to the actual addressee of his discourse, Agathon (as if by chance): this is to teach you that if you are obsessed with what in the discourse of the psychoanalysand concerns you, you do not understand yet. (Lacan, *Proposition of 9 October 1967*, p. 7)

It is, indeed, only because he is effectively "nothing" (*ouden on* [in no way or not at all a being or creature]) that Socrates can tell Alcibiades to mind his own business: this business is the young Agathon, the object of his desire (Plato's *Symposium*, p. 49). Yet it is also because the analyst incarnates a desire that is beyond all forms of exchangeable goods—the desire of the Other—that he can capture the subject's desire. In his seminar, *Desire and its Interpretation*, Lacan specifies in very Socratic terms that "The desire of the analyst is in a paradoxical situation. For the analyst, the desire of the Other is the desire of the subject in analysis, and we must guide this desire, not towards us, but towards another. We mature the subject's desire for someone other than us" (*Le séminaire VI*, 1 July 1959). This is a far cry from the principle of abstinence and analytic neutrality.

This lateral transference, which the analyst must arouse, is here, as in Plato, the very basis of the transference. The transference is a mask, and as Freud notes, it is not a false love, but is, instead, the love that contains the very essence of the pathological deceitfulness that can also be found in normal phenomena: the analyst incarnates the idol by proxy. He gives someone else—who is having difficulty in desiring—an occasion for loving, and then directs this desire onto an object: one that Freud calls a "true" object. Yet then, far from liquidating the transference, the desire of the analyst seeks to perpetuate it. The transference, in its essence, is lateral. The "true" object, however, which Freud situates in terms of reality—unlike the object of the phantasy—is utterly opposed to the subject's ideals, and particularly to his notion of the good. Agathon is, without question, the very picture of idiocy and futility, "the least likely object to attract the desire of a master" (*Seminar XI*, p. 255). However, it is this very futility of the *eron* that is the essence of the *agalmata*, whose dazzling splendour block out the horror of castration.

Socrates knows both that he does not have what Alcibiades is looking for in Agathon and that he has only attained the status of an idol because he parades his knowledge. Yet he can also occupy this place all the more easily by not giving any sign of his desire, and furthermore, the objects contained inside the body of Silenus will not be given up. That is, Alcibiades's love exists only in relation to the strategy that Socrates has set up, that of the semblance: "While deceiving them into thinking of him as the lover, he brings it about that he is the beloved rather than the lover" (Plato's *Symposium*, 222b, p. 53).

In short, the *Symposium* sets out the conditions for this experimental love, which make Socrates the "precursor of psychoanalysis" (Lacan, *Écrits*, p. 699). It is true that Lacan, not without a hint of irony, gave this label to Socrates at a time when it was still necessary to remind analysts of what constitutes the mainspring of the transference:

> Thus by exhibiting his own object as castrated, Alcibiades flaunts
> the fact that he is imbued with desire—a fact that does not escape

Socrates's attention—for someone else who is present, Agathon. Socrates, as the precursor of psychoanalysis, and confident of his position at this fashionable gathering, does not hesitate to name Agathon as the transference object, bringing to light through an interpretation a fact that many analysts are still unaware of: that the love-hate effect in the psychoanalytic situation is found outside of it. (*Écrits*, p. 699)

Everything happens as if the analyst's desire enables the patient to locate the object of desire beyond the mirages of love; this object can be found precisely because its sign is missing in the Other. Lacan explicitly states that "Castration is the altogether new mainspring Freud introduced into desire, giving desire's lack the meaning that remained enigmatic in Socrates's dialectic, although it was preserved in the recounting of *The Symposium*" (*Écrits*, p. 723).

Thus it appears that the dialectic of desire revolves not so much around knowledge as around the object. The marvels contained inside the body of Silenus, to which Alcibiades compares Socrates, are only present in a negative way. Their presence is relative to an absence, the absence of Socrates's desire, or rather the sign of his desire: the phallic object. "It is because Alcibiades has not seen Socrates's prick [...] that Alcibiades the seducer exalts in Socrates the *agalma*, the marvel that he would have liked Socrates to cede to him by avowing his desire" (*Écrits*, p. 699).

The charming objects, whose phallic brilliance is correlated to castration, thus highlight the dialectic of desires, since one desire is always relative to another. Yet this only serves to draw our attention to another dialectic: that of desire and the object, in which the object depends not only on the desire of the Other but also on castration.

The objects that are associated with the first dialectic—the objects of desire—need to be distinguished from the function of the object *a* as cause of desire; this object, rather than being a signifier, emerges when the latter falls. This is why the analyst is able to incarnate this object once he has effectively been stripped of his knowledge.

The dialectic of desire thus leads from the object of love, via the object of desire, to the object of jouissance. The *agalmata* become the pivots of a process that leads Lacan to highlight the role, not so much of Socrates's desire—which, as we shall see, is reduced to hysterical desire—as of the object.

Socrates the hysteric

I shall now consider more specifically the enigma of Socrates's desire. One of the ambitions of this book to resolve the problem of Socrates's relation to psychoanalysis, since this problem orients Lacan's teaching well beyond the 1960s. He still refers to Socrates in his "Proposition of 9 October 1967 on the Psychoanalyst of the School" and in *Radiophonie*.[4] Yet the accent has now changed, for Socrates is no longer situated in the analytic, but rather in the hysterical discourse, the discourse from which "science takes its impetus" (*Radiophonie*, p. 436). Lacan indeed explicitly refers to Socrates in *Radiophonie* as an "hysteric who confesses that he is acquainted only with what concerns desire" (*Radiophonie*, p. 436). If we compare the two discourses in question here, we note that, in the discourse of the hysteric, the divided subject is in the position of the agent:

$$\$ \rightarrow \frac{S_1}{S_2}$$

Socrates's feigned irony "constrains the master to produce knowledge" (*Radiophonie*, p. 436). His desire is, in a sense, an hysterical desire. His desire for the desire of the Other allows us, for convenience, to situate him in the hysterical discourse since he slips away from being desired as an object *a*. It is, on the contrary, precisely as a desiring subject that he enables Alcibiades to locate his own desire as being the desire of the Other: an unconscious desire that points to his division as a subject. His request for knowledge has been exposed for what it is and is then redirected onto the axis of his desire: "If the transference is that which separates demand from the drive, the analyst's desire is that which brings it back" (*Seminar XI*, p. 273).

When Lacan explicitly says in the *Four Fundamental Concepts*, that "Behind the love known as transference, is the affirmation of the link between the desire of the analyst and the desire of the patient," we can conclude that the analyst does not want his patient to be his object *a* (*Seminar XI*, p. 254). Does he himself desire, then, to be this object?

In a sense he does, since it is the mechanism of the *agalma* that is contained within him that allows Socrates to help Alcibiades transform his love into libido: "The *agalma* in the *eron* proves to be the motor force by which desire changes the nature of the lover. In his quest, Alcibiades spills the beans regarding love's deception and its baseness (to love is to want to be loved) to which he was willing to consent" (*Écrits*, p. 723).

However, as we have seen, Socrates is the one who desires (*erastes*), and the master's relation with the hysteric cannot serve as a paradigm for analytic discourse. Alcibiades is not a neurotic and is not afraid of castration. Socrates himself does not have the slightest intention of being an object *a*, and slips away from this position in order to occupy the place of the semblance. Therefore, as long as Lacan does not make the analyst into an object *a*—into the object-cause of desire rather than into a signifier—there could be a strong similarity between the hysteric's desire and the analyst's. Indeed, the latter could only be conceived of in terms of hysteria, so that the Socrates-effect arrived there at precisely the right moment. However, once Lacan has formulated a theory of the object *a* in which the analyst himself incarnates the object, the question of the latter's desire is posed in completely different terms: does the analyst want to be in the place of this refuse "so as to embody what the structure entails, namely allowing the subject, the subject of the unconscious, to take him as the cause of the subject's own desire" (Lacan, *Television*, p. 15)?

Socrates's hysterical relation to Alcibiades is thus not in itself sufficient to situate him in the analytical discourse. Socrates, unlike Freud, does not make the whole process of psychoanalysis hinge "on the genital act" (p. 300).

The characteristics that, according to Lacan, confer on Socrates a certain similarity with the analyst are generally considered to be the attributes of wisdom: an indifference to worldly affairs, which Lacan calls the renunciation of the service of goods. Socrates's desire for death in the *Phaedo* should accordingly be considered in this perspective. As for Freud, we shall see that the question is not repressed.

Socrates's desire is thus situated at the crossroads at which all these questions meet. Indeed, the analytic relation, far from constituting a pleasant pastoral in which two desires happily emulate one another, requires the role of a third party. In Plato's *Symposium*, it is Agathon, Alcibiades's object of desire, who occupies this position.

The object of desire, as the linchpin of the transferential relation, introduces a dissymmetry between the two desires. Yet Lacan, by accentuating this function of the object over the course of his teaching, ultimately operates a reversal: the analyst himself comes to occupy this position. As soon as the analyst is dislodged from the place of the

Other in order to occupy the position of the object cause of desire, he is thus no longer in the field of the Other as such. He is only there in so far as he is missing from it and merely constitutes a semblance of the object.

This reversal raises the question of the psychoanalyst's desire in different terms. What is up for discussion here is the question of the analyst's jouissance in occupying this position; another operation proves to be necessary in order to grasp the emergence of this jouissance, and this is what Lacan tries to formalize from 1967 onwards. This operation is called the pass and aims to transmit to others the experience that has led the analyst to occupy this position. It is this complex process that we shall now examine.

Notes

1. This expression is borrowed from Jacques-Alain Miller.
2. "... ὅς οὐδέν φημι ἄλλο ἐπίστασθαι ἢ τὰ ἐρωτικά" (*Plato: Symposium* (Cambridge Greek), 177d, p. 23).
3. Lacan uses the term "simulacrum" (see the Greek text).
4. See also *Écrits*, p. 699.

CHAPTER EIGHTEEN

The de-being¹ of the analyst

The desire for death

Freud, during his final period, refers to the *Symposium* once again in *Beyond the Pleasure Principle,* in relation to his theory of the union between Eros and the death drive, undermining the idea that the *Symposium* is merely a precursor of Christian asceticism (p. 58, note 1).² His references to Socrates, although few in number, give us a sense of a continuity between Socrates and the analyst. In both cases, the signifier of death is at play in the definition of desire: Freud's "realism" does not hide from us his conception that death is the master signifier of analysis. Just as what lies beyond the phenomena of repetition can be considered as a good criterion for the end of analysis, it would also be reasonable to ask what is the relation between two different concepts of death, or rather, of life. One of them tends towards inertia and repetition, and the other towards death as the principle of an erratic and metonymic desire, a desire for "something else".

A life whose meaning is not ultimately determined by death is, in Freud's opinion, of no more interest than, in Goethe's words, "a succession of fair days" (cited by Freud in *Civilization and its Discontents,* p. 76). The desire for immortality that characterizes obsessional neurosis is a desire for death, since, according to Lacan, the obsessional identifies with the dead master (see *Écrits*, p. 258). Certain texts of Freud's about death lend support to the theory that there is a strong affinity between neurotic repression and the negation of death.

In "Our Attitude towards Death" (part two of "Thoughts for the Times on War and Death"), which in many ways evokes the perspective adopted by Maurice Blanchot in *The Space of Literature*, Freud discusses the relation that, because we are unable to represent our own deaths, we have with the death of others: "It is indeed impossible to imagine our own death; and whenever we attempt to do so we can perceive that we are in fact still present as spectators" (p. 289).

Freud argues that, far from accepting death as an unavoidable real, we have grown accustomed to considering it as purely accidental, that is, not "natural, undeniable and unavoidable" (p. 289). In contrast, however, to the Epicureans, who think that death is of no more consequence than a dream, Freud states that death is the real element that makes life serious. Death gives meaning to life: "Life is impoverished, it loses in interest, when the highest stake in the game of living, life itself, may not be risked" (p. 290).

In contrast to the sensible attitude that one should simply get on with life, Freud cites the Hanseatic League motto: *Navigare necesse est, vivere non necesse!* (To sail is necessary, to live is not necessary!)—which lends a tragic dimension to this necessity (p. 290).

It is hardly conceivable, however, that Freud's intention was to offer a philosophical approach to the fear of death. He merely argues that if death has the power to give meaning to life, this is due to the ephemeral and transitory character of beauty and desirability. In his article "On Transience", he explicitly links the value of things to the fact that they are condemned to disappear (p. 305). In a conversation with "a taciturn friend and […] a young but already famous poet", he objects to the latter's despair at the elusive quality of natural beauty and his scepticism at the idea that there can be any pleasure in something so short-lived.[3] The countryside, the poet laments, is merely a semblance of life that must inevitably succumb to winter. Freud, however, retorts sharply that "I could not see my way to dispute the transience of all things, nor could I insist upon an exception in favour of what is beautiful and perfect. But I did dispute the pessimistic poet's view that the transience of what is beautiful involves any loss in its worth" (Schur, p. 302).

He concludes that "Limitation in the possibility of an enjoyment raises the value of the enjoyment" (p. 302).

This passage offers a valuable indication of the analyst's relation to death, which not only contradicts the idea that Freud was naturally pessimistic but also casts a rather different light on the question of poetic "melancholia". The sadness aroused in the poet by the "transience" points to a state of mourning; the projection of this subjective state onto nature suggests that he is unable to accomplish it successfully. According to Max Schur, who refers to this passage in *Freud: Living and Dying*, "All this beauty was giving 'these two sensitive minds' a foretaste of mourning, against which they were revolting" (p. 303). This explains why Freud's arguments are powerless to convince his companions:

> Mourning, [...] however painful it may be, comes to a spontaneous end. When it has renounced everything that has been lost, then [...] our libido is once more free (in so far as we are still young and active) to replace the lost objects by fresh ones equally or still more precious. (p. 303)

In this text, "On Transience" (*Vergänglichkeit*), which was written in 1915, Freud rather surprisingly compares the loss of love objects to the devastating disasters of war. Freud's intuition here is that nothing is absolutely irreplaceable and that there is no object that cannot ultimately be exchanged. This highly realistic bias amounts to believing that a love-object only acquires its "value" from the fact that it can be lost. This certitude that the object has value only as a substitute implies that a process of mourning has been successfully accomplished on the basis of an original loss. Of course, this "being-for-death", which we are unable to assume, evidently has a more Heideggerian character than Freud's reasonable assertions. Yet the debate is perhaps elsewhere: at the level of a certitude. We know that things are mortal and yet we do not want this knowledge; our knowledge of death is thus profoundly affected by the unconscious, which knows nothing about death. Freud's analysis of the refusal of death should also be considered in relation to the refusal to accept femininity, that is, imaginary castration. It is not by chance that once Freud has argued that "every one of us is convinced of his own immortality", he then goes on to cite a number of examples in which the individual's relation to woman becomes the criterion of his knowledge about death (p. 289). A superficial flirtation, for instance, may be better than "real love", the loss of which would be too cruel.

It might seem astonishing that Freud makes the erotic value of our attachments depend on the signifier of death. Yet this would be to forget that this construction necessarily implies the signifier of beauty. All beauty, through its perishability, secretly harbours the amputation of the Other, an amputation that is simply another name for castration. Fundamentally, as Freud says, enjoying life and accepting death are philosophical clichés that must be demonstrated. If, indeed, Freud treats the fear of death as "analogous to the fear of castration", it becomes clear that mourning should be conceived as an acceptance of castration in the Other (*Inhibitions, Symptoms and Anxiety*, p. 130). Nature can be an *analogon* of the Other, for the ephemeral quality of its beauty points to its perishable character.

The refusal to mourn coincides with a refusal to accept the Other's castration. The key to melancholia—the inability to put an end to mourning—is to be found in the subject's relation to woman and the refusal of femininity. Psychoanalysis thus constitutes a constant questioning of our attitude to death. Freud clearly states that it is about time that we "recognise the truth" and take as our motto the following saying: "*Sis vis vitam, para mortem*. If you want to endure life, prepare yourself for death" ("Thoughts for the Times on War and Death", pp. 299–300).

This call to respect the most fundamental of truths should not be considered as a requirement imposed by "reason". It is not reason but jouissance that gives the subject this warning. Being already dead does not suit the superego, which pushes towards jouissance.

When Freud says that the drives are essentially conservative and seek to re-establish an earlier state of affairs, he does so in order to include the sexual drives in this definition and to make the death drive the dominant force in the life of the drives—beyond the pleasure principle that necessarily tests the limits of life.

The desire of the psychoanalyst can be compared to the quiet and yet insistent voice of the unconscious, which "does not rest till it has gained a hearing" (Freud, *Future of an Illusion*, p. 53). Yet should it not also be related to the real of the death drive, which besieges us silently and relentlessly? For this drive, there is neither day nor night. As Freud explains at the end of *Beyond the Pleasure Principle*, "The death drives seem to do their work unobtrusively" (p. 63). This definition might, in many respects, be said to apply to the analyst, whose cadaverous position incarnates the signifier of death as the absolute Other.

On the other hand, if we accept that silence is a speech that says nothing, then many formulas concerning the superego could also be applied to the presence of the analyst. The symbol of all symbols, the superego has the property of destroying the thing itself and thereby of pointing to the limit of the signified at the very edge of all speech (see Lacan, *"Le symbolique, l'imaginaire et le réel"*). Finally, this symbol of all symbols points to a space that is now empty: that of the phallus, which has fallen from the status of the signifier of the all-powerful analyst, and has been reduced to the object *a*.

It is hardly surprising that on the final page of "The Direction of the Treatment"—a page that is devoted to making Freud's desire manifest—Lacan relates the signifier of desire, the phallus, to the logos that divides the subject and reduces him to a mere lack in being (*Écrits*, p. 537). How can the analyst bear to be amputated in this way?

The objectivization of the analyst

Freud expected the end of analysis to provoke a vacillation of being, which is nothing other than the acceptance of symbolic castration. The analyst, in Freud's work, is supposed to have finished mourning for her loss of being, and the patient is invited to join her in this place.

Lacan, however, does not always use the expression "desire of the analyst", in the sense of a subjective position, and his use of the formula varies considerably from one text to the next. Without going into an exhaustive study of the question, let us briefly examine how Lacan deals with the question that Freud had raised.

In his *Four Fundamental Concepts of Psychoanalysis*, Lacan throws light on the mysterious "link between the desire of the analyst and the desire of the patient" (*Seminar XI*, p. 254). This encounter is logical; there is no need to distinguish two separate desires belonging to two separate individuals, for the structure of discourse implies a single subject: the subject supposed to know. In order to construct the desire of the psychoanalyst, what must be added is the signification that is contained in this knowledge, a signification that the patient has been awaiting. The analyst is implicated in this knowledge, since she can decide whether or not to reveal this signification, thus laying bare the all-powerful character of the desire of the Other.

Lacan thus separates the trans-phenomenal function of the subject supposed to know from the person of the analyst, who should on no account identify with the former: "He is supposed to know that from which no one can escape, as soon as he formulates it—quite simply, signification. Signification implies, of course—and that is why I first brought out the dimension of his desire—that he cannot refuse it" (*Seminar XI*, p. 253).

There is even an opposition between knowledge and truth, for the truth-effect produced by the analyst undermines the function of knowledge:

> This privileged point is the only one by which we can recognize the character of an absolute point with no knowledge. It is absolute precisely by virtue of being in no way knowledge, but the point of attachment that links his very desire to the resolution of that which is to be revealed. (*Seminar XI*, p. 253)

To the extent that the analytic operation is linked to meaning (*sens*) and to signification, the function of the analyst's desire is indispensable.

Yet does this theorization not disappear in light of Lacan's developments on the question after 1964? In his seminar, *The Other Side of Psychoanalysis,* he radically transforms the analysand-analyst relation so that there is no longer room for the analyst as "subject".[4] Since the analyst is considered to incarnate the object *a*, there is now only a single subject, that of the phantasy, ($ ◊ a). Further, if the analyst is located in the place of the object, then the question of her desire relates specifically to the analysand's passage to the place of the analyst. Two questions now spring to mind. Does the analyst actually want to be in this place of the object? and what happens in analysis in order for this passage to occur?

Freud's conception of the analyst as subject is very different from Lacan's theory of her position as object. For Freud, who defines the analyst as "objective", rather than as having been turned into an object, the signifier of the analyst, however divided and alienated, actually exists. Indeed, it is precisely this subjective alienation that characterizes the analyst's function. The analyst represents a subject, which makes the transference possible. The analyst's desire is thus naturally aroused by this intersubjective structure. One can grasp the logic that required Lacan to move from such a formula to the one that appears in his "Proposition of 9 October 1967" and, more clearly still, three years later in *Radiophonie*.

Lacan explains in his *Four Fundamental Concepts* that the aim of the analytic operation is to maintain the distance between the ideal and the object of desire (I and *a*) (*Seminar XI*, p. 273). Since the analyst incarnates this ideal, she must put an end to this idealization and fall from this role "in order to be the support of the separating *a*" (*Seminar XI*, p. 273).[5]

The principle that Lacan is promoting during this period relies on the radical refusal of any identification with the analyst.

The criterion for analysis is that the analyst, as subject, should come to occupy the right place. There is no reason, however, to consider that her jouissance is implicated in this, since she has to discard her own ego. Beyond narcissism and opposed to any position of mastery, the analyst's desire is a function that operates, rather than being a modality of the drive.

While Freud submits to this principle of renunciation, he does not hesitate to point out how difficult it is to give up the imaginary power conferred on him by his patients.[6]

Just as there are not two separate desires in analysis, so there is also no place for two objects, if the analyst takes the position, not of a subject, but of the object of someone else's phantasy. The analyst is in the role of a polyvalent object *a* that is required to conform to the wishes of a variety of different subjects. What desire, then, allows her to bear this amputation? "There is no better way of placing him objectively than in relation to what was in the past called: being a saint" (Lacan, *Television*, p. 15). What can possibly motivate an analyst to give up all hope of being paid on the basis of her merits, thereby renouncing distributive justice?

In addition, the promotion of the object *a* to the place of the semblance is enough to explain why the analyst cannot aspire to represent a subject. Her representative role is reduced to shreds at the end of analysis, when there are no longer any signifiers to represent her; this is her de-being. Her abject status thus raises the question, not so much about her desire as the "linchpin of the treatment", but about why she would "aspire" to occupy this position. Lacan concludes that the analyst is left with an alternative: to be either a saint or a crook.

There is clearly a link between this last definition of the psychoanalyst and the abject nature of analytic practice. The analyst's role as a semblance challenges the logic of the signifier but not that of the phantasy. There is, indeed, an opposition between the analyst's being and the function of the object *a*, since the analyst cannot actually *be* the object *a* (Lacan, "*De la psychanalyse dans ses rapports avec la réalité*", p. 358).

Up to a point, this position brings the question of the analyst close to that of the masochist. The latter, for his part, knows that there is no jouissance other than that of the body, or rather that of a body that has been divided up by the partial objects. The object *a* is, in other words, his *Dasein*. The analyst, on the other hand, cannot ensure her ontic consistency by subjecting herself to the jouissance of the Other, a jouissance that, as far as the analyst is concerned, does not even exist. She is ultimately "rejected"—in the etymological sense of being thrown out—into a condition of de-being. "What the analyst's 'I am not thinking' expresses is the necessity that rejects her into de-being" (p. 358).

This is the end of the analyst as "subject". Lacan has thus separated Freud's desire from the object *a*, but this still does not resolve the question of why the analyst wants to occupy this position.

In as much as every analyst repeats Freud's act, without having any guarantee of being an analyst except through the transmission of Freud's desire, it can be said that there is only one desire: Freud's. This desire is, nevertheless, transmitted in an hysterical mode, which does not exclude the narcissism of minor differences. Lacan notes this in 1964:

> What do we know of all this?—if it is only at the mercy of fluctuations in the history of analysis, of the commitment of the desire of each analyst, we manage to add some small detail, some corroborating observation, some incidental addition or refinement, which enables us to define the presence, at the level of desire, of each of the analysts. This was the band, as Freud put it, that he left behind to follow him. (*Seminar XI*, p. 159)

Lacan himself tried to subtract the analyst's desire from its hysterical origins. As long as the desire of the analyst was represented by means of the model of intersubjectivity, it could only be defined as the desire of the Other. Lacan, however, in the course of his teaching, moves from the question of the Other's desire to another question: "It is not only a question of what the analyst wants to do with his patient in the matter. It is also a question of what his patient wants to do with him" (*Seminar XI*, pp. 158–159).

If the analyst conducts the treatment to the point at which she would want her own fall as object a, the question would be displaced. Yet Lacan takes the analyst's desire to be enigmatic. Why would anyone want to occupy a position that is void of either the charm or delights of masochistic jouissance? This is why he says, in the *Four Fundamental Concepts*, that "The analyst's desire is not a pure desire" (*Seminar XI*, p. 276).

The psychoanalyst, however, desires this undesirable position. How can we possibly make sense of this paradox?

It must be concluded that the analyst recoils from occupying a position to which her act, however, fixes her. Lacan indeed goes so far as to state that "The psychoanalyst holds his act in *horror*" ("The Other is Missing", p. 135).

Showing up the idealistic aspirations that would make the act the response to an irresistible call of truth, this chiasmus between the psychoanalyst's desire and the horror that accompanies her act implies a radical discontinuity: that between what the analyst can claim regarding her act and the particular motive that can account for it in each individual case.

There is no formula that would establish any continuity between desire and the act or that would allow an examination of the motives for the act to precede the act itself. Therefore, an entirely new operation is required if we wish to grasp the subjective turn that has led an analysand to occupy the position of analyst.

This subjective turn is the limit of what the operation of the treatment can transmit, and it is only outside analytic treatment that one will find—or not—the logic that presides over it. This new operation is the pass.[7]

Notes

1. The sound of the word, *"désêtre"*, translated here as "de-being", resembles somewhat that of *"désastre"* (disaster). Serge Cottet's discussion will play upon this similarity (translator's note).
2. The death drive manifests itself in Socrates in the purified form of a request for death, a "suicidal tendency", which is another aspect of the hysterical qualities noted above. Also see Lacan's *"Joyce le Symptôme"*.
3. Max Schur, who quotes this passage, supposes (with Herbert Lehmann) that it refers to Lou Andreas-Salomé and Rilke (*Freud: Living and Dying*, p. 302).
4. See also Lacan's *Radiophonie*.
5. Note that even in his most "activist" writings, Freud emphasized the contradiction between the analytic position and an identification with

an ideal. As he writes, "However much the analyst may be tempted to become a teacher, model and ideal for other people and to create men in his own image, he should not forget that that is not his task in the analytic relationship and indeed that he will be disloyal to his task if he allows himself to be led on by his inclinations" (*An Outline of Psycho-Analysis*, p. 175).

6. "[W]hen a man is endowed with power it is hard for him not to misuse it" ("Analysis Terminable and Interminable", p. 249).

7. On this problem, which is too vast to be approached here, see Lacan's "Proposition of 9 October 1967" and Miller's "*Introduction aux paradoxes de la passe*".

CONCLUSION

My aim in this book has been to trace Lacan's conception of the analyst's desire—which he specifies as the very "pivot of treatment"—back to its original source in Freud's desire.

The definition of the analyst's desire has, however, revealed an aporia. In the course of these chapters, I have tried not to put a name on this desire, but rather to identify a number of its parameters. As it is with dreams, this analyst's desire can only be inferred by induction or, occasionally, by deduction. Because it is always situated between two signifiers, it is always the desire for something else. I should also point out that this desire has been constructed out of bits and pieces that had also been intended for other purposes.

My central purpose in this book has been to show that considering psychoanalysis to be "Freud's lucubration", as Lacan puts it, does not imply a reduction of psychoanalysis to the arbitrary whims of one individual. There has been a transmission to which the horde of Freud's followers, inspired purely by his desire for "the cause", bears witness.

Lacan promoted this concept in order to account for the difficult question of the relation between analysts themselves. A reference to Freud's desire was necessary in order to account for the fact that psychoanalysis *has* been transmitted. Just as it is thanks to Socrates that we have a soul, so too it is thanks to Freud that we have an unconscious. This is because Freud made a social bond out of the "unconscious at work", which hysteria shows us. He activated psychoanalysis by recognizing hysterical desire and making it into a discourse in which he himself was implicated as a subject.

It is, indeed, hysterics who lay bare the parasitic contamination of sexual life by the unconscious. From the beginning, they led Freud by the hand, guiding his desire to know towards the traumatic element in sexual life. Freud's passion for origins and his quest for a real that creates holes in the phantasy and for the primal scene of the *Urvater* confirmed the hysteric's position, for whom the desire of the Other constitutes the law. From his *Studies on Hysteria* to *Civilization and its Discontents*, Freud made himself the dupe of the hysteric's desire, going so far as to signpost, in his theory, the path he intended them to follow.

This origin might well have proved fatal to his discoveries. In wanting, as he himself said, to "lift repression", he exposed himself from the beginning to a risk: that of ending up with a theory that would make the unveiling of truth and a secret into the source of a new *Weltanschauung*. This did not prove to be the case.

Freud, unlike others, escaped being seduced by the "mysterious unconscious". Because he followed the hysteric as far as she would go, he never became intoxicated with sexual meaning (*sens*); privileging the real and chance over hermeneutics, he was able to push the analytic discourse into the realm of science. The "death drive", as he named it, sets a limit to the jouissance of meaning by pursuing knowledge to the very end, a knowledge that had to be produced if psychoanalysis was not to depend only on the phallic cause.

It follows that Freud's passions do not fit into the already mapped-out categories of the philosophers: truth, beauty, and the good. The desire for truth that characterizes Freud's ethic, the ethic of the "well-spoken" (*bien-dire*), collides with the passion for ignorance, which the clinic reveals, belying the naïve belief in a *Wissentrieb*. Freud himself spared his patients this "sadism of truth" and refused any "brusque" revelation to them of their own secrets.[1] An advocate of the saying that "The truth is sometimes best left unsaid", he was not, unlike Zola— a man whom he nevertheless admired—a fanatical believer in truth. While he does advocate, in his "New Introductory Lectures", a "submission to the truth", this is simply in order to denounce the prohibition of thought that, to his mind, characterizes religion.

Likewise, for Freud, there is no other form of good than that which enables a subject to pay the price for reaching the object of desire. Any compromise in this respect causes untold damage to the speaking being. Finally, by separating the truth of desire from any possible collusion with the ideal, Freud refused to accord to it any of the ornaments of beauty that, in his opinion, simply veiled the horror of death. These positions allowed him to avoid being mesmerized by the unconscious.

The psychoanalyst's desire is not a pure love for the unconscious. It is linked to the ambiguity that causes the psychoanalyst to view his knowledge with horror whenever he responds, by means of his act, to another's wish to "know the truth". Freud clearly did not make a religion of desire, for such a religion would always be thwarted by civilization. This is a fact. He did not, however, love psychoanalysis to the point of madness, and we have seen the extent to which the desire of the analyst escapes from the law of pleasure.

From the moment when Freud's desire to interpret was dulled, when his passion for the signifier met a stumbling block in the death drive and the negative therapeutic reaction, it is to what is beyond desire that one must look.

Lacan took the step that shifts the analyst's desire to the side of jouissance. From the moment when the analyst is no longer in the position of a subject but in that of the object, the problem is displaced from the treatment to another operation. Although the psychoanalyst's desire is clearly implicated in the former, it is only another operation that can account for the analyst's choice of occupying this place of the object. Lacan set up the operation of the pass in order to enable something of the change in subjective direction—a change that, in the course of the treatment, involves this transformation—to be transmitted.

Only the results acquired in and by this experience will enable the question of the psychoanalyst's desire to be renewed. Lacan put his final efforts into accomplishing this project.

Note

1. "Attempts to 'rush' [the patient] at first consultation, by brusquely telling him the secrets which have been discovered by the physician, are technically objectionable" (Freud, "'Wild' Psycho-Analysis", p. 226).

REFERENCES

Alexander, F. (1925). A metapsychological description of the process of cure. In: *International Journal of Psychoanalysis*, 6: 3–34.

Analyse nouvelle expérience Paris (Ed.) (1990). *Le tumulte: dossier.* In: *L'Âne*, p. 42.

Association mondiale de psychanalyse (Ed.) (1994). *Comment finissent les analyses.* Paris: Éditions du Seuil.

Assoun, P.-L. (1976). *Freud, la philosophie et les philosophes.* Paris: Presses universitaires de France.

Blanchot, M. (1982). *The Space of Literature.* A. Smock (Trans.). Lincoln, NE: University of Nebraska Press.

Blanton, S. (1971). *Diary of My Analysis with Sigmund Freud.* New York: Hawthorn.

Brabant-Gerö, E., Falzeder, E. & Giampieri-Deutsch, P. (Eds.) (1993). *The Correspondence of Sigmund Freud and Sándor Ferenczi.* P. T. Hoffer (Trans.). Cambridge, MA: Belknap Press of Harvard University Press.

Breuer, J. & Freud, S. (1895). Studies on Hysteria. *S. E., 2*. London: Hogarth, 1953, pp. 3–305.

Castel, R. (1973). *Le psychanalysme.* Paris: F. Maspero.

Certeau, M. de. (1975). *L'écriture de l'Histoire.* Paris: Gallimard.

Clément, C. (1974). *Le Pouvoir des mots: symbolique et idéologique.* Tours, France: Mame.

Cottet, S. (1978). Constructions et métapsychologie de l'analyse. In: *Ornicar?*, *14*: 25–35.

Cottet, S. (1981). Profession: homme aux loups. In: *L'Âne, 2*: p. 44.

Descartes, R. (1968). *Discourse on Method, and Other Writings*. F. E. Sutcliffe (Trans.). Harmondsworth, UK: Penguin.

Doolittle, H. (1956). *Tribute to Freud*. New York: Pantheon.

Eolia (Ed.) (1994). *La conclusion de la cure: variété clinique de la sortie d'analyse*. Paris: Eolia, diffusion Seuil.

Falzeder, E. (Ed.) (2002). *The Complete Correspondence of Sigmund Freud and Karl Abraham 1907–1925*. C. Schwarzacher, C. Trollope, K. M. King, A. Haynal & E. Falzeder (Trans.). London: Karnac.

Fédida, P. (1978). *L'Absence*. Paris: Gallimard.

Ferenczi, S. (1908). Introjection and transference. In: *First Contributions to Psycho-analysis*. London: Karnac, 1994, pp. 35–93.

Ferenczi, S. (1908). The elasticity of psycho-analytic technique. In: *Final Contributions to the Problems and Methods of Psycho-Analysis*. London: Karnac, 1994, pp. 87–101.

Fichtner, G. (Ed.) (2003). *The Sigmund Freud-Ludwig Binswanger Correspondence 1908–1938*. A. J. Pomerans & T. Roberts (Trans.). London: Open Gate Press, incorporating Centaur Press.

Freud, E. L. (Ed.) (1960). *Letters of Sigmund Freud 1873–1939*. T. Stern & J. Stern (Trans.). New York: Basic.

Freud, S. (1895). Project for a Scientific Psychology. *S. E., 1*. London: Hogarth, 1966, pp. 281–391.

Freud, S. (1898). Sexuality in the Aetiology of the Neuroses. *S. E., 3*. London: Hogarth, 1962, pp. 259–285.

Freud, S. (1900). The Interpretation of Dreams (I). *S. E., 4*. London: Hogarth, 1953.

Freud, S. (1900a). The Interpretation of Dreams (II). *S. E., 5*. London: Hogarth, 1953.

Freud, S. (1904). Freud's Psycho-Analytic Procedure. *S. E., 7*. London: Hogarth, 1953, pp. 247–254.

Freud, S. (1905a). Bruchstück einer Hysterie-Analyse. *Gesammelte Werke: V*. London: Imago, 1991, pp. 163–286.

Freud, S. (1905b). Fragment of an Analysis of a Case of Hysteria [*Dora*]. *S. E., 7*. London: Hogarth, 1953, pp. 1–122.

Freud, S. (1905c). On Psychotherapy. *S. E., 7*. London: Hogarth, 1953, pp. 255–268.

Freud, S. (1905d). Three Essays on the Theory of Sexuality. *S. E., 7*. London: Hogarth, 1953, pp. 123–246.

Freud, S. (1907). Delusions and Dreams in Jensen's *Gradiva*. *S. E., 9*. London: Hogarth, 1959, pp. 1–96.

Freud, S. (1908a). Creative Writers and Day-Dreaming. *S. E., 9*. London: Hogarth, 1959, pp. 141–154.

Freud, S. (1908b). Hysterical Phantasies and their Relation to Bisexuality. *S. E., 9*. London: Hogarth, 1959, pp. 141–154.

Freud, S. (1909). Notes upon a Case of Obsessional Neurosis [*The Rat Man*]. *S. E., 10*. London: Hogarth, 1955, pp. 151–318.

Freud, S. (1909a). Remarques sur un cas de névrose obsessionelle [*L'homme aux rats*]. *Cinq psychanalyses*. Paris: Presses universitaires de France, 1970, pp. 199–261.

Freud, S. (1910a). A Special Type of Choice of Object Made by Men (Contributions to the Psychology of Love I). *S. E., 11*. London: Hogarth, 1957, pp. 163–176.

Freud, S. (1910b). Five Lectures on Psycho-analysis. *S. E., 11*. London: Hogarth, 1957, pp. 1–56.

Freud, S. (1910c). Leonardo Da Vinci and a Memory of his Childhood. *S. E., 11*. London: Hogarth, 1957, pp. 57–138.

Freud, S. (1910d). "Wild" Psycho-Analysis. *S. E., 11*. London: Hogarth, 1957, pp. 219–228.

Freud, S. (1911a). Formulations on the Two Principles of Mental Functioning. *S. E., 12*. London: Hogarth, 1958, pp. 213–226.

Freud, S. (1911b). Psycho-Analytic Notes on an Autobiographical Account of a Case of Paranoia (Dementia Paranoides) [*Schreber*]. *S. E., 12*. London: Hogarth, 1958, pp. 1–82.

Freud, S. (1912/1913a). Totem und Tabu. *Gesammelte Werke*: IX. London: Imago, 1996, pp. 3–195.

Freud, S. (1912/1913b). Totem and Taboo. *S. E., 13*. London: Hogarth, 1955, pp. vii–162.

Freud, S. (1912a). Recommendations to Physicians Practising Psycho-Analysis. *S. E., 12*. London: Hogarth, 1958, pp. 109–120.

Freud, S. (1912b). The Dynamics of Transference. *S. E., 12*. London: Hogarth, 1958, pp. 97–108.

Freud, S. (1912c). Types of Onset of Neurosis. *S. E., 12*. London: Hogarth, 1958, pp. 227–238.

Freud, S. (1913a). On Beginning the Treatment (Further Recommendations on the Technique of Psycho-Analysis I). *S. E., 12*. London: Hogarth, 1958, pp. 121–144.

Freud, S. (1913b). The Theme of the Three Caskets. *S. E., 12*. London: Hogarth, 1958, pp. 289–302.

Freud, S. (1914a). On Narcissism: an Introduction. *S. E., 14*. London: Hogarth, 1957, pp. 67–102.

Freud, S. (1914b). On the History of the Psycho-Analytic Movement. *S. E., 14*. London: Hogarth, 1957, pp. 1–66.

Freud, S. (1914c). Remembering, Repeating and Working-Through (Further Recommendations on the Technique of Psycho-Analysis II). *S. E.*, *12*. London: Hogarth, 1958, pp. 145–156.

Freud, S. (1915a). Observations on Transference-Love (Further Recommendations on the Technique of Psycho-Analysis III). *S. E.*, *12*. London: Hogarth, 1958, pp. 157–171.

Freud, S. (1915b). Thoughts for the Times on War and Death. *S. E.*, *14*. London: Hogarth, 1957, pp. 273–300.

Freud, S. (1916). On Transience. *S. E.*, *14*. London: Hogarth, 1957, pp. 303–307.

Freud, S. (1917). Introductory Lectures on Psycho-Analysis. *S. E.*, *16*. London: Hogarth, 1963, pp. 241–463.

Freud, S. (1918a). Aus der Geschichte einer infantilen Neurose. *Gesammelte Werke: XII*. London: Imago, 2005, pp. 29–157.

Freud, S. (1918b). From the History of an Infantile Neurosis [*The Wolf Man*]. *S. E.*, *17*. London: Hogarth, 1955, pp. 1–124.

Freud, S. (1919a). "A Child is Being Beaten." A Contribution to the Study of the Origin of Sexual Perversions. *S. E.*, *8*. London: Hogarth, 1955, pp. 175–204.

Freud, S. (1919b). Einleitung zur "Psychoanalyse der Kriegsneurosen". *Gesammelte Werke: XII*. London: Imago, 2005, pp. 321–324.

Freud, S. (1919c). Lines of Advance in Psycho-Analytic Therapy. *S. E.*, *17*. London: Hogarth, 1955, pp. 157–168.

Freud, S. (1920a). Beyond the Pleasure Principle. *S. E.*, *28*. London: Hogarth, 1955, pp. 1–64.

Freud, S. (1920b). The Psychogenesis of a Case of Homosexuality in a Woman. *S. E.*, *18*. London: Hogarth, 1955, pp. 145–172.

Freud, S. (1921–1938). *Résultats, idées, problèmes, II, 5e Édition*. J. Altounian, A. Balseinte & A. Bourguignon (Trans.). Paris: Presses universitaires de France, 1998.

Freud, S. (1921). Group Psychology and the Analysis of the Ego. *S. E.*, *18*. London: Hogarth, 1955, pp. 65–144.

Freud, S. (1923a). Remarks on the Theory and Practice of Dream-Interpretation. *S. E.*, *19*. London: Hogarth, 1961, pp. 107–122.

Freud, S. (1923b). The Ego and the Id. *S. E.*, *19*. London: Hogarth, 1961, pp. 1–66.

Freud, S. (1924). The Loss of Reality in Neurosis and Psychosis. *S. E.*, *19*. London: Hogarth, 1961, pp. 181–188.

Freud, S. (1925a). An Autobiographical Study. *S. E.*, *20*. London: Hogarth, 1959, pp. 1–74.

Freud, S. (1925b). Some Additional Notes on Dream-Interpretation as a Whole. *S. E.*, *19*. London: Hogarth, 1961, pp. 123–138.

Freud, S. (1925c). The Resistances to Psycho-Analysis. *S. E., 19*. London: Hogarth, 1961, pp. 211–224.

Freud, S. (1926a). Inhibitions, Symptoms and Anxiety. *S. E., 20*. London: Hogarth, 1959, pp. 75–176.

Freud, S. (1926b). The Question of Lay Analysis. *S. E., 20*. London: Hogarth, 1959, pp. 177–258.

Freud, S. (1927). The Future of an Illusion. *S. E., 21*. London: Hogarth, 1961, pp. 1–56.

Freud, S. (1930a). Das Unbehagen in der Kultur. *Gesammelte Werke*: *XIV*. London: Imago, 1991, pp. 421–506.

Freud, S. (1930b). Civilization and its Discontents. *S. E., 21*. London: Hogarth, 1961, pp. 57–146.

Freud, S. (1931). Female Sexuality. *S. E., 21*. London: Hogarth, 1961, pp. 221–244.

Freud, S. (1932). My Contact with Josef Popper-Lynkeus. *S. E., 22*. London: Hogarth, 1964, pp. 217–224.

Freud, S. (1933a). New Introductory Lectures on Psycho-Analysis. *S. E., 22*. London: Hogarth, 1964, pp. 1–182.

Freud, S. (1933b). Sándor Ferenczi. *S. E., 22*. London: Hogarth, 1964, pp. 225–230.

Freud, S. (1937a). Die endliche und die unendliche Analyse. *Gesammelte Werke*: *XVI*. London: Imago, 1993, pp. 57–99.

Freud, S. (1937b). Analysis Terminable and Interminable. *S. E., 23*. London: Hogarth, 1964, pp. 209–254.

Freud, S. (1937c). Constructions in Analysis. *S. E., 23*. London: Hogarth, 1964, pp. 255–270.

Freud, S. (1937d). Der Mann Moses und die monotheistische Religion. *Gesammelte Werke*: *XVI*. London: Imago, 1993, pp. 103–246.

Freud, S. (1938a). An Outline of Psycho-Analysis. *S. E., 23*. London: Hogarth, 1964, pp. 139–208.

Freud, S. (1938b). Splitting of the Ego in the Process of Defence. *S. E., 23*. London: Hogarth, 1964, pp. 271–278.

Freud, S. (1939). Moses and Monotheism. *S. E., 23*. London: Hogarth, 1964, pp. 1–138.

Granoff, W. (1975). *Filiations: l'avenir du complexe d'Œdipe*. Paris: Éditions de Minuit.

Heimann, P. (1950). On counter-transference. In: *International Journal of Psychoanalysis, 31*: 81–84.

Jones, E. (1955). *Sigmund Freud Life and Work, Volume Two: Years of Maturity 1901–1919*. London: Hogarth.

Jones, E. (1957). *Sigmund Freud Life and Work, Volume Three: The Last Phase 1919–1939*. London: Hogarth.

Kardiner, A. (1977). *My Analysis with Freud: Reminiscences.* New York: W. W. Norton.

Kaufmann, P. (1974). *Psychanalyse et théorie de la culture.* Paris: Denoël.

Lacan, J. (1958–9). Le désir et son interprétation *[Le séminaire VI].* Unpublished seminar of 1958–1959, Paris.

Lacan, J. (1966a). *Écrits: The First Complete Edition in English.* B. Fink (Trans.). New York: W. W. Norton, 2006.

Lacan, J. (1966b). Response to students of philosophy concerning the object of psychoanalysis. In: J. Copjec (Ed.), *Television: A Challenge to the Psychoanalytic Establishment.* D. Hollier, R. Krauss, A. Michelson & J. Mehlman (Trans.). New York: W. W. Norton, 1990, pp. 107–114.

Lacan, J. (1968a). De la psychanalyse dans ses rapports avec la réalité. In: *Autres écrits.* Paris: Éditions du Seuil, 2001, pp. 351–359.

Lacan, J. (1968b). La psychanalyse : raison d'un échec. In: *Autres écrits.* Paris: Éditions du Seuil, 2001, pp. 341–349.

Lacan, J. (1968c). Proposition of 9 October 1967 on the Psychoanalyst of the School. R. Grigg (Trans.). In: *Analysis,* 6, 1995: 1–13.

Lacan, J. (1970). Radiophonie. In: *Autres écrits.* Paris: Éditions du Seuil, 2001, pp. 403–447.

Lacan, J. (1973a). L'étourdit. In: *Autres écrits.* Paris: Éditions du Seuil, 2001, pp. 449–495.

Lacan, J. (1973b). Note italienne. In: *Autres écrits.* Paris: Éditions du Seuil, 2001, pp. 307–311.

Lacan, J. (1973c). *Television: A Challenge to the Psychoanalytic Establishment.* J. Copjec (Ed.). D. Hollier, R. Krauss, A. Michelson & J. Mehlman (Trans.). New York: W. W. Norton, 1990.

Lacan, J. (1973d). *The Four Fundamental Concepts of Psycho-analysis [Seminar XI].* J.-A. Miller (Ed.). A. Sheridan (Trans.). New York: W. W. Norton, 1978.

Lacan, J. (1975a). *Freud's Papers on Technique, 1953–1954 [Seminar I].* J.-A. Miller (Ed.). J. Forrester (Trans.). New York: W. W. Norton, 1988.

Lacan, J. (1975b). Introduction à l'édition allemande d'un premier volume des *Écrits.* In: *Autres écrits.* Paris: Éditions du Seuil, 2001, pp. 553–559.

Lacan, J. (1975c). Le séminaire R.S.I.—séances du 11 et 18 février 75 *[Le séminaire XXII].* In: *Ornicar?,* 4: 91–106.

Lacan, J. (1975d). *On Feminine Sexuality: The Limits of Love and Knowledge [Seminar XX].* J.-A. Miller (Ed.). B. Fink (Trans.). New York: W. W. Norton, 1998.

Lacan, J. (1978). *The Ego in Freud's Theory and in the Technique of Psychoanalysis, 1954–1955 [Seminar II].* J.-A. Miller (Ed.). S. Tomaselli (Trans.). New York: W. W. Norton, 1988.

Lacan, J. (1979a). Joyce le Symptôme. In: *Autres écrits*. Paris: Éditions du Seuil, 2001, pp. 565–570.

Lacan, J. (1979b). L'insu que sait de l'une bévue s'aile à mourre: séminaire du 19 avril 1977 [*Le séminaire XXIV*]. In: *Ornicar?*, 17/18: 11–16.

Lacan, J. (1979c). The Neurotic's Individual Myth. J.-A. Miller (Ed.). M. N. Evans (Trans.). In: *Psychoanalytic Quarterly, 48*(3): 405–425.

Lacan, J. (1980). The Other is Missing. In: *Television: A Challenge to the Psychoanalytic Establishment*. J. Copjec (Ed.). D. Hollier, R. Krauss, A. Michelson & J. Mehlman (Trans.). New York: W. W. Norton, 1990, pp. 133–135.

Lacan, J. (1986). *The Ethics of Psychoanalysis, 1959–1960 [Seminar VII]*. J.-A. Miller (Ed.). D. Porter (Trans.). New York: W. W. Norton, 1992.

Lacan, J. (1991). *The Other Side of Psychoanalysis [Seminar XVII]*. J.-A. Miller (Ed.). R. Grigg (Trans.). New York: W. W. Norton, 2006.

Lacan, J. (2001). *Le séminaire de Jacques Lacan livre VIII: Le transfert 1960–1961 (Seconde édition corrigée)*. J.-A. Miller (Ed.). Paris: Éditions du Seuil, 2001.

Lacan, J. (2005a). *Le séminaire de Jacques Lacan livre XXIII: Le sinthome, 1975–1976*. J.-A. Miller (Ed.). Paris: Éditions du Seuil.

Lacan, J. (2005b). Le symbolique, l'imaginaire et le réel (8 juillet 1953). In: *Des noms-du-père*. Paris: Éditions du Seuil, pp. 9–63.

Lacan, J. (2006). *Le séminaire de Jacques Lacan livre XVIII: D'un discours qui ne serait pas du semblant, 1971*. J.-A. Miller (Ed.). Paris: Éditions du Seuil.

Laplanche, J. & Pontalis, J. B. (1968). Fantasy and the Origins of Sexuality. In: R. Steiner (Ed.), *Unconscious Phantasy*. London: Karnac, 2003: pp. 107–144.

Laurent, E. (1981a). L'effet-mère. In: *L'Âne*, 2: p. 30.

Laurent, E. (1981b). Une clinique de la sexuation. In: *L'Âne*, 1: 22–23.

Lebovici, S., Diatkine, R., Favreau, J. A. & Luquet Parat, C. (1956). La psychanalyse des enfants. In: S. Nacht (Ed.), *La psychanalyse d'aujourd'hui*. Paris: Presses universitaires de France, pp. 169–235.

Leclaire, S. (1958). À propos de l'épisode psychotique que présenta "l'homme aux loups". In: *La psychanalyse*, 4: 83–110.

Leclaire, S. (1967). À propos d'un fantasme de Freud: note sur la transgression. In: *L'Inconscient*, 1: 31–55.

Leclaire, S. (1971). *Démasquer le réel*. Paris: Seuil.

Lévi-Strauss, C. (1988). *The Jealous Potter*. B. Chorier (Trans.). Chicago, IL: University of Chicago Press.

Little, M. (1951). Counter-transference and the patient's response to it. In: *International Journal of Psychoanalysis, 32*: 32–40.

Lyotard, J.-F. (1977). De l'apathie théorique. In: *Rudiments païens: genre dissertatif*. Paris: Union générale d'éditions, pp. 9–31.

Mannoni, M. (1979). *La Théorie comme fiction: Freud, Groddeck, Winnicott, Lacan*. Paris: Éditions du Seuil.

Mannoni, O. (1969). *Clefs pour l'imaginaire: ou l'autre scène*. Paris: Éditions du Seuil.

Mannoni, O. (1976). L'athéisme de Freud. In: *Ornicar?, 6*: 21–32.

Mannoni, O. (1980). *Un commencement qui n'en finit pas: transfert, interprétation, théorie*. Paris: Éditions du Seuil.

Masson, J. M. (Ed.) (1985). *The Complete Letters of Sigmund Freud to Wilhelm Fliess 1887–1904*. J. M. Masson (Trans.). Cambridge, MA: Belknap Press of Harvard University Press.

McGuire, W. (Ed.) (1974). *The Freud/Jung Letters: The Correspondence between Sigmund Freud and C. G. Jung*. R. Manheim & R. F. C. Hull (Trans.). Princeton, NJ: Princeton University Press.

Melman, C. (1975). À propos des *Études sur l'hystérie*. In: *Lettres de l'École freudienne, 15*: 194–205.

Melman, C. (1978). Enfants de la psychanalyse. In: *Ornicar?, 16*: 63–71.

Meng, H. & Freud, E. L. (Eds.) (1963). *Psychoanalysis and Faith: the Letters of Sigmund Freud and Oskar Pfister*. E. Mosbacher (Trans.). London: Hogarth and the Institute of Psychoanalysis.

Miller, J.-A. (1977). Introduction aux paradoxes de la passe. In: *Ornicar?, 12/13*: 105–112.

Miller, J.-A. (1977–1978). L'orientation lacanienne. Unpublished seminar of 1977–1978, University of Paris-VIII.

Miller, J.-A. (1980a). *Cinco Conferencias Caraqueñas sobre Lacan*. Caracas, Venezuela: Editorial Ateneo de Caracas.

Miller, J.-A. (1980b) Réveil. In: *Ornicar?, 20/21*: 49–53.

Miller, J.-A. (1992). Petite introduction à l'au-delà de L'Œdipe: ouverture. In: *La Cause freudienne (Revue de l'ECF), 21*: 7–11.

Miller, J.-A. (1994). La passe de la psychanalyse vers la science: le désir de savoir: extrait du cours de 1989–90 "Le banquet des analystes": leçons des 6 et 13 juin 1990. In: *Quarto, 56*: 36–44.

Millot, C. (1979). *Freud anti-pédagogue*. Paris: La bibliothèque d'*Ornicar?*

Milner, J.-C. (1991). Lacan and modern science. Miguel E. Vatter (Trans.). In: *Journal of European Psychoanalysis, 3/4*, 1996–1997. http://www.psychomedia.it/jep/number3-4/milner.htm

Money-Kyrle, R. E. (1956). Normal counter-transference and some of its deviations. In: *International Journal of Psychoanalysis, 37*: 360–366.

Plato. *Plato's Lysis*. T. Penner & C. J. Rowe (Trans.). Cambridge, UK: Cambridge University Press, 2005.

Plato. *Plato: Symposium (Cambridge Greek and Latin Classics)*. K. J. Dover (Ed.). Cambridge, UK: Cambridge University Press, 1980.

Plato. *Plato's Symposium*. S. Benardete (Trans.). Chicago: University of Chicago Press, 2001.

Porge, E. (1978). Sur le désir de l'analyste. In: *Ornicar?*, *14*: 35–39.

Ribeiro Hawelka, E. (1974). Commentaire. In: S. Freud, *L'homme aux rats: journal d'une analyse*. E. Ribeiro Hawelka (Trans.). Paris: Presses universitaires de France.

Roazen, P. (1969). *Brother Animal: The Story of Freud and Tausk*. New York: Knopf.

Roazen, P. (1975). *Freud and His Followers*. New York: Knopf.

Roustang, F. (1982). *Dire Mastery: Discipleship from Freud to Lacan*. N. Lukacher (Trans.). Baltimore: Johns Hopkins University Press.

Schur, M. (1972). *Freud: Living and Dying*. New York: International Universities Press.

Stein, C. (1968). Le père mortel et le père immortel. In: *L'Inconscient*, *5*: 59–100.

Weiss, E. (1991). *Sigmund Freud as a Consultant: Recollections of a Pioneer in Psychoanalysis*. New Brunswick, NJ: Transaction.

INDEX

189

For Product Safety Concerns and Information please contact our EU
representative GPSR@taylorandfrancis.com
Taylor & Francis Verlag GmbH, Kaufingerstraße 24, 80331 München, Germany